I've known JMo for over 20 year
whatever you do, don't let on that
ever meet. Seriously, he'd hate ~~~~~~~~~~~~~ ~~~~ moving
and smart as a whip, he can be just a little bit intimidating — but I
promise you, it's all part of his charm. Underneath is a guy with a
heart of gold (do not tell him I said that), an unmatched loyalty to
the people he cares about, deep empathy, who rescues wildlife and,
let's be honest, sometimes people too.

This book is a wild ride through the chaos of growing up,
mental health, past traumas and life as a celebrity journalist, told
with the same sharp wit and unflinching honesty that makes JMo,
well, JMo. He doesn't sugarcoat anything, ever, and thank God for
that, because life's messy, and his story reminds us we're not alone
in the mess.

If you've ever wondered what it's like to straddle the line
between entertainment and existential crisis, this is the book for
you. And if you get to the end thinking, 'Wow, what an incredible
human being,' remember, don't tell him. He'd rather keep you
thinking he's just a bit of a rogue.

—**Chelsea Bonner**

A huge congratulations mate on this fantastic read.

Your journey is one that should be written about and one
you should be so proud of. I have no doubt this book will go on
to inspire many young boys and girls. Thank you for an honest,
genuine and authentic friendship. I look forward to sharing many
more experiences with you.

This is an essential read — a powerful and life-changing
journey that hits it out of the park. It's a gift to yourself that you'll
cherish forever.

—**Michael Clarke**

Take this book home! It's honest, brutally raw, heartfelt and
ultimately uplifting — a ray of sunshine for anyone weathering
life's storms and seeking hope and strength.

—**Grant Denyer**

The first moment I met JMo I instantly adored him. We met at the start of my author journey when he wrote about my first book and could not have been more supportive, which meant so much, and he still is today. JMo really is an incredible friend to have! What I fell for, and why I have so much time, love and care for JMo, is because he is kind, thoughtful, caring, funny, honest, raw, intelligent, intuitive and has a big, beautiful, massive open heart. Something else I love about him is JMo owns his story and journey, and with this book he also can help others find acceptance and happiness, and love life just like he has. I could not be more proud or excited for this next chapter in JMo's life.

—**Sarah Di Lorenzo**

With love, gratitude, pride and a huge congratulations to the one and only JMo. I cannot believe we have been in each other's lives for almost 20 years? Thank you for being brave and sharing your truth with us all, warts and all. Your honesty, drive, self-exploration and determination is something to be admired, and I know by you sharing your story with us, it will be not only healing for you but it will be healing for many and will also set other people free. Your big heart and infectious personality is intoxicating and I am so proud of you for looking inside, doing the work, sharing your story and being an advocate for mental health. Congratulations once again my friend.

—**Casey Donovan**

JMo has spent his career writing about other so-called interesting people, but you're about to see that his story is even more interesting, compelling, dark and dangerous than those celebrities he writes about. There has never been a more important time for us to hear these voices, read these words and have these conversations.

Dr Jodie Lowinger is one of the best in the business and together, with this book, JMo and Jodie will change lives and help many find a better, safer, well-lit path.

—**Larry Emdur**

JMo's honesty and vulnerability is inspiring. His story is a beacon of light and hope for those who have struggled with mental health issues. I have no doubt this book will save lives.

—**Sam Frost**

Jonathon's bravery in sharing his story is inspiring! As someone who's been on my own journey, I know how hard it can be to break the silence and open up, but that's exactly what we need more of. The more we talk about mental health, the more we strip away the stigma, opening up space for real conversations and healing. Jonathon's raw honesty hits you right in the chest — he doesn't hold back, and it's clear he's opened up in the hope that his story will make others feel less alone in their struggles. This book is a lifeline for anyone feeling isolated by their own battles, reminding us that being human means facing our darkest moments and finding strength on the other side.

—Ben Gillies

Jonathon and I have known each other since the very beginning of both our careers. We have grown up in the industry throughout its many incarnations. He has always helped everybody else tell their stories to the world, and now it is his time to share his own! I have no doubt that his bravery and ability to communicate through his talent of the written word will connect, inspire and help so many others. I am so proud of you, my friend. Continued love and light on bringing strength to others through your vulnerability!

—Delta Goodrem

Jonathon writes like a trusted friend who understands your struggles because he's lived them too. He lays it all out — the mess, the trauma, the insecurities — and reminds you that you're not alone. This book is for anyone who's ever felt like they were the only one not holding it together, for those who've battled their own minds and need a reminder that healing doesn't mean being perfect.

—Jackie 'O' Henderson

JMo can bloody write. That's for sure. He sucks you into his stories. He is honest and authentic. *Mental As Anyone* is relatable AF. I needed this book.

—Tanya Hennessy

There are so few people in this world who have the ability to tell a story like JMo. The sincere vulnerability, honesty and care in everything he writes and with everyone he meets has long been my favourite thing about him.

JMo has been a dear friend for over a decade now, but there are things here even I have not known about the incredible life he has lived and the adversity he has faced.

I encourage you all to lap up every word of this precious book, for on a subject where so often we all fail to find the words, JMo always finds the faultless way.

—Erin Holland

Mental health is thankfully a topic that's being discussed more openly these days, but sharing personal struggles and journeys is still far from easy. I've had the privilege of speaking with JMo over many years during interviews at different points in our lives. Seeing him now share his own experiences so openly and honestly, with the hope of helping others, is truly inspiring. This book has the potential to make a real difference — whether by encouraging people to seek help or simply by sparking important conversations.

—Dami Im

We need more insightful, heartfelt and open conversations around mental health in this world.

In having them, we understand ourselves and each other better but perhaps most importantly, we feel less alone. A nuanced and personal deep dive into mental, acclaimed entertainment journalist JMo balances the stories of his own battles with mental health with insightful commentary and skills for life, by Dr Jodie Lowinger.

—Melissa Leong

Jonathon Moran's *Mental As Anyone* is such a heartfelt read. His honesty in sharing his own journey, along with Dr Jodie Lowinger's incredible insights, makes this book so special. It's full of strength, hope and tools to help anyone feel less alone and more supported in their mental health journey.

—Jessica Mauboy

Jonathon is as caring with his written words as he is in life, always reminding us that we are not alone, that he cares, loves and supports you, always.

I feel very lucky to be his friend and reading this book will allow you to feel some of his warmth, acceptance and understanding. It is important work because he shines a light in the darkest of places, which helps us all. He reminds us that we do not walk alone.

—**Edwina McCann**

Jonathon Moran fears that he is an imposter. Readers will soon disagree with his harsh judgement of his worth. JMo is not an imposter. He is a vulnerable, unique human being who has demonstrated the courage and grace to share his inner-most doubts and torment to help others. In my own life I have realised that I have only really been able to trust those who bear the scars of suffering to offer me help in healing my own wounds.

JMo bares his wounds and in so doing bares his soul. He tried to end his own life. I am so deeply grateful that he did not succeed. I treasure his friendship. I commend this important book to anyone who has struggled with fears of inadequacy, with deep depression and crippling anxiety. That is everyone who has one ounce of the honesty of this author.

—**Catherine McGregor**

In the spirit of owning every part of our story and sharing them to be free, this book is brilliant.

On the road to accepting who we are. Brave and honest is the way. This book proves it.

—**Kate Ritchie**

JMo … not good enough? Enough is enough! Just a bloody good, honest person, THAT is enough.

A must-read for anyone struggling with shame around mental illness. JMo's honest and plain-talking ways cut through the stigma of abuse and depression. I am proud to call him a friend.

—**Melinda Schneider**

I've known JMo for years now both in print and in real life — they can be worlds apart. What I've always appreciated about him is his honesty and transparency. He has an outward comfort in his own skin.

Back during COVID, JMo and I formed a unique friendship. We'd often run into each other in the empty halls of News HQ on Holt Street. It was a ghost town with only a small handful of us in the office, including JMo. I always appreciated the conversations we had during that odd time and respected him for his commitment to his work. He kept turning up — maybe he just needed to get out of the house, but either way I appreciated it.

That commitment says everything about the kind of person he is. Now, seeing him pour that same dedication into sharing his story is amazing. It takes serious courage to be this honest and vulnerable, to willingly put yourself out there for others. If leaning into vulnerability is the key to forming deep connections, healing and some even say success in life, then this book is truly a unique gift. It's not just about his life; it's about helping others find strength in their own truth.

Some of us need to be told how to live our lives, while others might not need direction at all. But sometimes, what we can all use is a road map, a guide to help us navigate those inevitable black spots, rough patches, and the most confronting dead ends. That's what JMo is offering in this book: a chance to learn something from his journey, to find hope, and to move on with courage.

—**Matt Shirvington**

Everyone has seen it. Most experience some form of it. But few have the courage to talk about it. We need more of this. Jonathon has the guts to go there and we can all learn from it. Bravo my friend. This is an insightful, honest read in the mental health space.

—**Karl Stefanovic**

MENTAL

AS

ANYONE

MENTAL
AS
ANYONE

A toolkit for **surviving** and **thriving** on the **chaotic** **rollercoaster** of life

JONATHON MORAN
AND **DR JODIE LOWINGER**

WILEY

First published 2025 by John Wiley & Sons Australia, Ltd

ISBN: 978-1-394-33843-6

A catalogue record for this book is available from the National Library of Australia

NATIONAL LIBRARY OF AUSTRALIA

Registered Office
John Wiley & Sons Australia, Ltd. Level 4, 600 Bourke Street, Melbourne, VIC 3000, Australia

For details of our global editorial offices, customer services, and more information about Wiley products visit us at www.wiley.com.

Wiley also publishes its books in a variety of electronic formats and by print-on-demand. Some content that appears in standard print versions of this book may not be available in other formats.

This book contains excerpts from articles published in *The Daily Telegraph/The Sunday Telegraph*, including 'Mumsy moments with Madonna', April 20, 2008; '"Hang them suckers": Anthony Mundine's offensive anti-gay rant', February 9, 2018; 'Jonathon Moran opens up about how Charlotte Dawson helped him work through his depression and how her work helped break down a stigma', February 22, 2014; 'Fiona O'Loughlin reveals booze battle while on reality TV', October 14, 2020; 'Learning love's lessons', October 11, 2009. '"I was a wreck": Michael Buble cried over news his tour sold out', February 12, 2020; 'Going bald can be a blow to your self esteem but a hair transplant could be the answer', February 17, 2014; 'Star Wars princess in a lather over souvenir hunt', June 20, 2013; 'In bed with a true princess'. This book also contains excerpts from 'Swinton up for being the bad witch', AAP, December 22, 2005.

Cover design: Paul McCarthy

Cover image: © Getty Images / Aleksandra Konoplia
Cover and about the authors photo: Christian Gilles
Dedication illustration: © Maria/Adobe Stock

Set in 11.5/13.5pt Warnock Pro by Straive, Chennai, India.

For Alex, Trish, Ali, Stu, Jude, Liv, Chloe, Grace and Bella — you are and will always be my reason.

CONTENTS

ABOUT THE AUTHORS

Jonathon Moran

Jonathon Moran is an accomplished journalist with more than two decades' experience. Moran grew up in Canberra and studied a double major in print and broadcast journalism at the University of Canberra.

He is Chief Entertainment Writer/Editor at *The Daily Telegraph* and *The Sunday Telegraph* and host of the hugely successful *Mental As Anyone* podcast, which has seen the likes of Robert Irwin, Michael Clarke, Melissa Leong, Jackie 'O' Henderson, Ben Gillies, Tanya Plibersek and Guy Sebastian share their own mental health stories. He is also a successful radio host with his national *Confidential on Nova* show on the Nova network, clocking up more than a decade on the air.

Moran is also a media and celebrity commentator, having appeared on various television programs from *The Morning Show* to *Sunrise, A Current Affair* and even *I'm a Celebrity... Get Me Out of Here!*

Dr Jodie Lowinger

Dr Jodie Lowinger is an award-winning adult, child and adolescent clinical psychologist, anxiety and mindset expert, and business strategist who drives transformation in leading CEOs and organisations while connecting at the heart with parents, educators, kids and teens.

Growing up with a mother who experienced severe anxiety, she was the caregiver from a young age. Her experiences with anxiety led to a passionate interest in equipping every adult, child and teen with the tools to manage anxiety and thrive.

Through two decades of research and practice, including her work at Harvard Medical School, as CEO and Founder of The Anxiety Clinic, and as a coach to business leaders and elite athletes, Dr Jodie created the Mind Strength Methodology—a groundbreaking methodology based on neuroscience which is transforming lives on scale. The Mind Strength Method has recently been named by *The Australian* as one of the 50 Australian Inventions Changing the World.

As an international keynote speaker, podcast host, media commentator, app creator and mother of three, Dr Jodie is passionate about sharing her voice to create a better world.

FOREWORD
GUY SEBASTIAN

'I had no idea what I was in for.'

I've known Jonathon Moran for almost all of my 21 years in the music industry. Although I never called him Jonathon — he was always JMo.

I'll be honest: at first, I didn't really trust him. Not because of who he was, but because of what he did. He's an entertainment journalist, and that job comes with its own set of challenges. Writing about the good, the bad and the ugly is part of the role. Over the years, I had opened up to journalists who I thought were friends, only to wake up and read their words, feeling like they were enemies instead.

I understood their job, but that didn't make it any easier. So, to befriend someone like JMo, I had to take down a lot of walls.

At first, when I'd see him at interviews or on red carpets, I'd think, 'Wow, he's a lot.' He's flamboyant, fun, carefree — a bit of a bitch, but a really funny one. I admired his confidence and energy, but part of me held back, wondering if he might one day hurt me too.

But he didn't. He didn't just not hurt me — he loved me. He loves me, my family, and he's always been in my corner. He's the friend who always picks up the phone when I need advice. Slowly, the walls came down, and I saw JMo for who he truly is: someone with a heart as big as his personality.

When I think of JMo, I can't help but think of others in my life who radiated that same energy — fun, outgoing, the life of the party. My brother-in-law Andy comes to mind. He was the last person we ever thought would lose his battle with mental health. We never saw it coming.

I think of Luke, an incredible musician in my band. Not long ago, we toured Europe as a duo, laughing the entire way at his wicked sense of humour. Months later, he, too, lost his battle.

Out of that heartache, my wife and I started The Sebastian Foundation. Through it, we fund Open Parachute, a youth mental health program reaching hundreds of schools across the country. It's our way of turning pain into purpose.

When I went on JMo's podcast, *Mental As Anyone*, I was excited to talk about mental health and hear his perspective. Then I learned he was writing this book. I was thrilled for him but had no idea what I was in for.

The stories within these pages — his pain, his triumph — tore my heart out. I discovered so much about my friend that I never knew. He's endured challenges that would cripple the strongest among us, yet here he is, sharing his journey with raw honesty in the hope that it might help others feel less alone.

JMo refers a few times to feeling inferior to the 'footy-heads'. But as you read this book, you'll realise, as I did, what true strength really looks like.

I've always tried to live by the metaphorical phrase, 'Never judge a book by its cover'. But ironically, this book is an exception. The title, *Mental As Anyone*, captures a universal truth: mental struggles don't discriminate. No matter how strong, fun or carefree someone appears on the outside, they might be fighting battles we can't see.

This book is a powerful reminder of that. The honesty within these pages will make you pause and reflect on the hidden struggles of those around you. It's also a testament to resilience and the importance of compassion — for others and for ourselves.

Thank you, JMo, for showing us what true courage looks like.

FOREWORD
GUS WORLAND

What does a hero look like?

With many dozens of Hollywood films now deep in the Marvel universe, we see 'hero' representation through their endless superpowers. Superhuman strength. Speed. Agility. Night vision. Energy blasts. Levitation. Heat Generation, and so many more.

But in my experience in life, heroes can be fragile too.

My hero, Angus, was my first superhero. He was smart, good-looking, successful, a good husband and father. He took his own life.

Even our greatest heroes are 'mental as anyone'.

I know how brave JMo has been to take off his 'superpower' as a leading journalist and have the courage to be vulnerable. I thank him for telling his truth, his story.

What you are doing here in this book, JMo, by sharing (very bravely) your extraordinary and confronting truths, is giving all humans the chance to be vulnerable and 'mental'.

Now, that is a true human SUPERPOWER.

This book is REAL — fair dinkum — and in JMo and Dr Jodie Lowinger's words, you have a guide for you to have the courage to commit to being so vulnerable.

Your vulnerability could help save a life — maybe your own, maybe the life of someone you love. This book is raw and honest, very much so. It comes with no judgment — some of the words are painful to read, it is confronting. But this is pain with a purpose.

We lose nine Australians every day to suicide.

Suicide is the number-one cause of death in this 'lucky country' for young men, seven out of those nine.

Enough is enough. No more!

Gotcha4Life was my start to looking after my village.

This powerful book is JMo's hug to you, his contribution to the village.

Let's work together.

1. No one wants to die.
2. People are tired and in pain but need a hero's hand.
3. And they can be hugged.

We all love someone — think for a minute and in your head picture the one person you love the most — they are 'mental as anyone'. You are 'mental as anyone'.

Read this book, and take the tools to love your superhero within.

Being a Marvel superhero and saving the world is a big task, but saving one life, one friend, one hero is 100 per cent doable in your village.

Your village will be 'mental as anyone', but let's use the tools here to make your village Gotcha4Life.

Gus xxx

CONTENT WARNING

Please note that some chapters in this book delve into subjects that some readers may find uncomfortable, such as sexual and physical abuse, trauma, drug addiction and suicide.

INTRODUCTION

Putting pen to paper or finger to keyboard is a truly cathartic thing. However, despite 20-plus years of journalistic experience, it doesn't come naturally to me to write or talk about myself. It goes against the grain of my early learnings in the trade — don't ever insert yourself into the story.

I have never been one to use big, complicated words. It is elitist and just another way of showing off. I find it wanky — pretentious, if you will. If you have to search for a word on Google or pick up a dictionary to find out what something means, then it's not a word I'm likely to use. In my experience, journalists who use obscure words are using them to show how smart they think they are rather than illustrating their actual smarts.

Of course, words can be and are beautiful, but I feel that it is more powerful to get your point across in short, sharp sentences than waffling on like an idiot. I am an entertainment journalist, not a university academic.

Each to their own, I guess; I just do not get it. Or more importantly, I am okay with using everyday words and don't feel less than for doing so. With this book, I tell my story in the most accessible way I know how, so don't expect any Shakespearean flourishes.

From the outside looking in, I have led a spectacular life. Business class travel, hobnobbing with Hollywood's biggest stars, financially stable, caviar and champagne at the ready. But the truth is that I'm just as troubled as the next person. To steal from legendary Aussie pop rock band, Mental as Anything, I am as 'mental as anyone' — or as mental as everyone, as I believe we are all a little crazy in our own way and I don't see that as a negative at all. Maybe we are born that way or maybe life does that to us, I'm not sure — but acknowledging our craziness, sitting with it even, can provide a lot of freedom, in my view.

> **I believe we are all a little crazy in our own way.**

Before we go any further, I feel I need to provide a trigger warning as parts of my story are not one for the faint-hearted. I go deep, really deep, and the content is sometimes graphic, covering topics such as sexual abuse, self-harm, violence, eating disorders, suicide and severe depression.

I've hit what I believe to be rock bottom, and I've got the scars and bruises to prove it.

I was first diagnosed with severe depression, anxiety and traits of borderline personality disorder at around 20 after my first serious suicide attempt.

I also harbour trauma from feeling rejected by my biological father.

You could say I have had a lot bottled up inside of me — a lot of trauma and a lot of joy. More than 40 years' worth to be exact. Sure, I've had plenty of counselling and psychologist appointments to process it all, but I have never truly expelled everything from my mind. I am not sure anyone does.

# # #

No matter how many different counsellors, psychologists or psychiatrists I have seen in my life — and I've seen many, trust me — a few basic themes come up every time.

Rejection, fear of rejection and not feeling like I am good enough are common features. After years of analysis, I have a pretty good grasp of why I think this way, but it does not make these thoughts go away.

I wasn't popular in high school — but am I truly that different from the footy-heads that bullied me? If so, what makes me different? In the end, hopefully, we all arrive at some point of resolution within ourselves in that we learn to accept and embrace what makes us all different because those differences can — and should, in an ideal world — unite us. Regardless of what is going on in our lives, community is vital and, as we are all 'mental as anyone', the fact we are all dealing with our own shit can undoubtedly bring us together. Plus, I want people to know you can hit the lowest of lows and still make it through to the other side. There is hope.

I have held that life view about my sexuality for as long as I can remember. I've had that view too about my mental health battles. And it is the same around drinking and taking drugs. I don't keep any of my battles a secret. (That openness may not be for everyone though, and I am most definitely not judging those who choose to deal with their demons privately.)

For me, I have just found it easier in life to be an open book. My theory is that if I have no secrets, no one can hurt me. I was never a drug addict, and I was never an alcoholic, but I did abuse both because they took away the pain of all the other shit that had been blowing around in my brain for so many years.

If I have no secrets, no one can hurt me.

Now, I choose not to drink and I choose not to take recreational drugs. I've tried everything (bar crystal meth and heroin), I'd say, or most of the party drugs anyway. I loved it at the time, it was fucking great. It made me feel a million bucks, but it was a sticking plaster to cover the shit that I was really dealing with.

People always think that because of my job I am 'somebody' — whoever or whatever somebody is. I don't say that in an arrogant sense. The reality is, I'm no more 'somebody' than the next person I meet at the supermarket. Just because I know famous people or I can afford to buy some nice things, it makes no difference when we are buried or cremated.

But my job has given me some interesting life experiences that have led me to this point, where I can share my experiences in a raw and truthful way.

In all my therapy and through all my trauma, I've learned that I am 'someone' just as much as anybody else is, and I have been blessed to see the good, the bad and the ugly in others — famous or otherwise — to learn they are 'anyone' too.

While undeniably alluring at first, and I have allowed myself to get caught up in the excitement of it all, tapping into the 'celebrity' world has affirmed these beliefs.

As a society, we idolise the rich and the famous when, in reality, we all know they are as flawed, if not more so, than the rest of us. I have seen this first-hand.

You might see yourself in my story. That's the aim of writing this book—hopefully some people will relate to the lighter side of things, while others might relate to the darker sides of my story and others the stuff in between. My whole view on how I live my life, and my contribution to society in general, is that if I am able to be honest about my truth—I am acutely aware that it is just *my* truth—if that helps just one person, then my job is done. By helping, I mean that if someone relates to my story or connects with it, hopefully it will help them feel less alone in their own life and with their own trauma and issues.

Mental As Anyone: Sharing my story

In public and in my job, I am generally known as a bubbly person, but in private, there's a lot of torment and trauma that I have not really shared with many people.

People have told me they are genuinely surprised by some of the things I've revealed on my podcast, which has the same name as this book, *Mental As Anyone*. In my podcast, and in this book, I am putting my full story on the table. Warts and all. Nothing will be held back.

Finding my voice publicly has empowered me. I feel better for speaking out because it has only affirmed my belief that we are all 'mental' in our own way. And so, I feel less alone now, which is a bloody great feeling.

All I ever really wanted in those times was to know things would be okay.

The core message I am hoping to convey by writing this book is that you can go through hell, experience all sorts of trauma and yet come out the other side a functioning human being. You may even end up happy like me. It is something I wish someone had told me when I was going through the darkest times of my life, because all I ever really wanted in those times was to know things would be okay.

Rather than going through my life in chronological order, I've separated the book into four key themes — sexuality, addiction, self-esteem, and life and death. I talk about each theme in its own part of the book, though naturally, many of the topics cross over, as you would expect them to. Life and its problems are not single-layered — there are multiple ways to look at everything, and so you'd expect that crossover when it comes to such complex issues and emotions.

In each part, I talk frankly about my personal experiences across these four broad themes, as they highlight the biggest areas in which I have struggled. In writing this book, I've discovered that my sexuality, my addictive personality, my lack of self-esteem, and my thoughts about life and death are all interconnected.

I look at sexual abuse and how being a survivor of this impacted my broader view on myself for many years. It wreaked havoc with my self-esteem and led to a pattern of self-abuse and addictions.

Losing my mum at a relatively young age is also integral to this story. She was my best friend and mentor, and her loss left a gaping emotional hole in my life that I have had to work hard to understand and accept.

Just as my issues are interconnected, I presume yours are too, which further highlights the common link we all share — while we may be battling different demons, we may be more alike than we realise.

To build on each part of the book, I've asked my friend Dr Jodie Lowinger to come on board to share some insights and practical strategies in each of these four areas that you can add to your mental health toolkit. Our hope is that you'll find some helpful tools that will support you on your mental health journey.

And remember, this book is meant to be a resource to help you and others. If you're triggered or feeling lost, don't be afraid to reach out to your loved ones and the likes of Lifeline, Beyond Blue, Kids Helpline or Gotcha4Life (see the Resources section at the back of this book for contact details).

Finally, I couldn't resist throwing in some celebrity yarns for good measure. These 'palate cleansers' separate the different parts of the book — and, I believe, highlight the fact that fame, money and celebrity don't quarantine anyone from their own struggles. We are all 'mental as anyone'.

So, strap yourselves in — here goes!

PALATE CLEANSER
Meeting Her Majesty — Madonna

It's an unwritten rule of journalism that interviewing the highest rung of celebrity talent is based not only on a journalist's level of seniority but, most importantly, the relevance and reach of the outlet you work for.

Australia's *The Sunday Telegraph* and *The Daily Telegraph* are top-tier outlets, but even so, getting access to the highest rung of talent is still not easy. Increasingly, publicists are going for easy win 'social media moments' with influencers over traditional media as it is a safe bet the subject won't be asked anything off script. Some of the big names don't even feel they need to do press interviews (which is fair) and because they speak so rarely, when they do talk, anything they say is a story — even if it is simply what they had for breakfast, what they're wearing or the car they drive.

Madonna for me was the holy grail of interviews.

The Madonna. Madonna Louise Ciccone.

I remember vividly dancing around the house in my sister's tulle skirt to her first album when I was just five. 'Borderline', 'Holiday', 'Burning Up', 'Lucky Star' — all bangers.

The thought of being in the same room as her made me weak at the knees. I don't get nervous around the celebrities I meet, and I've met many. But Madonna is top-tier royalty for me — and would be for most people. I might as well have been sitting down with the late Queen Elizabeth.

So, when Warner Music Australia's then publicity head offered me a chat with Madonna for her 2008 album, *Hard Candy*, it was like a gift from God. I felt like I'd won the Lotto. I'd lobbied for years to secure one of the slots with Madonna, and my time had finally come to meet the legend herself.

I was a year into my gig at *The Sunday Telegraph* under the editorship of Neil Breen and was determined to make it a good one. Sonia Kruger, then filing as entertainment reporter for *Today Tonight*, was the only other Australian flying to LA to take part in the junket. Kruger, of course, played Tina Sparkle in Baz Luhrmann's *Strictly Ballroom*, and I remember getting a buzz out of seeing her in her Qantas business class pyjamas on the flight.

Madonna was doing just a couple of hours of interviews for the whole world over two days. Television was one day, print the next. Osher Günsberg (then Andrew G or Andrew Günsberg) was based in LA and had a radio slot for Australia.

You know the scene in *Notting Hill* where William Thacker (Hugh Grant's character) finds himself in a film press junket with Hollywood actor, Anna Scott (played by Julia Roberts)? Comedy aside, that is exactly the awkward scenario when a journalist is sent into a room to interview an actor, singer or musician. Inevitably, in these clumsy moments, the journalist asks the talent the same questions they've been asked in the previous 15 interviews.

With Madonna, we were at a Beverly Hills institution, the Four Seasons Hotel. There was a mustering room — a hotel suite where media were able to listen to the album while refreshments were on offer. The famous American publicist Liz Rosenberg — who also looked after Cher, Michael Bublé and Stevie Nicks — was in the room. This was a big deal. Rosenberg herself was a big deal.

We exchanged polite chit-chat and, just before I went in, I was told another journalist from the junket had been kicked out of his interview for asking a stupid question. His question was something like, 'What would you (Madonna) do if you had four minutes to save the world?'

I didn't think that was too stupid a question, given '4 Minutes' (initially titled '4 Minutes to Save the World') was the lead single from the album and featured a guest spot from Justin Timberlake. Usually not one to write questions, I scratched that one off my list of back-up questions in case I lost my cool or train of thought.

Then, Rosenberg asked me what my joke was. Joke? Yes, joke.

She explained that Madonna will always ask for a joke in an interview. I wasn't sure if she was winding me up or telling the truth. My mind went blank, and I feared I would either faint, shit myself or vomit.

Funnily enough, before her interview Kruger admitted to me prior to going in that she hadn't slept for the two nights in LA and that she'd had terrible tummy troubles due to nerves. That image was one I would never forget.

Kruger, a veteran at that stage and a big-name TV star, recalled afterwards the horrifying moment she gave Madonna a gift. They were in a different room for their chat, where television reporters from whatever country would be cycled through for each interview while Madonna stayed in her place. When it was Kruger's turn, she offloaded a plush toy koala and a boomerang, holding them out to Madonna with excitement. I was told by Kruger that the singer didn't move an inch. Kruger then awkwardly placed the prized gifts on the floor at Madonna's feet and proceeded with her interview.

Even before this I never gave gifts to people I interviewed, although it was a common way for journalists to lighten the pre-interview mood. Some journalists were even on the payroll of different jewellery (or whatever luxury item) companies to try and get their product in the hands of a big name. I'd been offered that deal over the years, where a brand would offer to gift me something to wear, jewellery or something distinct, into an interview, and if the celebrity commented on it, I could gift it to them. That way, the brand gets their product in the hands of the star. I never took anyone up on the offer, despite being offered pretty good cash.

So, without a joke in my head — I can do funny things, but I have never been good at telling jokes — I made my way into Madonna's interview suite at the Four Seasons Hotel.

My adrenaline was pumping. This was my moment with a woman I grew up crushing on and admiring, and who I saw as a goddess. My biggest fear was that she wouldn't live up to my expectations — but she did, in every way.

Madonna was sat in what looked like a giant armchair in one corner, a double sofa next to her and a coffee table in the middle of the room. Her blonde hair was still wet, with two pins holding it back in a girlish bob.

She leaned forward with the sort of smile I would have expected from a doting older aunt.

'Have a piece of candy,' she said, offering me a sweet from a handbag cluttered with tissues, make-up and hair clips.

Here was the most successful female singer in history — who had built her reputation on sex, controversy and defiance — passing me a Werther's Original from her cluttered handbag.

Was I seeing a softer, more genuine side to the woman famous for her knack of marketing herself for almost three decades?

Or was it the opposite: very clever marketing? She was, after all, offering me a hard candy to begin an interview for her new album, *Hard Candy*.

Either way, it worked, and I was putty in her hands.

Despite her mumsy greeting, Madonna was dressed like the rock star she is — tight black pants, a designer black puffer jacket and yellow stilettos. A red Kabbalah bracelet dangled from her wrist.

A matching red BlackBerry rested on the chair beside her, and she played with it occasionally, scrolling through her messages. BlackBerrys were the thing back then. Around that time, Madonna had admitted that she and (now long-time ex-husband) Guy Ritchie were so reliant on the communication devices that they slept with them under their pillows.

Remember when I said that anything that someone with a certain level of fame says becomes a story? This was a cute line we could all relate to.

In my chat, Madonna admitted to feeling anxious, nervous and hopeful that people would like her then 11th studio album. Was she being humble, or was she genuinely anxious?

'Listen, I didn't know how any of it was going to turn out,' she said, sounding uncharacteristically vulnerable.

'Just because you get a bunch of talented people together doesn't mean anything good is going to come out of it, so thank God it did. I chose to work with Pharrell (Williams) and Justin (Timberlake) and Timbaland, knowing there was going to be a hip-hop, R'n'B flavour to it, but hopefully I was going to put my spin on it as well.'

Madonna explained the experience didn't come without its share of challenges and she had to be strict with her collaborators, especially in the studio.

'They're very opinionated. They're all stars in their own right. Pharrell and Justin are also vocalists, singers. They do live performances and sing on their own records, and I don't usually work with producers and songwriters who sing themselves. They had very strong opinions about how I should sing things, and usually nobody tells me how they think I should sing something, do you know what I mean? So that was a challenge.'

I was perplexed by this but also grateful to see the vulnerable side of a woman I'd idolised. She was only human, after all.

'Working with other strong-willed, strongly opinionated people is always a challenge,' she explained. 'You end up having to make compromises; sometimes people's feathers get ruffled. I said: "Listen, all you guys, you don't have three children waiting for you at home like I do. I can't work till three o'clock in the morning." So, once we got used to what everybody liked, we found a happy middle ground.'

Hard Candy debuted at number one in 37 countries. It sold millions of copies and while it received mostly favourable reviews, it wouldn't be considered one of her best. I, however, loved the album ... of course, I was always going to. *Hard Candy*, a flirtatious play on words, featured 12 stand-out pop tracks Madonna described as both sweet and dangerous.

Surprisingly, in an industry where overzealous publicists increasingly put restrictions on interviewers, nothing was off limits with Madonna. It was, however, suggested politely that Madonna wasn't keen on discussing her upcoming 50th birthday that year.

In the short time available for my interview, there was so much more to cover — so I didn't push the line.

I was there to represent her loyal Australian fans. It had been a long time since visits with her last tour — The Girlie Show World Tour in 1993, when her show at the Sydney Cricket Ground was rescheduled after being rained out. 'That was like a typhoon,' she recalled.

I remember the night vividly as along with my sister and a couple of girlfriends, we'd paid for a coach package from Canberra to Sydney to be in the audience that night, only to have to drive home in a seven-plus hour round trip due to the weather — and we did it all over again the following week.

To get her over the line for a return visit, I even offered Madonna a bed in my then Redfern apartment, telling her my housemate could bunk in with me and she could have her own room. She played along.

'Do I get my own bathroom? Are you neat and tidy? It has been a long time. It's the least I can do. Okay, all right, you've twisted my arm.'

I will never know if Rosenberg was playing with me about telling a joke to Madonna because I pre-empted any questions and jumped in with my own story that both shocked and amused the pop icon. It wasn't a joke, more of a story about my sad love life that she found amusing, once she understood it.

On a bender one night a year or so earlier, I had met this guy and he was hot, like ripped body, nice eyes, maybe a little short but he was a package I was into.

We did cocaine in the bathroom at one of the nightclubs on Oxford Street.

It was a real bender, and it was so fucking hot. In that moment of passion in the grubby bathroom stall, I asked him what he did for a living. He said he worked with the vision impaired. I thought, 'Wow, I've found a saint and a sinner in one hot guy.' We hung out a few times after that night. He'd always sleep at my place, and we saw each other on and off. I, like usual, fell head over heels for a guy I didn't really know.

One morning, we got up and it was raining so he said he couldn't go to work. 'What, blind people don't go out in the middle of the day when it is raining?' I asked.

He looked at me confused and said: 'What do you mean blind people?' And I'm like, 'Well, you said you work with the vision impaired.' And he said he did.

My view of vision impaired was working with blind people or training guide dogs or something equally important, so I couldn't understand the fact he didn't work when it rained. He then explained that he is the guy with a squeegee at the traffic lights washing your windows, receiving small change in a bucket. That was what he meant by vision impaired.

To be fair, he didn't lie. He helped people see through their windows who were vision impaired. That sad, funny story pretty much summed up my dating life for most of my adult life. And that is the joke I chose to tell Madonna. She is a queen of the highest order and was a little confused by my 'not joke', but she then seemed to find it funny and was super sweet. Perhaps she related to my story or felt sorry for me. Maybe she saw I was damaged, perhaps in a way she recognised. We are all damaged to some degree.

Thrilled I'd made it through the full interview without being turfed out, we wrapped our chat with a comment about how busy the next year will be.

Again, she showed a softer side to the character we feel we know her as.

'I am going to collapse in a heap. Then I am going to do a tour, then another film, then I am going to learn how to cook.'

Hang on, Madonna can't cook?

'No, nothing. Toast and scrambled eggs — that's all.'

It is these rare 'human' moments you aim for when you sit down with a celebrity — it makes them more relatable. In that moment, the picture of Madonna struggling to make anything more than scrambled eggs on toast was gold.

PART I

SEXUALITY

Sexuality is a complicated thing. For me, sex, sexuality and gender are intertwined, mostly due to my experiences in life — and to be honest, I find it hard to separate them as individual topics at all.

Sex can be empowering. Superstar singer Rihanna put it really well in a 2012 interview with *Elle* magazine when she said, 'Sex is power … it's empowering when you do it because you want to do it.'

Sex can also be painful — not necessarily physically, but emotionally too. That could involve having sex for the wrong reasons or being forced into a situation you're not comfortable with.

Our life experiences can help us unpack our emotions and interpretations of our sexual experiences so that we can best try and move forward. Ultimately, by seeking to understand ourselves better (and this can apply to all aspects of life), I've found we can have a more honest relationship with ourselves and our feelings around what are often complex and often triggering issues, where many of us carry a lot of baggage.

To be clear, this is my experience of sex and sexuality — and while I am a gay man, this is not a queer-specific book. My hope is that the stories are relatable to and for everyone.

1

Promiscuity

How many people have you slept with? To be honest, I'm scared to admit the real number.

The average number of sexual partners for men and women across the world is nine in a lifetime. Nine? Those figures date back to Durex's 2005 Global Sex Survey, which showed the highest scores for Turkey (an average of 14.5) and Australia (13.3). The lowest-scoring countries were India (3) and China (3.1).

For me, and I'm sure many others, that number is far from nine. I don't say that in any way to boast or brag. It is just a fact, and I wonder how many people are lying when they say they have slept with just nine people.

To guestimate accurately how many sexual partners I have had would require me to define sex. For me, that isn't full penetration, so I am classing sexual partners as people I've had sexual relations with. That means nudity, cumming — what I deem to count as sex.

Based on being sexually active from the age of 17, I would say I have had 'sex', however you define it, with more than 1000 people. That is a big call but one I suggest would be consistent with many gay males.

I base this figure on being 46. Let's say, hypothetically, I had sex with on average a different person each week from the age of 21 to 40 (20 years). That equates to 52 times 20, making the guesstimate figure 1040. That's conservative.

To be fair, I had relationships in that time, but I also would have had weeks where I had sex with multiple different people. Heck, there would have been nights in my late teens and early 20s where I had sex with multiple people in a day. I've never been diagnosed as a sex addict, but I have in the past wondered if it is something I've suffered from. It felt like an addiction.

Beats

In my early 'out' years, there were no online apps — beats were where you'd go for instant gratification. A *beat* is a place for gay men to meet for sexual acts. It is a long time since I've used one but I am told they are still a thing, although they are less popular given the rise of online dating and sex apps, which make it easier to seek out quick sex. Beats are usually public toilets, parks or other outdoor spaces. (The word beat is a parody of the 'police beat' walked by an officer of the law, or a prostitute.)

> **When I was coming out, beats were really the only option to meet other gay men outside of going to clubs.**

When I was coming out, beats were really the only option to meet other gay men outside of going to clubs. In Canberra, there were just two gay bars: The Meridian (which was literally the size of a large lounge room, with a small dance floor, a pool table, and a couple of bar stools and tables) and Heaven. While The Meridian was small, Heaven was a full-on nightclub, which was pretty intimidating, and plenty of heterosexuals liked to go there because it was a safe space to dance and have fun.

For me, I started out going to The Meridian, and as I 'earned my stripes' in the gay world and came to know myself better, I then started going to Heaven. You could talk at The Meridian, get to know people, and I guess this is where I started to really find a community of gay people to connect with outside of the instant gratification I found at beats. I'm still friends with several people from this time in my life.

I got into the beat scene a lot as a young guy, and I was always the chaser. I'd drive around Canberra's Lake Burley Griffin, where there was a route of public toilets where guys would congregate and 'get off'. (By a 'route' of public toilets I mean several toilet blocks around the lake.) Pretty much any male toilet block was a beat, though some were busier than others.

They were busiest at night-time, but I generally only went during the day. It didn't feel safe otherwise, and I didn't see the point if I couldn't see the person I was having sex with: I still needed to feel some sort of attraction to be aroused.

Beats were easy because they provided an outlet to expel that 'gay' energy and gain that validation of feeling wanted without too much emotional commitment. It was more about being wanted for me, feeling valued, than the sexual act itself. It really was that simple for me, and I truly believe my desire for instant gratification, to be loved even for just a minute, dated back to my experiences of being groomed and abused as a 13-year-old boy (which I talk about in Chapter 2). Sex was an exchange. The guys I met on the beat scene got what they wanted, and I felt a sense of validation, of being desired.

Beats are places where you can meet other young men experimenting with their sexuality. A guy would ride past on their BMX bike, curious to check out the action but unsure how to proceed. Another might be sitting in a nearby car, waiting and watching to see if they like the look of anyone who's arrived. Others would be nervous and jittery, as they looked around cautiously. The more you visited a beat, the more it felt like a bit of a study of human behaviour. It was an 'if you know, you know' kind of situation. And instinct played a big part too. I can almost smell that feeling of someone driven by sex — it is almost animal instinct, primal.

There were a few ways it would work out. One would be that you would sit in the toilet cubicle, where holes had been cut out previously. You would communicate with the guy in the next stall either by looking through the hole or by putting your foot under the cubicle partition. If you found the guy on the other side unappealing, you'd walk out. If you 'matched', so to speak, you would play with each other through the hole or meet in the cubicle together to get off.

The good thing was that you had the control to say yes or no depending on how attracted you were to the other guy. This is also why I preferred daytime beat activities as it gave me full control, or at least I felt in control in some capacity — despite hating myself for addictively frequenting them. I am sure some pretty hectic shit went down at night-time.

As well as public toilets, there were also beats in the bushland near the toilets, where guys would cruise each other, looking for a match.

It struck me how many married, so-called heterosexual men would frequent these beats. I couldn't understand it, but I also didn't overthink it as it would make me feel dirty and full of shame and guilt.

> **I don't feel that shame anymore.**

I don't feel that shame anymore. It is just a fact, something that I don't really talk about. Many gay men of my age experienced beats in some way.

Apps and websites: Gaydar and beyond

As I got older, the gay scene changed. I remember having to log on to the dating website gaydar.com on my computer. As mobile phones have become more prevalent, it has become acceptable to use online apps to meet guys. Describing beats now, it sounds pretty similar to the apps so commonly used by gays and straights today. The difference is you now scroll through your phone, swiping to arrange to hook up rather than hanging out at a beat to meet someone.

When Gaydar first appeared, you wouldn't discuss using the site even with your closest friends. Even though everyone was doing private meets, it was all a big secret no one talked about. You wouldn't put your photo on a Gaydar profile.

Nowadays, guys put their face and their arse in one profile photo and no one blinks an eye.

Experimenting and HIV

You could say I am a 'Tin Foil Gay' on the scale of how gay I actually am.

A male gay who hasn't had any sexual encounters with a female would be described as a Gold Star or Platinum Gay (a Platinum Gay is a Gold Star Gay who was born via C-section and so has never been in physical contact with a vagina). A Tin Foil Gay *has* had sex with a female. It isn't an official thing; it's more of a common term in the gay community.

The answer to the common question of whether or not someone has had sex with a female can range from 'eww' and 'yuk' (Gold Star Gay/Platinum Gay) to 'I tried it when I was younger' (Somewhere in the Middle Gay) or 'yeah, plenty' (Tin Foil Gay).

I've had sex with probably a dozen or more women over the years, mostly when I was younger. It isn't something I am proud of, nor am I ashamed of it either. It just is. You could say I experimented, which I think is a healthy thing.

Lurking in the background of my experience experimenting as a young gay man was the constant fear of contracting HIV. I came out in the back end of 1995, with the AIDS crisis having hit the community hard through the 1980s.

TV ads ran regularly when I was a kid warning about the dangers of contracting HIV and AIDS. The Grim Reaper ad campaign sits with me today whenever I think of that fear. Despite my promiscuity, which was almost something I felt I couldn't help, I was terrified of contracting HIV. Back then, it was a death sentence.

When I was 18, my mum introduced me to Hamish. A gay man who had been the year above me in high school, Hamish worked as a junior in Mum's office. Mum thought it would be good for me to have someone to talk to about the world of 'gayness'.

Hamish was absolutely gorgeous. Confident, sassy, funny, sexy. He had great skin and a lean, athletic body. Hamish exuded confidence for someone who had lived a very tough life.

Hamish came out as gay in Year 9 at Daramalan, the all-boys school I went to. His parents kicked him out of home and he moved to Sydney, where he lived on the streets for some time and worked as a male prostitute at 'the wall', a cruising street near St Vincent's Hospital that was a known spot to pick up gay hookers.

Sometime down the track, he was taken in by a gay couple that were in their 50s in Canberra. They insisted that Hamish went back to school to finish his education, after which he got a job in the public service — which is how he met my mum.

When I met Hamish, he was living in government accommodation and earning minimum wage. He was a real mentor to me — I felt I could ask him anything. He must have thought I was so naive and inexperienced. I'd never had a boyfriend, and my only real sexual experiences had occurred while being raped or when I was experimenting at beats. Despite feeling free around Hamish — I loved just hanging out with him as he danced around and regaled me with stories of his fabulously colourful life — I harboured so much shame at this time and so I never told him of my deep, dark secrets. To him, I was pretty much as innocent as Snow White.

We stayed friends for a couple of years. Sadly, not long after Hamish moved to Melbourne, he killed himself. Hamish was HIV positive, something he told me without any shame, but the pain of life got to him. He was scared of dying — back then, it was almost certainly a death sentence.

I think about Hamish often today. Gosh, it would have been wonderful if he had been alive a decade or two later to see PrEP (pre-exposure prophylaxis) become the norm. PrEP is a pill you can take to reduce your risk of contracting HIV. Many see it as a miracle pill because while you can still catch other STDs, you lower your risk of contracting HIV and, in turn, developing AIDS. And today, if someone were to contract HIV, it is no longer a death sentence. There are so many treatments that ensure people can live longer, healthier lives with a significantly lower risk of passing on HIV.

I envy the young men coming out today without that fear of sex and I think back to Hamish, wishing he was still alive today with the knowledge that people with HIV can live full and wonderful lives.

2

Experiencing Sexual Abuse

I am always second-guessing myself on this story. It is a chapter of my life that I have suppressed for so long because it is full of pain, so it is not something I ever talk about.

Logically, I know exactly what happened, but the details have gone through my mind so many times that it can be hard to distinguish between the facts and my feelings about what happened. My closest friends don't even know the full details thanks to the mountains of shame and guilt around what I did, and what I allowed to happen.

Even though I know it wasn't my fault, it is hard to separate myself from that guilt. I am sure it is the same for most survivors of sexual assault and predation.

Did I ask for it? Was I a willing participant? Did it feel good? These are questions I imagine any survivor of abuse asks themselves, which, in turn, exacerbates feelings of guilt and shame.

> **Even though I know it wasn't my fault, it is hard to separate myself from that guilt.**

The guy that sexually abused me was a man I will refer to by the pseudonym, Graham. He was about 10 years older than me. I was around 13 and would have been in Year 8 of high school when I met him. I was very clearly underage.

I would sometimes ride my bike to school and other days would catch the local bus home. I'd get the bus from Dickson shops to my house, which was about 20 minutes up the road. Dickson was a bit of a community hub and there were toilets at the bus stop.

The men's toilet block was gross, with concrete bricks, a harsh metal urinal and one tattered-looking wooden cubicle that looked to be falling apart. The walls were painted a deep, dark blue, not that you could see the paint through the writing on the walls. I can still smell the ammonia from the urinal and picture the graffiti. The toilets were cold and harsh. It wasn't a nice place. That said, I was fascinated by the sexual graffiti. I had known from an early age that I was attracted to guys, but I was hiding it; I was hopeful that through the graffiti, I would maybe meet someone my own age to share these feelings with — perhaps another teen who was exploring their sexuality. Alas, I met Graham, someone that physically and emotionally haunted me for years. To this day, he pops into my mind regularly.

The sexual graffiti said things like, 'If you want a good time, ring [phone number]' or 'Ring [phone number] for a blowy' (they were home phone numbers then, as mobile phones weren't a thing yet). There were also funny poems about sex and invitations to meet at a specific time and date for fun. Even if I didn't need to go to the toilet, I would sit there for ages reading the graffiti and thinking about who wrote it with their black permanent marker. What if I wrote something, asking to meet the reader at a certain time or date? Would someone show up? What if they did? I'd imagine the hot footy guys from my class being the ones writing on the wall, and then I'd fantasise about normal things, like a life where I could have a boyfriend. This was my *Heartstopper* (iconic British coming-of-age comedy drama book and TV series) or *Heartbreak High*.

There was a glory hole too, a few actually, set at different heights, where some mystery stranger had cut a hole to stick your dick or hand through.

A glory hole works like this. A guy in the cubicle looks through the hole while guys come and go from the urinal. When there's a match — that is, the two guys catch each other's eyes, or cocks — one of them strokes their cock or otherwise indicates that they are up for something more than just a piss, and then the other person slips into the cubicle and they get off. Or the person in the cubicle comes out and they might wank each other off at the urinal, with half an eye on the entry to the toilet in case someone comes in and busts them.

It really is that brutal.

This is all stuff I didn't understand until much later. I had no idea what a beat was at that point (refer to Chapter 1), and it was long before the arrival of online sites like Gaydar and Grindr and other 'dating' apps, where mostly closeted gay guys come together for sex.

Back then, I would just sit and read the graffiti and fantasise. Graham, a fat, blond, balding guy in his mid-20s, caught me one day. Once done sitting and reading in the cubicle, I went and waited for the next bus. I was wearing my distinct grey school uniform when Graham started talking to me. He started with light chit-chat and told me he knew what I was doing in the toilet. It shocked me. I had been found out. I was equally terrified and excited at the same time. I pretended I didn't know what he was talking about at first. Had I found a friend? Someone to share my fears and sexuality with? Could I trust him?

I couldn't. I had found someone that could see something in me that I'd thought was hidden, who somehow knew I was different from the other guys in my class, and he preyed on me for years to come. Graham told me he knew I was gay. He said I could talk to him, and that he would introduce me to other guys at Daramalan who were also gay. He told me the names of guys in my class and in the years above me that he also claimed to have 'friendships' with, but he said that I could not say anything to them as it was a secret, thus keeping the whole thing hidden. Sometimes I would look at these guys at school and wonder if he'd told them my name. I'd hope for a knowing raised eyebrow or smile, but nothing.

He preyed on me for years to come.

I was obviously extraordinarily naive, and desperate, and I stupidly thought he was legit. How else would he know their names and what grade they were in? Maintaining what I thought was an effective charade of being straight (heterosexual) and that he was mistaken, I sat and listened and asked questions. I was curious but tried to keep my cool. After a while, my bus came; I missed it deliberately and kept chatting, then got the next bus an hour or so later. I said goodbye and I remember jumping on the bus, with my Action school bus pass in my hand, full of adrenaline and excitement at the possibilities.

Some days later, Graham sprung me in the toilet. Nothing sexual—he just looked through the glory hole and saw me sitting on the seat with my school uniform on, devouring the messages in the graffiti on the walls. I went outside and again we sat and chatted. This time I confided that yes, I was indeed different, and while not saying I was gay, I admitted I was curious to find out more. Instead of getting the bus home that day, he drove me to his apartment in North Lyneham, two suburbs away from my house. It was there that he first asked me to do things I find it hard to think about.

This cycle went on for several years, until I was 17 and had a girlfriend. One day, he rang my home phone number. That number is etched in my mind. Luckily I answered, and he asked me what I'd have done if my mum or twin sister had picked up the phone and he'd told them our secret. Until this point, there had only been threats of him telling my mum or others what I'd done. It was a cat-and-mouse game that he played constantly to keep me on my toes. He clearly got a thrill out of it. The phone call was a real escalation in my mind. I'm not sure he would have followed through, and most likely he would have hung up had someone other than me answered the phone, but it had me scared shitless regardless, to the point of feeling vomit-sick, shaking-sick. I was terrified, petrified, ashamed. Guilty.

Enough was enough. The weekend after the call, I sat my mum and sister down and told them I was gay. I was extra emotional as I was on antibiotics for tonsillitis at the time. I had a fever and felt like shit, but I somehow found the courage to tell them my story and, by doing so, it took away my fear of being found out.

Ignorance, or pretending it wasn't real, had made the guilt easier to bear.

They weren't surprised at my being gay, although I did always have girlfriends and was sexually active with them. Overwhelmingly, I remember my mum expressing her guilt that I wasn't able to tell her sooner what I had been going through, what I had been feeling. I told her about Graham, how he got me to do things with him. Mum cried. We all cried. I spared her the gory details, mostly because I was embarrassed — and if I actually said out loud what had happened, it would make it more real to me. I was disgusted at myself. Ignorance, or pretending it wasn't real, had made the guilt easier to bear.

Given my mum had experimented with her sexuality when she was younger, I knew she would be okay with me being gay. It was all the other stuff that I felt bad about. The beats. Graham. The shame. Mum told me that afternoon while sitting at our 'good' dining table that she didn't care about me being gay, her only fear was that it could and most likely would be a lonely life. This was in 1995, and by this time I was in my final months of Year 12 at Hawker College in Canberra. I'd not long broken up with my girlfriend. Mum wasn't being critical of homosexuality, she just felt it was a difficult path, which it was and has been at times. Discrimination was rife still then and is today. Heck, marriage equality only became a reality in 2017, more than two decades later. She was right — my journey wasn't going to be an easy one, but I have no regrets.

By telling my mum and sister, by coming clean and coming out, I felt an immense sense of pressure easing from my body, both physically and mentally.

For all those years, Graham's abuse took many forms. He would bribe me and say if I stood there naked or masturbated, he'd cum on me. Or if I lay there naked, he'd masturbate on me. I felt worthless lying naked on the floor with this morbidly obese, fat, ugly man masturbating over me. The shame. The guilt. I can still smell his musty apartment. Afterwards I would feel filthy, worthless, disgusting, although for the briefest moment, if I was to cum, I would feel like someone wanted me and I was worth something.

This self-worth issue has long been something I've battled with. Sex from then on, and only until relatively recently, became a transactional thing. He'd give me presents to make me feel better. He'd promise to introduce me to other gay guys at my school, but he never came through. He told me he'd introduce me to famous people too. He never did.

One time, I remember vividly being at Graham's apartment. I would have been in Year 10 at the time. Yet again, I lay there as he masturbated over me. Fat. Ugly. Gross. I felt disgusting. The promise was that if I did what he wanted, he would give me a Take That book, and then he said he knew people that would introduce me to them when they came to Australia. Robbie Williams, of course, was in Take That, and I loved him. Surprisingly, Graham did give me the Take That book after he came. I rushed home. I can't remember if I walked or rode my bike, but it was cold, cold enough to make it look like smoke's coming out of your mouth.

Robbie Williams was the most famous of the Take That crew, and at one time he was a British pin-up for both women and men. I've met him several times over the years. We aren't exactly mates — I've just done the press interviews a few times with him when he's had new music or something to promote. But every time we've crossed paths, I think of Graham.

Jumping forward from my teenage self, many years later I found myself on the red carpet with Robbie Williams at Australia's big music awards, the ARIAs. It should have been such a special moment. It was. I was filming for *The Daily Telegraph* for a Facebook Live video, so it was captured on screen forever — Robbie Williams kissed me smack-bang on the lips on the red carpet during our interview. It was a career highlight moment — fun, inappropriate and naughty — and I loved all four seconds of it. The only thing was that all I could think of at the back of my mind was fat, ugly Graham masturbating over me. Robbie's kiss was a moment I celebrated on social media, but inside it ripped me apart because Graham was all I could think of.

To this day, I often think about what Graham did to me and what I allowed him to do. It fills me with a mixture of anxiety, fear, dread and embarrassment. I don't have any regrets, as what I went through and all my life experiences so far have made me the person I am today — flawed, but wiser for what I've endured. I have long had these weird pangs of guilt though, and I have asked myself over and over how it happened and why.

Was I asking for it? If it wasn't consensual, then why did I sometimes cum too? How could I orgasm? Didn't that mean I was asking for it if I was complicit in the act? Sure, I was underage, but cumming felt good. Maybe I deserved it. Was I a willing participant?

These feelings, thoughts and emotions haunt me even now.

# # #

From the moment I could get a part-time job, I did. I did a paper run as my first job, and when I was at university I worked at the department store Target in the Canberra Centre, part of the Civic town centre. First, I worked in confectionery, stocking the lolly shelves, and then I went on to work as a weekend lay-by supervisor. It was a great job; I loved it and the people I worked with. It wasn't too stressful either — I remember struggling with hangovers in the back area behind the swing doors where the packages would be stacked, and where the customers couldn't see us. We would take it in turns to serve customers.

One day, it would have been a Sunday morning, I felt rotten. I was 19 and in my first year at university studying journalism at the University of Canberra — double majoring in print and broadcast to be exact, with a cross institutional elective of German language at the Australian National University.

This one Sunday morning, I remember feeling like shit, hungover. I sat resting in a big black tub that we would use to pack customers' lay-bys in between serving people. There were just two of us working. The bell rang and I rushed out to the front, not looking at who was there. I put my log-in code into the register and looked up, and Graham was standing in front of me. I froze and I must have gone pale, then I said I would be back in a second. I walked back in shock and asked my colleague to go and serve as I commenced to vomit into a large, green garbage bin. I was totally frazzled. It wasn't alcohol-induced spew but adrenaline-pumping fear-vomit.

It brought back all the deep, dark feelings of shame and guilt.

This was the first time I'd seen Graham in a few years, and it confirmed in my mind that I hadn't been making up the shit I thought had happened to me.

# # #

While I have not seen Graham in the flesh since, I did track him down electronically.

In 2015, more than two decades after I saw him at the store counter, I confronted him. It is a moment I am proud of because it was my chance to take back control.

I saw his profile pop up on Facebook a couple of times. Each time it was a triggering thing for me, and I think understandably it caused me a lot of angst. We had several mutual friends and acquaintances on social media too. At this point in 2015, someone had set up a reunion event page for The Meridian, the local gay bar that was so much a part of so many coming out stories in Canberra. I noticed that Graham had commented, indicating he was going to attend the reunion, and so I plucked up the courage to stalk his account. In doing so, I summoned the strength to message him directly on Facebook.

He didn't even know who I was, or he said he didn't anyway.

At 9.21pm on 9 April, 2015, I wrote in a direct message:

> *Saw you come up on the Meridian reunion page. Reaching out to say you should be ashamed of yourself for taking advantage of me and no doubt countless other Daramalan boys back in the day. You're lucky you're not behind bars as what you did constitutes sexual abuse of a minor. Shame on you!*

Immediately, he responded:

> *What the fuck mate think you have the wrong person.*

My reply read as follows:

> *Nope it's you — Graham XXXXXX. I remember vividly you luring me to your place in North Lyneham and taking advantage of me on the promise of introducing me to other young gay teens when you had no intention of ever doing so. Plus, I still have the Take That book you gave me in exchange for sex — which was illegal as I was a minor. You should be behind bars and at the very least you're lucky not to be publicly shamed for what you did.*

Graham replied again:

> *If that is so I cannot remember as it was not the proudest days of my life I was a drug user and not the person I am today.*

My next response:

> *Just so you know, the pain you caused me was immense and what you did to me was horrific. Funnily enough I don't wish you pain anymore but I will never forget what you did to me. I do hope I do not bump into you at the Meridian reunion.*

Graham replied:

> *I was sexually abused as a child many time so I do if that the case and ended up in a unit to help me. I still undergo help for this drugs and sex is all I knew as a young guy being homeless from 14 it was the way of finding acceptance for the world and that I am sorry for if I so the pain I course I am sorry for and please forgive me for any pain I may have done. I did not know better.*

To that, Graham blocked me on Facebook, robbing me of any opportunity to respond further.

I wasn't angry at that point, although my heart was beating at what felt like a million miles a minute and I was full to the brim with a mixture of anxiety and adrenaline. I had finally confronted this guy.

About an hour later, as I sat there on the couch thinking about what had just transpired, another message popped up from Graham. Frustratingly, as he had blocked me, he could undo that and message me but I couldn't respond.

> *Jonathan I am sitting here with a very sunken heart — I am so sorry for any thing I course you — if this is the case. All I can say is sorry for the pain I coursed u. I can not believe I did what was done to me to you. Those years of my life a so painful for myself as well. I committed suicide*

and ended up very fucked up—please forgive me and I pray that you have healed and moved on. I pray that all have turn out better for you. Than for me.

Clearly, Graham hadn't committed suicide because he was right there messaging me. The guy couldn't even structure a basic sentence. For fuck's sake. Fuck him. 'What a loser,' I thought at that time. I was understandably angry, emotional … I could feel my pulse racing.

I don't take any pride in saying that but if I am truthful, I did want to know he had suffered in his life. That may make me a bad person and I should have felt pity for him in that moment, but right then I was full of rage. I continue to have those mixed feelings, which again brings more guilt and shame, but overwhelmingly now (today anyway) I am happy he has also experienced pain.

That was the last I heard from Graham as he again blocked me, yet again, stopping me from responding.

In the end, while I still bear the emotional scars of what he did to me, I only really feel pity for him now.

I am a survivor and I will not hide my story, in the hope that sharing it helps others.

I have come out the other side with some degree of success and, while depression is a part of my life for now and forever, I know others have not been so fortunate. For them, I will continue to speak up.

3

One, Two, Three ... Like a Virgin

The way I see it, I lost my virginity three times.

By losing my virginity, I mean I had a sexual experience where there was either penetration, or where either or both of us had an orgasm.

Obviously there is Graham, the guy who sexually abused me for years from the age of 13. We never had penetrative sex — not that that makes a difference. It was still sex, as bodily fluids were exchanged. We both came. I saw that as an exchange. I gave him what he wanted, although he never gave me what I wanted, or needed, which was to be connected with other guys around my age having the same thoughts and feelings. I do class this as sex though, and in a way it was the first time I lost my virginity — my innocence, if you will.

My first lust/love was a guy called Mark (not his real name). He was the same age as me, although we went to different schools. We had been friends since Year 4, when our shared interests were *Star Wars*, Lego and biking. As we got older, our relationship changed. It was always a friendship but, looking back, I think I fell in love with Mark, as I feel I did with other male friends over the years. I saw him as my best mate, but I also had strange feelings about him that I didn't quite understand at the time.

It didn't worry me that I had those feelings at that young age; later though, when I felt strong connections to male friends that confused me, I struggled to understand what was going on and I pushed those feelings down. It was almost like I enjoyed the pain of rejection — in the sense that I thought I fell in love with my mates — but what it really did was reinforce my sense of feeling worthlessness.

Mark happened to live just down the road from Graham's apartment, where I'd had my first non-consensual sexual experience some months earlier. Ironic, hey? I couldn't help but think of Graham and fear seeing him as I rode my bike to or from Mark's house; I was ashamed of the grubbiness of what I had been drawn into with Graham. I was happy with Mark, but I hated the constant reminder of Graham whenever we were together at Mark's place. It was a strange feeling that I internalised and didn't fully deal with at the time.

I had known I was different from an early age.

Despite going to different schools, Mark and I were inseparable. We would hang out at each other's houses after school and have sleepovers on the weekends. We would just do stupid kid things. I was about 13 at this point.

I think Mark was my first love. Maybe not love, but I definitely felt lust in a 13-year-old, innocent kind of way where you don't really know or understand what sex or sexual love is.

I certainly liked him a lot. He was tall and lanky, sort of geeky, but cool as well. He had big, brown saucer eyes, matching brown hair and a huge smile, with what I remember to be perfect white teeth. He was smart but also athletic in a runner sort of way.

We were friends, but I think we both recognised it was more than that.

I had known I was different from an early age. I was attracted to guys, while not sharing that in any way with anyone. I wasn't sure if Mark felt the same way, but I knew we were closer than what might be considered normal. What is normal anyway?

I slept at Mark's house this one night. I think it was a Saturday because we didn't have school either side. We were in his room, with a trundle bed thing on the floor next to his bed for me to sleep on. Like usual, we were up talking about anything and everything, playing games, laughing a lot. We were shooting the shit, doing whatever it is 13-year-old kids do at a sleepover. His mum, who like my mum was also a single parent, was in her room.

I'm not sure how it happened, but Mark and I started giving each other massages. He was on the floor with me at this point and everything started moving very fast. Our hands fumbled everywhere under our pyjamas. We both had hard-ons. It was sexy but awkward. Neither of us knew really what was going on, other than that it felt good. We stroked each other's penises, touched each other's chests. We didn't kiss. It was exciting and scary at the same time. Adrenalin pumped to the point I felt like I was going to explode. And then we did, we both ejaculated at the same time. I am sure neither of us even knew what an orgasm was. Up until that point previously, my sexual experience had been limited to Graham cumming on me but I had never cum. With Mark, it was full of emotion, fast, intense. Because it was my first real orgasm, it was the most intense I think I've ever had.

It shocked us both. I stood up and rushed to the toilet, where I looked down and saw white semen on my stomach. I wiped it off with toilet paper and flushed it down the loo, desperate to get rid of any evidence. It was cold that night. I walked back to the bedroom on the tips of my toes, trying not to wake his mum, if we hadn't already with our climactic orgasms. Mark was back in his bed pretending to be asleep.

Much to my devastation, that was the end of our friendship. We never spoke again, not really. Sure, we crossed paths, and I think he dated my sister for like two weeks at some point between Year 7 and Year 10, but he and I were never, ever a thing again, friendship or otherwise. Our romance, friendship — whatever you could call it — was over, and I was devastated.

I don't regret that first 'real' sexual experience — quite the opposite, in fact. In my mind it is a shame we couldn't have done it again and truly explored ourselves in a really lovely, innocent way, but it just didn't pan out that way.

I think Mark is straight and married with kids now. Who knows if he ever experimented with any other guys? I often wonder if ours would have been a great love story, if things had turned out differently. That experience cemented in me that I was gay — that I liked boys more than girls. Or did I? Was it a phase? The confusion at that age is oh so real.

#

I was never a footy or sporty type in high school, nor was I one of the popular kids.

Maybe it was because I was brought up by a single mum and my twin sister was my best friend, but I always got along with girls. I had girlfriends all through high school right up until I came out at 17, towards the end of Year 12. Dating girls became a bit of a game to me (which might seem sick from the outside looking in now). By game, I mean I was doing the normal experimenting stuff teens do anyway, but I had that added mind-fuckery of knowing I wasn't heterosexual while also not being able to experiment with guys.

It was all an act, which is painful to admit now.

One day, I got busted by my sister while I was on a trampoline with a girl. We never had sex but we played around doing other stuff. For me, it was part challenge and part trying to feel my way through what was right for me. I feel bad for not showing more respect for the girls I hung out with and, looking back, I am ashamed to admit I was manipulative. I knew how to get what I thought I wanted; I needed to be friends with these girls. I did care for them, but I was so caught up in my own little selfish web of pretending to be straight, trying desperately not to be gay (and associating those feelings with Graham) that I didn't show as much respect as I would have liked. I think I over-compensated for being gay by acting straight with girls. I'm not sure I was any different in the way I treated girls than any of the other boys my age, but I knew I wasn't into girls sexually. It was all an act, which is painful to admit now.

In Year 11, I met a girl called Sarah (not her real name). She was gorgeous and smart, and just lovely in every way. I really liked her — I loved her, even. She was best friends with another girl that dated one of my best mates, Simon. The four of us would double date, hang out on weekends, and get drunk together on the local oval near whoever's house we were hanging out at on a given night. Those were the days of house parties, as we were obviously too young to be going out to clubs (I didn't get a fake ID until I was 17 for my Year 12 formal, which was confiscated as I tried to get into the notorious Canberra club, the Private Bin).

Sarah was my first female love. I lost my heterosexual virginity to her. She was special, my stereotypical high school sweetheart.

Oh, how I wished I was straight so I could live a normal life with Sarah. She was the dream girlfriend in so many ways. She was respectful, caring, and thoughtful, and didn't expect or want me to be like the other footy-head or sporty guys. She seemed to love me for me, only the me she knew wasn't the true me. I was in hiding, scared to reveal my true self.

I don't have many regrets in life but the way I treated Sarah is one. I regret not treating her with the respect she deserved. I did love her, but I also kept my true self from her and that was wrong. Later, when I did come out, I didn't even have the balls to tell her directly — she found out through friends, which is unforgivable. In my defence, I was young and naive, and coming out as gay back then was very different to what it is now. I should have been kinder though, as she was a woman I loved.

On the day we lost our virginity together, we snuck home to her parents' house during a lunch break from Hawker College. In Canberra, Year 11 and Year 12 are referred to as 'college' and public schools are separated into high school — Years 7 to 10 — with college being the final two years of school, including your HSC equivalent. After a tormenting four years at all-boys school Daramalan, Hawker College was a chance for me to be free. I was no longer hiding, trying to fly under the radar day in and day out as I had at Daramalan. I was free to be whoever I wanted to be, and so I reinvented myself as one of the cool kids. Well, maybe not cool, but somewhere in between. I was more confident and had a core group of mates, who I am still friends with to this day. We sat somewhere between the sporty guys and the dags, and I loved life at college. I wasn't put in some pigeon-hole of being a dag just because I wasn't into sport. I felt free after years of being on the outer.

Sarah's parents weren't home. We snuck into her room and fumbled around mechanically, as if re-enacting what we had seen in the movies. Down to our undies, we rolled around on her single bed. I got out a condom that I had got my hands on from somewhere. The sex was planned, awkward and uncomfortable. It wasn't romantic, nor was it spontaneous and explosively sexy, like with Mark those few years earlier. After the deed was done, we put on our clothes and rushed back to school, where my friends teased me for having a bright red face. I was pretty chuffed with myself but also full of self-doubt and loathing, for I knew I was living a lie. I also felt I had disrespected Sarah, which she didn't deserve.

The 1997 flick *Chasing Amy* remains a favourite for me, not because of director Kevin Smith's genius filmmaking but because of what the film represented. I was 19 when it came out: I was blown away by the fact it was a mainstream movie dealing with real issues of sexuality, ones that I felt too. Apologies to anyone who hasn't seen the film by giving the plotline away... Ben Affleck plays a straight guy who falls in love with a lesbian woman, played by Joey Lauren Adams, much to the disappointment of his best friend, played by Jason Lee. The movie showed me that relationships aren't black or white; everything in life is a shade of grey. A gay man could fall in love with a straight woman. A lesbian woman could fall in love with a straight man. Life is complex, it always is.

This film made me think of the Kinsey Scale (also called the Heterosexual-Homosexual Rating Scale), which is used in research to describe the level to which a person identifies with a particular sexual orientation. Named after Alfred Kinsey, who created the scale, a zero on the list would be exclusively heterosexual and a six would be exclusively homosexual. The idea is that few people are 100 per cent either way and that we all float somewhere in between.

> **Very few people are truly one way or the other, right? Not on paper, anyway.**

The Kinsey Scale is something I have thought a lot about through life. It is something concrete to refer to with regard to sexuality. It made me feel like we are all in this together. Very few people are truly one way or the other, right? Not on paper, anyway.

Based on this, and the fact I've had sex with several women (and also bearing in mind that I am a Tin Foil Gay), I'd put myself down as a four on the Kinsey Scale. That would make me mostly gay, but it also considers that I believe sexuality is a fluid thing. Hey, I could fall in love with a woman one day, and do the whole white picket fence thing. Hell would more likely freeze over, but anything is possible.

4

Kissing Boys ... and the Occasional Girl

It is the first question people ask when they find out I'm a celebrity journalist — who is the best and who is the worst I've met? They use the words best and worst but really what they want to know is who is the most famous and who is my least favourite. It puts them one step closer to that person in a 'six degrees of separation' sense and we are all, whether we admit it or not, fascinated by celebrities.

Ultimately, what people want to hear is the gossip. Who is gay? Who is straight? What size is their penis? All the stuff you don't necessarily read in the magazines or online!

They also want to know if I've hooked up with anyone famous.

'I wish,' I tell them, which is the truth. Oh, the stories I would tell ... if only I had such tales to regale them with.

There have been a few celebrity encounters, though nothing serious. I am sharing these stories not to gloat or brag but to paint a full picture of someone trying to understand sex and sexuality.

You have a guy (yours truly) who essentially felt worthless his entire life, someone who sought risky and sometimes dangerous sex at beats for instant gratification to feel some sort of validation, in the hope that the intimate act or fleeting sense of intimacy would bring calm to someone who never saw any value in their life.

I felt that the sexual act was a way of finding peace and value in myself. If someone else thought I was worth snogging, maybe I wasn't a piece of shit, despite my inner voice telling me just that.

The fact is we idolise celebrities, be that athletes, movie stars, singers, stage entertainers or TV hosts, so they aren't just 'someone else' in this context, even though they are of course 'mental as anyone'.

That potential for brief validation for me, when I saw very little value in myself, was so much greater when someone I, or others, would deem a celebrity felt I was worthy of such an encounter or any affection at all really.

Schoolboy crush

The first almost hook up — well not even almost, you could say I was just naively hopeful — was with an actor named Lara Cox when I was in Year 7.

She wasn't famous at the time; she did dance classes with my sister after school. Lara went to Merici College, the all-girls sister school to Daramalan College, my all-boys high school in Canberra. (My sister went to a different school — she was far more disciplined than I was, and our mum felt the stricter schooling at Daramalan College would help me.)

I would often go into the big ol' CBD of Canberra and wait for my sister to finish her dance class, and then we would catch a bus home together with her friends. I had a major crush on Lara, who would later become a big TV star, playing the lead role of Anita Scheppers in *Heartbreak High* (the original, not the new Netflix version).

One afternoon, Lara sat down with me on the steps outside the dance studio and I asked her if she would be my girlfriend. We would have been around 13 years old. She was very nice about it and politely said no. I was mortified and didn't meet my sister after dance class from then on — or not for a long time, anyway. For the rest of my time at high school, every time I saw her I would blush and look away. I was embarrassed by the knockback; analysing the interactions now, I think it reinforced my own lack of self-worth.

Today, Lara and I are friends, on Facebook anyway, and we sometimes exchange messages. Recently, I reminded her of the fact I'd asked her out and she honestly couldn't remember — she laughed awkwardly, and I joked that she had turned me gay. It is funny how a moment that was so pivotal to me is something she barely remembered.

Pashing on the dance floor

Fast-forward to the mid-2000s, to a crazy night out on the tiles with one of the most famous faces from Aussie reality TV at the time. This guy was one of the ones that went on to have career longevity.

He and I met through his show and were friendly — never best mates, but friendly as we mixed in the same work circles and would bump into each other at events.

I assumed he was 100 per cent straight. Back then, the starting point was assuming people were straight. But you know how the saying goes — don't assume, it makes an ass out of u and me (ASS-U-ME).

> **Back then, the starting point was assuming people were straight.**

No expense was spared for the opening night of the 2004 *We Will Rock You* stage musical at The Star's Lyric Theatre. He was a guest, as was I, having covered the red carpet with a who's who of celebrities frocking up and rocking up for their moment in front of the camera.

Ben Elton wrote the script, while Queen's Roger Taylor and Brian May did the music. They flew in for the opening, which was a must-attend on the calendar.

Michael Falzon, who has since died tragically of cancer at the age of just 48, led the cast as Galileo, with Kate Hoolihan as Scaramouche and Annie Crummer as Killer Queen.

The production itself was great, but that wasn't the best part of the night. The afterparty was where it was at. This was back in the days where they would spend big bucks on the parties — whereas now, even though I don't drink, you're lucky to get a voucher for a complimentary glass of house wine in the foyer of a venue after a show on opening night.

It was early days for this famous fella, but he was well and truly on his way to becoming a big star and was instantly recognisable. He was hot.

He had what Gen Z would call 'rizz' (meaning charisma).

For whatever reason, he and I gravitated towards each other that night. I really have no idea why. He was hanging out with a mate of his, a very good-looking, blond-haired guy, as well as a female publicist mate, who I was also close with. Those were the days I would work hard and party even harder.

Free booze, good stuff too (French champagne), meant we were all pretty pissed — and relatively quickly. I'd done my work earlier in the night, so it was pens down (meaning nothing could be written from the goings on inside) and time to party.

It was a cracking party by any measure. Social media wasn't a thing then so people could get away with a lot more, and they did.

Back when I drank, I would drink until I passed out. It isn't something I am proud of. It is simply fact. This was one of those nights. I was dancing with the reality TV star, his mate and a publicist I knew. How we got to the subject (or how we could hear each other enough to communicate the story) I don't know, but the mate revealed that he'd had pearls inserted under the skin of his penis. That's right, three pearls just under the skin on the shaft. I was confused until he showed us there and then on the dance floor. Yep, he unzipped his jeans and pulled out his cock. The publicist and I even touched it. According to him, it felt better during sex. My mind was blown.

Being an overly sexual person then, and to a lesser extent now, I was fascinated. I'm not sure how it happened but the reality star and I then pashed hardcore in the middle of the dance floor in front of everyone. This went on all night. It was just a thing, a fun thing. And I loved every minute of it. I was in for the long haul that night, who wouldn't be? We both knew it was naughty but we didn't care. It was fun and nothing was stopping us.

(For the record, the dictionary definition of pashing is to 'kiss and caress amorously'. In Australian slang, it simply means kissing with tongue.)

We went our separate ways after a brief fumble on the way home, and I briefly allowed myself to fantasise about dating him. Maybe I wasn't as ugly, heinous and unlovable as I thought? Someone so handsome and so hot in every aspect had kissed me. Full of hangover guilt and shame the next day, I texted him — I'm always the keen one in the dating space — but he made it very clear it was a one-off. He wasn't rude, it was just a one-off fun thing. I was paranoid for a few weeks after that night someone might write something about our hot and heavy moment. It would have been a pretty juicy story — TV star pashes a guy on the dance floor at the party of the year. I also felt anxious about him thinking that I would tell someone about it — as well as the shame of people finding out I'd actually thought I'd had a chance with this guy.

In my head, I believed that if someone of his level of fame could find some form of attraction and value in me, maybe I wasn't as gross as my brain told me I was. That momentary joyful high was almost euphoric, but the counter to that, the anxious pit of paranoia and lack of self-confidence I then found myself in, was where my mind ended up taking me. It was an ugly cycle that didn't do me any favours mentally.

Afterparty antics

My ultimate celebrity pash may shock some because the guy in question is a high-profile ex footballer. It is no surprise to me, or others, that rugby league blokes like to get drunk and kiss each other for a laugh. They also get naked, dance around and do other stupid stuff. For some reason they find it funny to kiss each other.

For me, on this one night, I was happy to be at the receiving end of not one but a whole night's worth of kisses.

It was the after party following the 2011 season of *Australia's Next Top Model*, hosted by Sarah Murdoch, and with Alex Perry and the late, great Charlotte Dawson as judges.

Charlotte, who died tragically by suicide in February 2014, was a close friend and introduced me to this footballer at the bar of the Piano Room in Kings Cross.

The footballer was a star recruit for one of Australia's most elite football teams. He was a star on the rise and when Charlotte introduced me, she said he likes to kiss boys. I laughed and before I knew it, our tongues were locked as we stood at the bar in front of a whole room of celebrities, media and modelling industry people. This was pretty much at the start of the party so not everyone was as well imbibed as us, although I would have pashed him sober or drunk, any which way. He was fresh on the scene and he made a big impression that night, kissing not just me but at least one guest that I know of — she was much older. We kissed on and off all night. Call me opportunistic or maybe I am just a good kisser — I like to think the latter — but I made sure I was in the right place at all times to maximise potential interactions. It wasn't just a party pash, for me anyway, and he got into it for sure. It didn't feel like a footballer kissing just for a laugh, although I am sure that is what it was. The novelty was fun. He, by the way, is a very good kisser too.

I must have thought I was the duck's nuts, the cat that ate the cream that night, and for a brief moment, I allowed myself to fantasise about dating this guy. It was brief but hot and heavy, and lots of fun.

Intimacy for me has always been a way of feeling like I am worth something.

Intimacy for me has always been a way of feeling like I am worth something for even a small moment. In that moment, I thought that if this A-grade football player, or anyone else that was famous, could kiss me, maybe I wasn't ugly and worthless, which is an opinion I held about myself for way too long.

5

Business Potential:
Penthouse Couples

To illustrate the pecking order of where I sat on the Daramalan College 'cool meter' — and there was one — let's just say it wasn't high. Of course I had friends, but I most definitely was not cool by any stretch of the imagination.

I was the guy that would get to school at 8am, but it wasn't to study — instead, it was because there was a bit of a competition between myself and a few other guys in differing grades.

Each night, our school's security team would do the rounds, leaving yellow cards about the size of a business card in each door to prove that they had been locked and checked at the end of each day.

To make sure the yellow cards were not blowing as rubbish all around the school yard, the office manager at the front desk set up an incentive scheme for students: for every 50 cards you would collect and hand in to reception, you would get a large Mars chocolate bar. The aim was to get to school as early as possible to collect as many cards as you could. It was a big school, so it wouldn't be impossible to collect 100 cards in a day, probably more. I used to save up my cards and collect my Mars bar winnings once a week. That shows just how cool I was at school!

Several of us were in on the racket, so there was a bit of competition between us. After a while though, word got out. As a lot more students got involved in the great Mars bar bonanza, it became a waste of time getting to school early. Boys would be riding their bikes to school earlier and earlier each day to beat other kids to the cards.

Eventually, I gave up on the chocolate prize and found another way to score some loot. I had another racket going on, a dodgy racket with another guy from school. This guy was Croatian and much cooler than me. He was into soccer, which was a rung below rugby league at Daramalan College but still sporty, so definitively further up the food chain than me in the cool stakes. He was never a real friend, but a guy that I would sometimes catch the bus to and from school with. Our deal was to steal pornographic magazines from the local newsagent and sell them to horny teenage boys at school. We would steal the magazines after or before school when the newsagency was busy with morning and afternoon trade. We would then sell them for $20 or more apiece. We were in Year 8 or 9 of high school and had a captive audience of randy teenagers. We thought we were pretty cool little entrepreneurs.

I liked to steal *Penthouse Couples* because I could look at the men and the women. It was a double bonus for me as I thought it was a good cover so people wouldn't realise I was gay. While other guys in the class focused on the boobs, bums and vaginas, my attention was on the ripped abs and throbbing cocks.

Porn allowed me to escape the real world. Remember, this was before the internet and mobile phones. We had a computer at home, but I was hardly going to sit at the desk in the study right next to the kitchen watching gay porn. At least if I had a *Penthouse Couples*, I could hide that and when safe to do so, pull it out to do my business. If it was discovered, it wouldn't be a big deal cos there were women in there too.

My mum hated porn in general because she felt it degraded women. I understand that argument, but it is also a helpful way for people to find their sexuality. It certainly was a good thing for me and at that time, my desire for gratification and to allow myself to fantasise about an alternate universe where I could be sexual with a man was more important to me.

We made pretty good cash selling those magazines. We would go into the newsagent to look at the magazines, usually in our very clearly identifiable school uniforms because it was before or after school. We would pick up three magazines, with *Penthouse Couples* stashed between two others, and walk around the store. When we were out of sight of the shop assistant at the cash register, we would slip the desired magazine under our jumpers, or tuck it into our pants or shorts, and walk out. Other times we would stash the magazines in our big school bags, which were again identifiable as they were black with the school logo emblazoned in red across the front.

Stupid, right?

This went on for a couple of months — let's just say my thieving career began pretty quickly and ended just as fast. I guess you could say we became complacent. On one occasion, I went to steal some magazines with my 'business partner' from school. He got his magazines and walked safely out of the shop, while I had mine in hand, ready to stash and go. This one time I was cocky I guess, and I hadn't realised that the owners had installed a double-sided mirror at the back of the shop — they could see into the shop, but we couldn't see them in the office. I was putting a magazine under my jumper when someone shot out of the office where they had been watching me carry out my crime. The owner chased me out of the store, grabbed my arm and dragged me through the shop and into the back office. It was humiliating. I crumbled and told him everything. He rang my mum, fortunately — not the police. Of course, I lied to my mum and told her that I was just looking at the magazines and that the shop owner had incorrectly accused me of stealing, but I'm sure she knew the truth.

The porn mag racket made us cash, but that was more of a side benefit as it give me a way to escape through porn. It allowed me to discover parts of myself I didn't know how else to explore. I certainly wasn't going to ask some guy in my class on a date. Instead, I'd masturbate to ridiculously ripped, hot blokes while dreaming of being good enough.

So therein lies my career as a criminal, a dodgy crook — and not a very good one at that.

6

Faggot: Flying Under the Radar

My years at Daramalan were mostly spent trying to fly under the radar, aside from the time I had my porn mag racket going on. I was at Daramalan from 1990 to 1993 (years 7 to 10) before I went to Hawker College for my final two years of school. I wasn't brought up Catholic, and my mum didn't believe in God. I was sent to a Catholic school for discipline and structure, I guess.

I got that discipline, and a lot of bullying … so much bullying … all of the bullying. One kid bit me on the shoulder and called me out for being a faggot in the playground, which wasn't ideal or fun. I hadn't declared my sexuality to anyone, nor did I really know I was gay at that point. ('Faggot' was a generic derogatory term used for anyone that didn't fit the footy-head norm at our school.) The word is still used today, and while I generally have a 'sticks and stones may break my bones but names will never hurt me' approach to these things now, it still hurts to hear this word in particular and it immediately puts me into flight-or-flight mode.

Classrooms at Daramalan were run mostly by what anyone would consider to be fairly strict and conservative teachers (especially by today's standards), and the playground was under the control of footy-heads who tormented anyone not considered sporty or manly in their eyes.

I fitted into the 'not manly' category but always did my best to overcompensate. I was a fuller-figured Fraulein in my high school days. Daramalan was a big rugby league school, and I played tackle rugby in years 7 and 8. We weren't allowed to play tackle rugby because of the obvious risk of serious injury but we did anyway, and teachers mostly turned a blind eye. Chunky as I was, I would get the footy and run through as many of my classmates as possible, and I have to say was pretty good at it.

However, it didn't help me appear manly when in years 9 and 10, I registered for the Rock Eisteddfod Challenge dance competition. But this class, under the guidance of Mrs Angela Dunn, an amazing woman I'd describe as a saviour over those years and a friend to this day, was an escape and the only real safe place I experienced in my four years at Dara.

My sporting days ended in Year 8 when I hurt myself pretty badly in a gymnastics class. Our teacher fitted the mould of what I'd call a footy-head himself. He was buff-ish, sporty, and I used to perv at his toned, tanned legs and muscled chest in his tight shorts and t-shirt. I looked forward to those classes for that reason, until one day I was injured. We were doing a round-robin style gymnastics circuit. Not being the most naturally athletic kid, I was awkward at best. Our teacher was stationed at what would have been the most dangerous stop, a mini tramp in front of a pommel horse. On the count of three, we'd run, jump on the tramp and do a flip over the pommel horse. Only when it came to be my turn, our teacher got distracted and turned just as he was supposed to flip me over.

I was rushed to hospital after landing on my neck. Everyone heard the crack rip through the gym. There, they put a heavy-duty plastic neck brace on me. I was terrified as my cousin, who is 11 years older than me, broke his neck playing rugby at high school when he was 15. He is quadriplegic as a result.

The school called my mum. The fear in her eyes was intense as I lay there in the emergency department getting scans. I had to piss into a bottle as they rolled me on my side and we awaited the X-ray results. Luckily, it was only a small fracture. Nonetheless, it was a fracture, and I had to wear a foam neck brace for several months, which was most definitely not cool.

You can imagine how well that went down at a boys' school run by footy-heads who already had me in their sights. I might as well have drawn a target on my back. I was the butt of all sorts of jokes. They'd tap me on one shoulder then step to the other, laughing as I turned the wrong way, all the time calling me a fag and a poof. ('Poof' was another term they'd use for someone not considered sporty or super cool. Gosh, those days were fun.)

'That's so gay,' I hear kids still saying today, unaware of the pain the word can cause. It makes my skin crawl.

Flying under the radar with a great big neck brace on wasn't easy and I never really lived it down. To this day, my neck flares up regularly and the constant pain is there. I often wish we'd pursued the school for compensation over the incident given it still impacts me to this day.

Donkey Dick

I had a science teacher named Mr Lyons. Everyone would call him Donkey Dick Lyons, because, well, you can guess, he appeared to have a massive penis, and everyone knew it.

It was huge, like ginormous, and literally appeared to hang down in his pants like a horse's giant schlong, in a way that would surely have been anatomically impossible for a human. It was so big it looked like he'd had specially made pants with extra crutch space to accommodate the size. For pre-teens it provided much amusement and laughter, hence the nickname.

In the Year 7 and 8 science classroom we had these chest-height, laboratory-style desks with a tap and sink at the end, the kind you'd get out the Bunsen burner on. They were like stand-up desks with high stools. At the beginning of science class, Mr Lyons would check who had done their homework. If you hadn't done it for any reason, even if you had a legitimate excuse or a note from home, he would call you up to the front of the room and embarrass you.

I was usually pretty good, too scared to be singled out, so I nearly always did my homework. I spent high school trying my best not to stick out, making myself as small as possible to avoid attention. One time though, I was one of a group of about five of us who didn't do our homework. We were told to get down on our knees on the cold linoleum floor and hold our hands out straight, palms up. Mr Lyons then stacked textbooks on our hands. It only happened to me a couple of times, but it was a regular occurrence at the beginning of each class as he started a lesson by checking who had finished their homework. If you hadn't, he would make you kneel there for the entire class. The books felt like they weighed a kilo each and we'd end up with five or more on our puny, pubescent-boy arms. If we strained or fell back or the books would fall, he would whack us hard on our arses with a long, thick ruler as he patrolled the room.

That wouldn't happen today. In the Australian Capital Territory (ACT), corporal punishment (the use of physical force to correct or punish a child's behaviour) has since been banned.

He seemed to get a kick out of seeing us squirm uncomfortably, way more than any teacher should. Those of us not kneeling would laugh awkwardly, happy we weren't getting the attention. It was funny in a sick way.

Another time, a loud and popular, leader-of-the-pack, footy-head guy farted loudly, much to the amusement of us teenage boys. Mr Lyons' punishment was to get him to squat up on the high desk in front of everyone in the class and bounce around squatting until he farted again as a way of embarrassing him.

This love/hate back-and-forth that Mr Lyons kept going with the students equally amused and terrified us. I found his behaviour both strange and fascinating.

Who would believe us, and who would we tell if we were to complain?

Looking back now, I guess he was trying on the one hand to keep us on our toes and on the other to be funny with some of the students. It would have ingratiated him with the footy-head boys he probably fancied. I don't recall anything sexual, but it was very odd — and we all knew it. But he was the boss, and who were we to question authority? That's how it was back then. Besides, who would believe us, and who would we tell if we were to complain?

A 2007 article in *The Australian* newspaper with the headline 'College has a "sad history" of sex abuse' detailed the 'sad and tragic' history of sexual abuse at a prestigious private Catholic school in Canberra. This was Daramalan. Its school motto was *Fortes in Fide*, meaning 'strong in faith'.

At the time the story came out, then-Principal David Garratt issued a statement calling for former students to come forward with stories of abuse. I wasn't abused but I knew we weren't treated right. The late journalist, Ean Higgins, claimed to have dozens of former students who had been abused by Mr Lyons (Paul John Lyons).

I learned only recently that Mr Lyons' behaviour was something other teachers were aware of, and I've been told others had made their own complaints. My Year 7 Coordinator apparently went on the record at the time to say he and two other teachers had reported Mr Lyons in the late 1980s.

The Australian's 2007 newspaper article on Mr Lyons states: 'Mr O'Brien made it clear that until he found out about Lyons being charged in 2000, he did not have any evidence he sexually abused Daramalan boys, but that he had regarded Lyons' behaviour as inappropriate for a teacher.'

Mr O'Brien also said he believed many former students deserved 'an apology, compensation and possibly psychiatric help'. This statement made by my coordinator to the media so many years later surprised me, as I was not close with this teacher at the time and did not feel that he was a friendly ear that I could have gone to during those days.

Later, when I was around 19 or so, I would see Mr Lyons at The Meridian (one of only two gay bars in Canberra at that time). Canberra was an even smaller place back then than it is now — a little over 300 000 people lived there then. There were very few other people my age 'out' and gay. They used to refer to me, and the two or three others in my age group, as 'fresh meat' and we were hot property for a couple of years (until we got 'old' in our 20s).

But that is how I've always thought — I'm not good enough.

Mr Lyons would pop up every now and then to play pool, and I would chat with him. I was going through the stage of being as gay and out there as possible — wearing tight flared pants, platform shoes and cropped tops, with my hair dyed a different colour each week. At some point I stopped seeing Mr Lyons at the bar. He didn't come out anymore and someone told me he had been charged with sexually abusing school kids. Strangely, my first thought was, 'Why didn't he abuse me?' I felt so shit, as if I wasn't even good enough to be abused by my teacher. How fucked up is that? But that is how I've always thought — I'm not good enough — and the circumstances didn't stop those thoughts from arising.

A few years later I found out Mr Lyons had killed himself before going to trial. He was a champion shooter, and he shot himself in the head. I felt sorry for him. The same 2007 article in *The Australian* stated Mr Lyons committed suicide in 2000, days after being charged with the indecent assault of a 15-year-old student.

In a police interview, Mr Lyons admitted to taking the teenage boy and other students to his home in 1989 — when I was in Year 6 of primary school — where he would show pornographic movies, massage the students and have them masturbate him.

In a police interview he stated that his actions had plagued him.

He said he had 'stacks' of other boys stay at his home over the years and that it would usually involve him 'rubbing' them.

Good people do bad things, bad people do good things.

Funnily enough, when I think of Mr Lyons now, I feel shame for him. Also, pity. Mostly, thinking of him reminds me of being abused myself. Of course, his crimes were heinous and someone should have stopped them from happening, but I'm a shades-of-grey guy — good people do bad things, bad people do good things. Selfishly and in a fucked-up way, I still sometimes wonder why he didn't prey on me.

Surprisingly, I liked him. He was different, and maybe I related to him because he was an outsider — and, while I didn't know or understand it at the time, he was also gay and tormented inside. I just find it hard to separate the good and the bad qualities I saw in Mr Lyons.

It may seem hard to compute, but Mr Lyons was a good teacher in many ways, even if he was obviously really shit in so many others. I liked him at school. He was not your normal teacher, although despite his nickname, he dressed professionally and acted mostly like a typical, middle-aged, conservative teacher. He was strict but also kind, and I felt seen and safe within his discipline in an odd way I can't explain.

Kids looked up to him because he was clear and matter of fact. He was harsh but fair, and funny at times. He cracked jokes and made us laugh while teaching a subject that could be pretty dry at times.

I can't help but wish he had used those qualities for good, nurturing positive relationships with the boys instead of taking advantage of them. He was kinder and more nurturing than some of the other teachers. He was ugly, really ugly, with a fat squashed nose, so when I looked at him, I could tell he wouldn't have had an easy time as a school kid himself. That's why I was conflicted, even though he had also made some of my own times in the classroom tough going. While most would describe me as outgoing now, I was terrified of standing out back then. Mr Lyons taught in a dangerous way that kept me on edge, so while I mostly toed the line on homework and I didn't misbehave, he did pick on me occasionally.

Mr Lyons taught at another boys' school across town called Marist College and was also the subject of allegations there. Another Daramalan teacher was later charged and found guilty of inappropriate conversations and of touching students. He got off lightly though, I believe, fined and with a suspended sentence. He also taught at Marist before Daramalan. Obviously not all teachers at Catholic Schools are abusers, but I have absolutely no doubt from my lived experience that countless cases of abuse were covered up over the years. It has been widely reported that with

Catholic brothers, if they did something 'wrong', they would be sent to another Parish. That seemed to be the formula — they were given a glowing reference and sent on their way to another school, where they became someone else's problem. Does it happen today? I am not sure — but with sexual abuse cases consistently an issue, I would suspect so.

Principal Garratt wasn't in the job when Mr Lyons' abuses took place. Father Denis Uhr was principal from 1989 to 1997 and Father Robert Irwin for the five years before him. Garratt did, however, apologise publicly and express sympathy to the victims and their families. He also encouraged former students in need of help to contact the school.

Allegations of child sexual abuse against the late Cardinal George Pell many years later brought up a lot for me about this part of my story. He was Australia's highest representative in the Catholic Church as one of the then-Pope's top aides. Cardinal Pell, who died at the age of 81 in 2023, was convicted and spent more than 400 days in prison before a full bench of the High Court overturned his convictions. In January 2025, it was reported that two men had been granted compensation by the federal government's National Redress Scheme for the abuse they accepted the men endured from Cardinal Pell dating back to the 1970s, when he was a young priest in Ballarat.

Obviously, it reminded me again of my own experiences of sexual abuse due to Graham, but it also made me think about the cases we've never heard about. Just how many people were abused in school situations over the years, particularly in religious institutions?

It may sound jarring, but I feel as if Mr Lyons was a scapegoat in a way — if he is blamed for the abuse, no one will look at all the other abusers who have gone through the ranks of the school. That's not to take away from the hideous things he did — it just was and is complex. It makes me think of *The Keepers*, the award-winning Netflix documentary series about nun Sister Cathy Cesnik, who was murdered after asking questions about the suspected sexual abuse of female students at Baltimore's Archbishop Keough High School. In my opinion, the Catholic Church here and abroad has deliberately and systematically covered up countless cases of abuse to protect the religious institution. While I wasn't abused there, I didn't get through unscathed.

My four years at Daramalan — a testosterone-fuelled, angry, boys' school — were mostly horrific. It was not a happy time. I have a handful of mates I am still friends with from those days — and a teacher, Mrs Dunn. But mostly those days and years were filled with fear, and I have very few fond memories of that time.

Footy-heads ruled the roost. Every day was a struggle to fly under the radar from the bullies and the teachers who enabled them to maintain the status quo.

7

Conflicting Views

Someone saying they don't mind if a person is gay so long as they don't 'do it' in front of them is a curious thing. Offensive, even.

It is something I've heard so many times over the years I couldn't honestly count.

Can you imagine someone saying, 'I don't mind if you have blond hair, so long as you don't have blond hair in front of me.' Alright then, I'll just scalp myself, shall I?

What does 'doing it' in front of them even mean, anyway?

Is holding hands as a gay couple 'doing it'? Kissing a person of the same sex on the cheek? Kissing them on the lips, even? Hugging someone of the same gender? Or do they mean actual carnal knowledge... fucking?

I suppose my belief system around religion and politics is similar on the surface — who am I to judge someone based on their faith or what political party they align with? If someone doesn't force their opinion on me or hurt anyone in the process of following their beliefs, I am fine. Be as you will.

Who am I to judge someone based on their faith or what political party they align with?

But the 'don't do it in front of me' argument goes further as it is a heteronormative way of saying someone is 'okay' with a person's sexuality, so long as they are not exposed to it in any way.

But, wow, fuck that. Are they really cool with it? The answer is absolutely not — it is inherent in the wording. They want to distance themselves; they don't want to have anything to do with anyone's sexuality unless it is the societal norm (heterosexuality).

This was the stance of legendary Indigenous Australian rugby league personality and boxer Anthony Mundine when we spent time together in South Africa before and after he went into the 'jungle' to compete on the popular reality show, *I'm a Celebrity… Get Me Out of Here!*

He is known for being outspoken on many things. In fact, I truly believe he makes certain points just for impact — whether he actually believes what he's saying, or not.

That doesn't make it okay, even if it made for great television. And perhaps it has kept him in the spotlight for too long.

Mundine has been vocal about his Islamic faith. I am totally fine with that. Why wouldn't I be? He can even 'do it' in front of me, despite the fact I oscillate between agnostic and atheist beliefs. Where I struggle, is when someone with a large platform, such as Mundine, shares these views in a way that can cause real harm and pain to people.

Regarding TV drama *Redfern Now*, which was critically acclaimed, Mundine had previously come under fire for homophobic comments he made about the series featuring a gay character. At the time, he wrote on Facebook: 'That ain't in our (Aboriginal) culture and our ancestors would have there (sic) head for it! Like my dad told me, God made Adam and Eve not Adam and Steve.'

But what would he say to a struggling teen in a remote Indigenous community that is suicidal because they feel lost within themselves around their sexuality or gender?

I don't need to tell you what he would say because he shares his views so openly to anyone who will listen. It makes for a good headline too, so he gets a lot of airtime.

But the irony of a homophobe sitting there during an interview and telling me, an out homosexual journalist, that being gay is an abomination, is not lost on me. He has also spoken against contraception and abortion.

I see Mundine as a walking contradiction, which is why I had to share this story. And while I found the whole thing very unsettling at the time and I struggled with being a part of amplifying his views, I have always felt my job as a journalist is not to censor.

⚛ ⚛ ⚛

Our interview ran in *The Daily Telegraph* and online on 9 February, 2018 and, for context, same-sex marriage had been approved just a few months earlier after what was a pretty difficult time for the queer community and its allies.

The headline of that incendiary interview was, 'Hang them suckers': Anthony Mundine's offensive anti-gay rant.

During the interview, he appeared to support the death penalty for gays, saying it was the only way for society to deter homosexuality. He also claimed homosexuality was banned in Aboriginal culture.

Mundine has stated on record that he believes in polygamy, and that he is entitled to multiple wives. It is rumoured that he is the father of seven children with four different women.

It was and remains fascinating to me that someone can have such relaxed views around sex and relationships when it comes to themself, but when it comes to the way others choose to live their lives, including in terms of sex and their sexuality, they become so judgemental. That disconnection is extraordinary to me.

In the interview, he asked, 'If we were to live in a society, just like in Aboriginal culture, that homosexuality is forbidden and you do it and the consequences are capital punishment or death, you think you are going to do it? Or think twice about doing it?'

There is no record I can find of homosexuality being punishable by death in Indigenous Australian culture.

Mundine then added the same fate should befall paedophiles. 'Hang them suckers,' he said.

Asked to clarify if he meant gays should be executed, he replied: 'The paedophiles mainly, hang them suckers and let's see if they have the balls to do it again.'

So then was he likening homosexuality to paedophilia? Or putting us all in the same box?

'If you are going to be gay, do it behind closed doors, that is how it used to be,' he told me in the interview.

'I talk the truth... I don't care if you are gay or not, it doesn't worry me because the creator will judge you later.'

Thank you, Anthony, but I don't need your approval. I am doing just fine without it.

Mundine later claimed his comments were 'twisted' or misquoted, although it all played out in the interview that ran online and was filmed for video. You can find it on *The Daily Telegraph* website (dailytelegraph.com.au) if you want to decide for yourself.

I am grateful that *The Daily Telegraph* also published a subsequent opinion piece I wrote, in which I explained that I had found Mundine's comments hurtful. While I've been used to hearing slurs about my sexuality my whole life, these felt like a cricket bat to the head. It was difficult because Mundine was so fervent in his beliefs and yet he clearly knew I was a gay man sitting in front of him.

Conversely, Mundine has done a lot of good during his life. He's worked with various charities, and there is much he has said about Indigenous Australians that I agree with. Not that he needs my approval or commentary, but I genuinely believe he could be a real leader in that area.

I am all for the free exchange of opinions. It is important to hear and try to understand different perspectives, even when those opinions differ from yours. Remember, opinions are like arseholes — we've all got one.

With this in mind, while I don't like or agree with certain political agendas — I consider myself I guess to be more centre left — it is important that everyone's views are reflected in any arena, even if only to show how ridiculous or damaging they might be.

The world has sadly come to a place where we can't discuss any issues, even things that aren't controversial in any way, for fear of being cancelled. If we can't talk about almond versus macadamia milk, how can we dissect real issues?

In listening to others, whether you agree or not, we are able to better understand the world we live in and the challenges that other people face. While some will never shift their opinion, many will, so it's helpful to make space for a middle ground on some issues.

I grew up in a house where my mum educated me on her beliefs. As an adult, I've taken that information and learned to better understand why I feel the same way, if indeed I agree. And, to be fair, there were some things we would disagree on. That is okay, and it wouldn't lessen her viewpoints in any way.

Without opinions and society evolving over time on fundamental issues like gay rights, abortion and the right to vote, we wouldn't be where we are now. Obviously, that comes with new generations seeing the world differently too, but they see it differently because they are free to constructively fight for the things they believe in.

I may describe Mundine's views as extreme, but they have been a reality of my life as a gay man for as long as I can remember. I wish they were seen as extreme but, unfortunately, I fear they are not that uncommon at all.

In fact, over recent months there have been several times I've been called a 'faggot' walking down the street here in Sydney. That is the world we live in today and it isn't always one I feel safe in.

8

Discrimination

'Have you engaged in male-to-male anal sexual intercourse?' This is a question I had to answer recently when applying for life insurance.

I was asked because I admitted to being a sexually active gay man. Discrimination is part of daily life when you are gay, openly or not. I'm used to it as a 42-year-old who has been out since the age of 17.

Sometimes discrimination is subtle, sometimes it is in your face.

The horrific events of the 2016 Orlando gay nightclub shooting really sparked this thought in my mind. There were 49 people killed and 53 others injured in the mass shooting inside Pulse nightclub. That was a hate crime. Initially, it was thought to be a gay hate crime. Instead, it was later found to have been a terrorist act in retaliation for the killing of an Iraqi militant a month earlier.

For me, it will always be a gay hate crime because of where and how it happened. I don't think it was a mistake that shots were fired in a gay nightclub. Reading people's comments and posts on Orlando really affected me in a way I wasn't prepared for at the time, and made me reflect on my own life as a gay man.

I once read a piece explaining how being openly gay comes with fear, the pressure of having to check if it's safe to be who you are, to be affectionate with someone you care about. Even though I've been out for more than 20 years, I still look over my shoulder to see if it is safe if I want to kiss or hold hands with my partner.

I can't help but feel jealous of the freedom straight people have to engage in such simple, carefree, public displays of affection. It is this subtle, everyday discrimination that my mum was referring to when I came out and she said it was going to be a hard path. It was exactly what she was warning me about and what she feared I would experience.

This has changed a lot since marriage equality was passed, but it is still a subconscious thing for me to ask myself, 'Is this a safe space?'

It is an oppressive feeling, almost like a huge physical weight on my shoulders, and it's a feeling I've only recently come to understand.

I feel it every day. It is an oppressive feeling, almost like a huge physical weight on my shoulders, and it's a feeling I've only recently come to understand.

When I first came out at 17 and started going to clubs at 18, I was an in-your-face gay. I'd wear tight pants, a crop top and sometimes platform shoes. I felt that if I was so out there, loud and proud and visibly so, it would force change and encourage more acceptance in society. Nowadays, I am an everyday gay — probably more on the daggy side than cool but nonetheless much more relaxed and not trying to fit into any mould of what a gay person feels they should be.

The oppressive feeling is mostly a subconscious thing — a mixture of shame, embarrassment and fear that has crept into almost every part of my life without my realising. It arises in the most normal of experiences, leading me to question myself. I don't think these things openly, they are just thoughts that exist at the back of my mind. When I pick out a supermarket bag, is it too colourful, will it stand out? Is my t-shirt too 'out there'? Is my haircut gay?

So, when I was sorting out my life insurance, perhaps I shouldn't have been surprised by the discriminatory line of questioning. But it hurt me to the core and made me feel that guilt, shame and embarrassment I was all too familiar with. It is a sickening feeling, but it is ingrained inside me.

I was sat with a financial advisor, who was filling in an online automated form for total and permanent disability and life insurance — yes, I'm getting old — and I was being asked standard questions about all aspects of my health. I felt slightly uncomfortable when asked about my mental health and having to disclose that I've been on antidepressants for more than 20 years.

Then the questions came to my relationship status and the question about male-to-male anal sexual intercourse. Upon answering yes, I was asked to provide further information.

Further information? Can you believe that? What did they want to know? I'm a top, if that is what they wanted to know. I use protection and, yeah, sometimes I have sniffed a bit of amyl. I'm probably more vanilla in bed than many people; I would have said I was pretty normal in the bedroom.

Under a section called Lifestyle Activities, I was asked: 'We'll need more information on this and some of the questions can be quite personal. We can continue now or we could send you a form. Which would you prefer?'

I chose to continue on the spot. I didn't really have a choice — I wanted to get it done as quickly as possible as I needed to sort this for my mortgage and other financials. Plus, why not? I've got nothing to hide.

The questions continued:

- Am I in a mutually monogamous relationship?
- How many partners have I had over the last 12 months and over the last three years?
- Do I always use a condom?
- Please provide dates and results when you were last tested for HIV antibodies, hepatitis B, hepatitis C, other sexually transmitted diseases (STDs).

These are not the sort of questions they would have asked my heterosexual twin sister. She's considered safe purely by virtue of the fact she doesn't have sexual relations with people of the same sex.

Sure, this might have been an appropriate line of questioning in the middle of the AIDS pandemic but now, surely not.

But still I'm asked the questions, even though, according to recent reports, roughly 35 per cent of new HIV infections are not attributed to men who have sex with men. In other words, people in the heterosexual community that practise unsafe sex also have a significant risk of HIV infection. And speaking for myself, I have always played it safe. The 1980s and 90s Grim Reaper AIDS campaign is forever entrenched in my mind.

Things are changing, but I currently can't give blood through the Red Cross if I engage in 'at risk' sexual activity over the previous three months. 'At risk' activity includes sex with another man if you were assigned male at birth. I am in a healthy, monogamous relationship with a man, so that rules me out.

Surely testing has changed since the 1980s and anyone receiving blood from the Red Cross or other suppliers shouldn't need me to disclose whether or not I am a practising homosexual. Alas, no, if you are gay, you cannot give blood to this day. The irony is, if I lied and said I was straight, I could give blood.

I wanted to storm out of the meeting, but I was told these are questions all insurers ask. So if I wanted insurance, I had to put up with the discrimination. I have no idea how my answers would influence my premium — whether or not answering yes to being gay and having sex with guys made my premium rise.

But I was and still am outraged — that as a gay man I'm subjected to these questions. It's not okay that I, and others, are made to feel this way.

Your TOOLKIT for SEXUALITY
DR JODIE LOWINGER

Sexuality is multifaceted. It includes your *gender identity*, or your internal sense of being male, female or non-binary. For some people, their gender identity aligns with the sex they were assigned at birth (cisgender), while for others, it doesn't (transgender, non-binary, or gender-fluid). For those who identify outside the gender binary, life can feel like a constant push-pull between authenticity and societal pressures. Navigating that tension can be exhausting and challenging.

Sexuality also includes your *sexual orientation* — who you're attracted to physically and emotionally. Your sexual orientation is a deeply personal aspect of your identity and can include attraction to people of the opposite gender, the same gender, multiple genders or no gender at all. Sexual orientation is often categorised into broad labels, though it exists on a spectrum and can vary widely among individuals, with some preferring not to label it at all as they feel that no label quite fits. Some people identify as *heterosexual* (straight), where they are attracted to people of the opposite gender; *homosexual* like JMo (gay or lesbian), where they are attracted to people of the same gender; *bisexual*, where they are attracted to people of more than one gender; *pansexual*, where they are attracted to people regardless of their gender; *asexual*, where they experience little or no sexual attraction to others; or *queer*, a broad term encompassing a variety of identities. For some, their experience of sexuality is fixed and unchanging. For others, it's fluid, shifting and evolving over time.

Your sexuality is also about your *sexual behaviour* — what you do or don't do when it comes to sexual activity. Your sexual behaviour may not always align with your sexual orientation. For example, someone might identify as heterosexual but have same-sex experiences, or vice versa. JMo has had sex with men and women but identifies as gay, for example. Or someone might be attracted to multiple genders but prefer one over the other in practice. That doesn't make their identity any less valid.

Some clients I've worked with have worried about whether their behaviour 'matches' their label. However, the thing about labels is that they're tools to help you understand yourself, not boxes to trap you in. They're there if you need them, but you're not obligated to pin yourself down to a particular label, especially if your feelings or experiences don't fit neatly into a box.

Sexuality can evolve throughout your life, influenced by your experiences, environment, culture and biology. For example, someone might decide to come out about their attraction to a different gender later in life, or a person who once identified as asexual might experience sexual attraction in a new way after a significant relationship. This can feel liberating or confusing, depending on the stage you're at in your journey. Your time in history can also play a part. JMo came out at a time when HIV/AIDS was a serious issue and homosexuality had not long been legalised in Australia. And today, for queer people, conservatism is on the rise, which can impact someone's journey.

As a clinical psychologist at The Anxiety Clinic, I've spent years helping people explore, understand and embrace their sexuality. In this section, we're going to unpack what sexuality is, explore the challenges you might face, and identify ways you can support yourself or others.

Becoming secure in your sexuality

Sexuality doesn't exist in a vacuum — it's connected to your mental health, self-esteem and overall sense of wellbeing. When you feel confident and secure in your sexual identity, it can boost your mental health and strengthen your relationships. But when there's shame, confusion or conflict, it can contribute to anxiety, depression or feelings of isolation.

One of the biggest challenges I see when working with people who are struggling with their sexuality is the impact of society's expectations. You might be feeling different or sensing that you don't quite fit in with the people around you. Feeling different can be isolating, but it's also a sign that you're tuning into your authentic self. And while it might not feel like it now, that's a good thing.

If you think you are experiencing an identity crisis, where you may be questioning who you really are, this can feel overwhelming, especially if there's a sense that your feelings don't match society's expectations. Questioning your sexuality might also bring up a fear of rejection, being judged or not knowing where you fit in. However, asking these questions means you're exploring and responding to your needs at various stages in your life. You are building awareness around what is going on for you and the underlying reasons for this, and responding with appropriate action. You don't have to have all the answers right now. Give yourself the time and space to figure it out at your own pace. For JMo, that was at age 17, but others might come out later in life.

Culture can also play a large role in shaping how we see and express our sexuality. For some people, cultural or religious beliefs create a sense of safety and clarity around their sexual identity. For others, these same influences can lead to confusion or conflict. For example, some people may struggle with reconciling their own feelings with the respect they feel for their family, community or faith.

Many people carry the weight of shame around their sexuality. This might be due to early life experiences or societal messaging. You might feel guilty about your desires or your sexual orientation — or even your lack of interest in sex. Keep in mind that shame thrives in silence. Talking about these feelings with a trusted friend, partner or therapist can help release some of those feelings of shame.

Then there's the experience of coming out — one of the most vulnerable, and potentially liberating, experiences a person can go through. But it's also deeply personal. For some, it's a joyful moment of self-expression, while for others, it's an experience filled with fear — especially if safety or acceptance isn't guaranteed.

One of the hardest challenges is rejection or discrimination. Whether it's rejection from family, discrimination at work or judgement from strangers, it hurts. And it's okay to grieve the loss of the support and/or respect of others when you feel rejected. But don't forget there's a whole community of people out there who will celebrate and support you for exactly who you are.

Experiences of trauma, like abuse or coercion, can be tremendously challenging and deeply impact how sexuality is experienced. For those who've experienced sexual abuse or grooming, sexuality can feel tangled up in pain, fear and confusion. You might wonder if your feelings or preferences are 'real' or a product of what happened to you. It can take time to rebuild trust, safety, and a sense of control over your body and choices. Therapy can be an invaluable resource here, offering a safe space to process and reclaim your sense of self. The right evidence-based psychological treatments can be highly effective in liberating you from the impacts of trauma. Sexual trauma can often deeply impact your sense of self-worth, but no matter how hard it might feel, you are worthy of seeking out the help you need. The key is to not suffer in silence when healing from trauma is well and truly possible.

A toolkit for navigating sexuality

Exploring your sexuality or navigating the aftermath of sexual trauma can be challenging but there are proven ways to help. Whether you're in a place of certainty, confusion, or somewhere in between, take time for self-reflection. Be kind to yourself.

Wherever you are in your journey, you're not alone. If it feels messy, complicated or daunting, remember that you're not broken or weird — you're human. Whether you're wrestling with feelings of shame, trying to make sense of your past or figuring out where you fit in the spectrum of human sexuality, this toolkit of things you can try, tweak or take at your own pace is here to help.

If you're in the middle of questioning or discovering something new about your sexuality, it can bring up some deep anxiety or life challenges. Working through these experiences with a skilled mental health professional can be tremendously helpful to manage these challenges.

A fundamental tool is self-compassion. *Self-compassion* means treating yourself like you would a close friend — offering kindness instead of criticism, understanding instead of blame or judgement. Ways to practise self-compassion include acknowledging your feelings. It's okay to feel confused, angry or scared. Give yourself permission to sit with those emotions without rushing to 'fix' them.

Practise challenging your inner critic. When that voice in your head says, 'You're broken' or 'This is your fault,' get some distance from that voice. Think of it like a bully trying to boss you around. Instead of directly battling your inner critic, take a step back and observe it with curiosity rather than judgement. Treat those negative thoughts like background noise; acknowledge them, but don't engage with them. You might even give your inner critic a name to create psychological distance, recognising that it's just a voice in your mind, not the ultimate truth. Then, gently redirect your focus to what truly matters: your values, the effort you're putting in and the actions within your control. If something is beyond your influence, practise acceptance, allowing it to be there without letting it take over. This shift helps you move forward with clarity and purpose, rather than getting stuck in self-doubt.

Write a letter to yourself. Start by imagining you're writing to a friend who's going through exactly what you are. What would you say to comfort and encourage them? Now, say those things in a letter to yourself.

See if you can practise naming and normalising your feelings. It's not weak to feel, it's human to feel — and allowing yourself to name your feelings is a step towards processing and accepting them, and taking helpful action. Psychologists call this *affect labelling*, and research shows it can help reduce the intensity of emotions. When you name a feeling, like sadness, fear or shame, it activates the thinking part of your brain and helps you process it more effectively. Emotions aren't 'good' or 'bad', they're just signals. Naming your emotions gives you a chance to understand and respond to your own needs rather than hating the way you feel or trying to block and suppress your emotions, which can make you feel worse.

Learn mindfulness and practise grounding techniques. For example, practise placing your feet firmly on the ground and focusing on the sensations of stability. Try the '5-4-3-2-1 technique': see if you can name five things you can see, four things you can touch, three things you can hear, two things you can smell, and one thing you can taste. Spend five minutes focusing on your breath, noticing the rise and fall of your chest. If your mind wanders, that's okay — just gently bring it back to the present moment.

Try using a journal and writing down what you're feeling right now. Where do you feel it in your body? It might be in your chest, in your stomach or somewhere else. Can you respond to those feelings with kindness and compassion?

When life feels heavy, sometimes the best thing you can do is pause, breathe, and focus on self-care. Some simple self-care strategies include moving your body — go for a walk, dance in your kitchen or try yoga. Movement releases tension and boosts mood. Surround yourself with things that make you feel good, whether it's cozy blankets, candles or a playlist of your favourite songs.

Start to explore and get curious about your identity. Instead of judging your feelings, approach them with curiosity. Ask yourself questions like 'What feels authentic to me?' 'What labels (if any) feel right, and why?' and 'What do I need to feel safe and comfortable in my relationships?'

It can be helpful to build a supportive community where you can be your authentic self, or to explore your feelings in therapy and through journalling. Seek strategies for self-acceptance to replace shame with understanding. No one should have to navigate this stuff alone. Whether it's friends, family or a therapist, having people in your corner makes all the difference. Online or in-person LGBTQIA+ groups can provide a sense of belonging and connection. Look for stories, role models or people who resonate with you. Seeing others navigate similar experiences can remind you that you're not alone, and that your path is valid.

See if you can practise patience. It's okay to not have it all figured out. Give yourself permission and time to reflect and evolve.

There's no right or wrong in coming out. If coming out or opening up feels overwhelming, allow yourself to start small and begin with someone you trust deeply. Not everyone will understand or support you, and that's on them, not you. Protect your energy by focusing on relationships that feel safe and affirming.

Reframe shame into strength. Shame has a way of making us feel small, broken and unworthy. But as mentioned, shame can only thrive in secrecy. When you bring it into the light by talking about it, writing about it or challenging it, shame starts to lose its power. Strategies to combat shame might involve sharing your feelings with someone you trust. Sometimes, just hearing someone say, 'That makes sense' can be a game changer. Remember, you're not defined by what happened to you or by anyone else's expectations. You are enough.

If you've experienced sexual abuse or grooming, your sense of self, especially your sexual identity, might feel tangled up in those experiences. It's not uncommon to question your feelings or even blame yourself. It's important to stand up to that bullying inner voice of self-blame. Seek support from a mental health professional trained in trauma-informed therapy. In my experience with my clients, the right scientifically supported therapy can liberate people from the shackles of trauma, helping individuals to process painful life experiences and get on with the life that they want to live.

Progress isn't always linear, and that's okay. See if you can change any self-critical habits with positive self-talk. Write down one thing you're proud of each day, no matter how small. Remind yourself of everything you've overcome to get to this point. You're stronger than you realise.

Navigating sexuality, trauma and identity is hard work but it's also deeply meaningful. Every step you take towards understanding yourself, healing your wounds and embracing who you are is a step towards a deeper sense of fulfilment. Remember that you don't have to do this perfectly, and you don't have to do it alone. Lean on your support system. And most importantly, keep showing up for yourself. You're worth it.

How to help a loved one who is questioning their sexuality

If someone you care about is navigating the journey of questioning their sexuality, power to you for wanting to show up for them. Not everyone has the willingness to lean into a conversation that can feel vulnerable. The fact that you're here, reading this, means you're already on the right track. Here, I talk about how you can support them in a way that's compassionate, respectful and grounded in understanding.

Remember, you don't need to have all the answers, but you can be a steady, safe presence in their lives as they figure things out for themselves.

Create a safe space. Your loved one might be feeling exposed, anxious or unsure of how you'll react. Coming to you with their feelings may be a big deal for them. Your job is to honour that trust by creating a safe space where they feel seen and heard. Listen first. Let them share their thoughts without interruption. Resist the urge to jump in with advice or assumptions. Validate their feelings. A simple, 'That must be really hard' or 'Thank you for trusting me with this' can go a long way. Most importantly, avoid judgement. Even if you're surprised by what they share, keep your reactions neutral and supportive. They're already grappling with enough uncertainty. Keep in mind that this isn't about you having the 'right' response. It's about meeting your loved one where they are, without rushing them towards a conclusion. They might be questioning, exploring or just reflecting. Some things you might consider saying are, 'It's okay to not have all the answers right now,' 'Your feelings are valid, no matter what they are' or 'I'm here for you, no matter what.'

It can be helpful to educate yourself. You don't have to be an expert to be supportive, but taking the time to educate yourself shows your loved one that you care and are dedicated to learning more. Learning LGBTQIA+ terminology may be a helpful place to start. Understanding these concepts can help you avoid unintentionally saying something dismissive or incorrect. Reading or listening to others' experiences can also give you insight into what your loved one might be feeling. Seek out resources for family members who will offer excellent tools and tips for supporting someone questioning their sexuality.

If your loved one is open to talking, asking thoughtful, non-judgemental questions can help them feel supported and understood. The key is to keep the focus on them, their feelings, their experiences and their journey. Questions to ask might include, 'How are you feeling about all of this?', 'Would it help to talk things through, or would you rather I just listen?' or 'How can I be of the best help right now?' Avoid overloading them with questions — remember, it's not an interrogation. Give them space to share what they're comfortable with.

Be cautious of not jumping to conclusions about their sexual orientation, preferences or identity, and respect the pace of their progress. This journey is theirs. Some people need time to figure out how they feel before they're ready to talk about it, and that's okay. Your job isn't to rush them to a 'resolution'; it's to walk alongside them at whatever pace feels right for them. Practise being patient. If they're not ready to talk, let them know the door is always open when they are. And acknowledge and celebrate small steps, even if they share just a tiny piece of information.

It's essential to check your own biases. We all carry biases, whether we're aware of them or not. Maybe it's something you learned growing up, or maybe it's tied to your own experiences with sexuality. Whatever it is, it's important to recognise those biases and set them aside. Questions to reflect on might be 'Do I have any assumptions about what my loved one's journey "should" look like?', 'Am I projecting my own fears or beliefs onto their experience?' or 'How can I create space for their truth, even if it's different from my own beliefs?'

Your loved one doesn't need you to 'fix' anything. They don't need solutions, advice or a step-by-step guide to figuring out their sexuality. What they need is someone in their corner who believes in them, supports them, and reminds them that they're not alone. Remind them of their worth — and the fact that they are loved just as they are — and celebrate their authenticity.

If your loved one feels stuck or overwhelmed, helping them to find resources can make a big difference. This might include:

- Finding a clinical psychologist they can work with who's experienced with LGBTQIA+ issues to provide a safe space for exploration
- Connecting them with in-person or online support groups, where they might experience the validation of connecting with others who have been through similar experiences
- Looking for podcasts and other material that covers relevant content.

Finally, recognise that supporting yourself is also important. Supporting someone through a vulnerable journey, regardless of what it is, can be emotionally intense, and it's okay to feel a little out of your depth sometimes. Make sure you're taking care of yourself along the way. You might want to talk to a therapist who can help. Allow yourself to learn as you go, be open to feedback and embrace a willingness to grow. The most important thing you can do is to keep showing up. Be there for your loved one through the ups, downs and in-betweens. Your presence, patience and love mean more than you realise. Authentic statements like, 'I'm here for you, no matter what,' 'You don't have to figure this out alone' or 'You are enough, exactly as you are' will have a powerful impact.

Supporting someone as they question their sexuality isn't about having the perfect words or knowing all the answers. It's about being present, listening with your whole heart, and letting them know they're loved unconditionally. This journey is theirs, but your support can make all the difference. Trust that your care and compassion are enough.

Reflection prompts

Reflection is a powerful tool for connecting with yourself and making sense of things. These prompts aren't about 'finding the answer' or 'getting it right'. They're about giving yourself space to listen to what's going on inside. So, grab a journal, or just sit with these questions in your mind, and see where they take you.

For individuals struggling with their sexuality

1. How do I feel about the labels I've used to describe myself? Do they feel empowering, limiting, or somewhere in between? Are there other words I've been curious about but haven't explored yet?

2. When in my life have I felt most like myself? What was it about that moment or experience that felt so true?

3. What scares me about embracing my sexual identity? What would it look like to take one small step in that direction? (Try to visualise the action required to take that small step.)

4. If no one in the world could judge me, how would I describe myself? Without fear, expectation or pressure, who am I?

5. What has my past taught me about love, trust and boundaries? Are there lessons I want to carry forward? Are there beliefs I need to let go of?

6. What am I holding onto from my experiences of abuse or trauma? How is it shaping how I see myself or my relationships?

7. What would it feel like to forgive myself for things that weren't my fault? What would I say to a younger version of me who didn't know any better?

8. What moments from my past bring up feelings of shame, and why? What would it look like to replace that shame with self-compassion?

9. Who in my life makes me feel safe and understood? How can I spend more time with them, or lean into those connections?

10. Have I been honest in my relationships about who I am and what I need? If not, what's holding me back?

11. How do I handle rejection or misunderstanding from others? What healthy actions help me bounce back when I feel hurt?

12. What does healing mean to me? Is it about letting go, building something new, or both?

13. What do I need right now to feel more at peace with myself? Is it rest? Self-compassion? Permission to take things slow?

14. What's one small step I can take today towards understanding or accepting myself?

15. What kind of life do I want to create for myself? What would it feel like to live authentically, unapologetically?

For individuals supporting a loved one who is struggling with their sexuality

1. What emotions come up for me as I support my loved one in embracing their sexuality? How can I make space for both their experience and my own feelings with kindness?

2. In what ways has this journey challenged or expanded my understanding of identity and relationships? What have I learned so far, and what do I still want to explore?

3. Are there any fears, uncertainties or discomforts I'm experiencing? How can I acknowledge them without letting them get in the way of offering support?

4. How has my relationship with my loved one evolved through this process? What moments have strengthened our connection, and how can I nurture more of those?

5. What support do I need as I navigate this? Are there conversations, resources or personal reflections that could help me feel more grounded and confident?

Some of these prompts might bring up big feelings, and that's okay. If you feel overwhelmed, take a break or reach out for support.

PALATE CLEANSER
Golf Course Stakeout – Robbie Williams

I have been on a lot of work trips, too many to count. Most of them have been pre-organised, pre-approved junkets covering a film festival, visiting a movie set or television show, or interviewing a music star.

These trips are usually wonderful experiences that are pretty organised and orderly. My favourite trips though have been the unpredictable ones where things didn't always go to plan, or where I have unexpectedly had to pack my bag and jump on a plane or hop in a car to cover a breaking story. This story is about one of those last-minute, unexpected nothing-went-quite-to-plan trips.

It was the 60th birthday of Michael Chugg, a legendary Australian music promoter. He is a big personality in the industry, and he splits his time between Australia and Phuket in Thailand. A bunch of people were flying to Phuket for a multi-day party to celebrate, and some big-name stars were rumoured to be flying in.

Chuggy, as he is affectionately known, is a gruff man with a raspy smoker's voice and a deep belly laugh. He is a softy at heart but also a tough, no-bullshit businessman. He is much loved in the same way as the late Michael Gudinski was for his mammoth contribution to the music business.

After weeks of umming and ahhing as to whether to go (from a work perspective), I was heading to Phuket. Initially, Chuggy had invited me himself. I was chuffed at the invite and the possibility of a front-row seat to the party of the year. The thought was that I could get some cracking stories for the entertainment section, with rockers like Jimmy Barnes heading to the party. But it was the big international names we were really interested in. For starters, there was talk of Robbie Williams going, as well as Keith Richards from The Rolling Stones. The story pitch to my boss was getting inside the party of the year with this legendary, iconic music figure that no other media would be attending.

Chuggy's right-hand woman, Amanda Pelman, a publicist, artist manager and producer who was a judge on reality TV show, *It Takes Two*, was organising this party. She was lovely, but she wasn't overly impressed on the phone when I told her that Chuggy had invited me — instead, she offered to send us some pictures. In the end, the decision of whether to go was left to my deputy editor at the time, the great journalist and media figure Helen McCabe, who decided it was better for us to be there than not. You've got to be in it to win it. (This was in the days where we had a little more money in the budget. It wasn't the glory days of the 80s and 90s, but there was certainly more cash to throw around than there is today.) And so, I joined photographer Anthony Reginato on a flight to Phuket that left that afternoon, not knowing what we were going to get story-wise because technically we'd been uninvited.

We had booked into the same five-star resort where many of the guests were staying. But we were there to work, to get a good story — not to hang out in our villa at the resort.

I was young and naive, full of bravado and bolshy excitement as I was trying to make a name for myself — and Anthony and I were on the chase. Our adrenaline was pumping and it was fun, like an old-fashioned, stakeout-style news story where we had to open the doors for ourselves and figure out where to find the story.

A full itinerary of activities was organised for the guests — swimming, boat trips, dinners, shopping. I knew a few of the guests at the party so they fed me bits of information, telling me what the itinerary was and who would be going where and when. A dinner in Phuket town had been organised for the first night. A bus took guests from the resort to the restaurant so Anthony and I followed them around, doing our thing.

It was all very strange, fish-out-of-water stuff, being in another country on a stealthy, paparazzi-style job. We didn't see anyone famous, which had me a little worried, but I had heard Keith Richards was flying in by private jet and I could hardly imagine him hopping on and off a tourist bus for dinner. There were a few music industry executives but no one particularly famous, and certainly not Robbie Williams.

The next day, the guests were scheduled to do different activities. Some of the blokes were down for golf, and a contact of mine messaged to say a Rob Williams had signed the registration form at the golf club. We leapt into action, with Anthony registering for a beginner's golf class for the day, with his camera equipment stashed in his backpack so he could pull it out and shoot at the drop of a hat. I stationed myself on the outside perimeter, mostly in the car park, but I did many loops of the golf course that day!

We spent eight hours sweltering in the heat and humidity. The sun was oppressive, and by the end of the day Anthony and I were burnt to a crisp — we hadn't packed sunscreen and we didn't have time to go to a convenience store for fear we would miss Robbie Williams strolling past.

My golf-playing contact had turned his phone off so there were no further updates from inside the camp. You can imagine our disappointment when we finally got in touch with him that night. He was back at the resort sipping a glass of pinot while we were still in the bushes at the golf course. As it turned out, Robbie Williams *had* been invited to Chuggy's celebration, but he didn't make it over from the United Kingdom. The Rob Williams playing golf was not the Robbie Williams of Take That fame but Rob Williams from Perth. That was a tough call back to the office to let them know we hadn't succeeded!

Not all hope was lost. With the actual birthday party being held the next night, we still hoped someone big might show up. Amanda went all-out for the party, taking over a whole residential precinct nearby with the streets closed off and a stage set up. It certainly looked like a party a celebrity would attend.

We were running on very little sleep and pure adrenaline. Amanda eventually felt sorry for us and gave us access to the party for a two-hour window, where we could take some pics, get some quotes and then bugger off. And we still had the hope of spotting a big-name guest. Alas, that wasn't to be the case, though veteran music TV host Molly Meldrum was there, frocking up in drag for a surprise stage appearance, while videos from various famous faces from home were played on a big screen. Gudinski and his wife Sue were also there, but it was mostly executives, roadies, music people and friends Chuggy had collected over the years.

In the end, we had a story that ran on, say, page 42 of *The Sunday Telegraph* as a small piece up the back of the news pages, with a picture of Michael Chugg with Molly Meldrum. It was hardly the top tier we'd been hoping for but at least something ran. (For perspective, the better the story, the further up the front of the paper it would run. And it would be better to run on an odd-numbered page because that is where the reader's eyes are drawn when they open the paper.)

The whole trip was a bit of a disaster and not one of my proudest moments in journalism. Three days in Phuket sounds amazing; in reality, it was a disaster and would have cost thousands of dollars for both of us to cover the story. It was one of those instances in my career where I just wanted the world to swallow me up and disappear.

PART II

ADDICTION

I believe I have an addictive personality—but there is a whole lot more to addiction. In my experience, addiction always masks something much deeper. The problem is not so much *what* you're addicted to but what has *driven* you to the substance or issue in the first place. Whether it's chocolate or cocaine, I have realised how important it is to work through and understand what drove me to the point of addiction in the first place. This isn't easy in any sense of the word.

I am a work in progress as I'm constantly finding new things to obsess about and become addicted to. And while I've done a lot of work on my recovery—regular therapy, check-ins with my GP, being hyper-aware of my behaviours—and I've never been in rehab so to speak, I have been forced to make some tough choices that I believe ultimately have been about choosing life over death and protecting my mental wellness over destructive patterns of behaviour.

These realisations came in my mid-30s as I leaned into alcohol and drugs to cope with traumas of the past. It was easier to explain away (to myself and anyone else) my partying going through those earlier 20s years when everyone seemingly was doing the same. Plus, I had the added situation where my work meant I could be out and about at events with all of the trappings of substance addiction any night of the week.

This is my perspective on addiction, and I know everyone is different.

9

A Wake-Up Call

Charlotte Dawson was a larger-than-life former model, turned magazine beauty editor, turned television star on one of the hottest shows on the box — *Australia's Next Top Model*. It was during her time as a TV star that Charlotte became a dear friend, away from the red carpets and fake reality of that world.

She had grown up in New Zealand and lived the high life in Europe and New York as a model before settling in Australia. She had been married to disgraced Olympic swimmer Scott Miller and always had been unlucky in love, despite the fact she was a glamazon of the highest order.

Our friendship was a private friendship, not one that we paraded on social media or used to any advantage. She never asked me to write stories about her, and I didn't ask her for gossip or stories. We felt safe around each other. She understood my work world; I understood hers. Perhaps we gravitated towards each other because we were both damaged and we could see that in each other — we had both suffered trauma, so we shared a common enemy. In that way, we were kindred spirits.

> We had both suffered trauma, so we shared a common enemy. In that way, we were kindred spirits.

Charlotte attracted a lot of damaged souls — she was seen as a mother-type figure to many. She was vivacious, fun and funny, friendly and warm. She was outspoken and people admired her for that. Anyone who knew her, loved her dearly.

It was Charlotte who gave me the strength to be open about my mental health issues. Friends and family knew, of course, but it wasn't something I'd shared outside that. It was a huge deal to speak publicly. It also came as a relief. It's such a shame that I only found this strength after Charlotte's death in February 2014. Until then, I had largely kept my struggles private.

Minutes after learning of her death, I sat in front of my computer at News Corp's *The Sunday Telegraph* headquarters in Sydney and shared the story of my relationship with Charlotte and why she was so important to me and so many others. I felt physically sick and weakened by the news, and I was writing about my feelings to get the pain out of me. I was sobbing at my desk as I wrote, struggling to type through the tears.

I wrote:

> *Not many people in the public eye speak out about their personal experiences with depression. Charlotte did and she helped me enormously. See, I too suffer from depression and have done for years. I've been in hospital with it and experienced the lowest of lows. While I've never really hidden it, it's not something I've advertised.*

Charlotte and I shared similar demons — addictive personalities, dark depression and an unfortunate understanding of what it was like to be a victim of sexual abuse.

Whatever people say, there's a massive stigma associated with depression.

Whether you are right or wrong, once you admit to suffering from mental illness, people always put you in a box. They tread carefully and whatever happens, any issues are always attributed to your illness. You can see it in people's eyes.

We never really spoke about it publicly, but Charlotte helped me immensely with my depression. Charlotte and I had an understanding that didn't need to be talked about. We'd look in each other's eyes when we were at social events together and both of us knew the fake smiles masked something deeper.

It helped me to know she was going through it too. When I was at my lowest points, whatever the reason would be, she was there for me. She'd coach me through it on the phone.

We would talk for ages and she told me everything would be okay.

Now that she's gone, I'm not so sure.

It has been more than a decade since Charlotte took her own life. It was a massive wake-up call for me. It remains a tragedy that I reflect on often, almost daily.

All or nothing: My addictive personality

When I used to drink alcohol, I would drink until I passed out or vomited my guts up so badly I'd burst capillaries around my eyes. There was never an in between. I was all or nothing, and I still am in many aspects of my life, which I don't think is always a bad thing. I can't even drink a cup of tea without being excessive — I need two tea bags instead of one because I can't find any tea that's strong enough. And I drink probably eight of those a day.

There are many reasons I don't drink alcohol or do drugs anymore. Charlotte is one of them. A few months before Charlotte died, I was on a bender. It was an all-nighter and I called her in the morning, around 8 am, saying I was wide awake and still going from the night before. I had snorted that many lines of cocaine that I was high as a kite and had no intention of going to sleep any time soon.

There are many reasons I don't drink alcohol or do drugs anymore. Charlotte is one of them.

Charlotte, being motherly as she always was, told me it was going to be okay and that I should come over. And so I got in a cab and I did.

She offered me something to eat, a hot drink and a welcome hug. Of course, I couldn't eat. I didn't stay long as I was filled with anxiety from the partying and cabbed it back home, took a sleeping tablet and slept off my bender.

This was a little example of how Charlotte nurtured me. She calmed me down and made me feel everything was going to be okay in her caring, motherly way. I know she did the same for others. During and after benders like these, she would coax me down from the imaginary ledge in my mind.

Charlotte too would call me when she was at her low points. She was a fierce and glamorous woman in life and on television. She said it how she saw it but, as stated, she was nurturing, motherly. Charlotte took on online trolls with ferocious gusto — it was her mission and, despite her tough exterior, she felt every word of hate that was levelled at her. Behind closed doors, like all of us, she struggled with her own demons of depression.

My worst time with these benders was after my mum died, so from 2009 onwards. By bender, I mean I'd go out for one quiet drink that would end in a two-day endless party with no sleep and lots and lots of alcohol and party drugs. When I'd be on one of these bender highs, life was wonderful... until it wasn't. Inside, I didn't care about myself — to the point of being recklessly stupid. Each and every one of those benders was a cry for help. I was desperate but didn't know how else to escape and cope with the noise in my head and the pain that felt almost like a knife piercing my chest.

I was always up for a party — as I never saw value in my own life, my attitude was 'why not live on the edge and push myself to the limit'? It took no coaxing and if I was in, I was all in. I genuinely didn't care if I lived or died, save for the fact that I didn't want to hurt my sister and nieces.

Having gone through her own mental health stuff, I felt Mum deeply understood what it felt like to have a brain that wasn't quite right. Without her there to talk to, and without the ability to kill myself, I took on any self-destructive behaviour that came my way.

Alcohol: The gateway to addiction

People find it so strange that I don't drink alcohol now. They just don't understand it. When I tell people I don't drink, they look at me like I'm an alien or I've got two heads.

I truly believe many of us are too reliant on alcohol, but I don't judge — in fact, sometimes I envy those who can stick to only having a couple of drinks. Sadly, this legal substance is a gateway drug, if you like, to other drugs and substances that can be misused, so for many people it is responsible for as much if not more harm than many of the other drugs it leads to.

For me, alcohol led to cocaine and any other party drugs I was either offered or could find at a club or on the streets at 3am. Even though I knew it was bad for me, I could never say no when I was having a big night.

However, I don't think I was an alcoholic or a drug addict. I could go weeks, months even, without touching a drop or snorting a line. But boy, did I love that feeling of freedom when I did drink or do drugs — where the pain couldn't get to me. It was as close to being freed from my emotional shackles as I felt I could get. I used to love that orange-peel taste down the back of my throat when I snorted a line (that's what it tasted like to me, anyway), and then the numb tingling before the initial buzz hit.

It was as close to being freed from my emotional shackles as I felt I could get.

I also loved the process of snorting a line. I felt like a superstar and would wankily prefer to roll up a $50 or $100 note to get my fix. It felt somehow less trashy, more Hollywood, than a common $5 or $10 note. It was decadent in a stupid, funny way. We are raised in a society where money means success, so there was probably an element of flaunting those $50 notes or trying to look like a 'baller' because it made me feel like I was worth something. I drew some sort of value from that moment. The thought seems laughable and preposterous to me now.

But I was trashy at those points. The irony of using a high denomination bank note made it all the more silly. I was in on the joke. I *was* the joke, in my head at least. It was all about punishing myself. I didn't see myself as anything more than some skanky disgusting loser with no purpose or worth. I saw myself as a piece of dirt in the gutter, so when I say trashy, I mean it in the harshest of ways. I felt I didn't deserve any better.

There was also an element of playing a role, like I was in a movie playing out someone else's life on screen — that of an out-of-control drug addict.

Perhaps I wasn't an addict, but I was deeply troubled. And it was very rare for me to knock back the offer of a line of cocaine when I was in my heyday of partying. I was in my early 30s, had a reasonably high disposable income and felt invincible. In my job as an entertainment journalist in Sydney, I could find a party to go to every night of the week. Sure, Sydney isn't New York or London, but there was plenty going on. Sundays were the worst days for me because I worked Tuesday to Saturday and had Mondays off. I would be the random guy dancing with strangers, becoming best friends with people I'd never met before and would never meet again. I would party alone if I had to, meeting people while out at legendary gay nightclub ARQ, staying until closing time and offering any strangers still wanting to buzz to come back to my house to keep the party going. Then I'd have these out-of-body experiences, where I'd step back and look at what I had created. I would see ten, maybe 15 people at 1 pm in the middle of the day, full daylight, high, snorting cocaine and drinking in my backyard. And I would barely know any of them, if I knew them at all.

For those moments, I felt invincible. I was the happiest guy in the world. Until I wasn't, and then I was a blubbering mess on the phone to whichever of my closest friends were unlucky enough to pick up the phone when I called. My twin sister lived in Jakarta in Indonesia at the time and would get those calls. I wouldn't usually admit to being on drugs, although I am sure she could tell.

It wasn't fair on her. I would cry and cry and cry about my life, the trauma and about how I had been sexually abused, how my mum had died, I was fat, I was ugly, I hated myself, I was going to be single forever. All that self-pity crap that I genuinely believed because I didn't have any self-worth.

At that point, the only thing keeping me alive was my sister and her three daughters.

From the outside looking in, I would have been seen as highly successful, travelling the world business class, with famous friends in my phone and my little black contact book. I had what many would consider a dream life. But at that point, the only thing keeping me alive was my sister and her three daughters — her fourth wasn't born yet. Without them, I saw no point and no value in my life. In reality, I was one line of cocaine away from killing myself.

The self-destructive behaviours of abusing drugs and alcohol were just another way of masking the depression. If I was high, and partying, I could let that pain go for that moment. When the party eventually ended, I would be left alone, feeling even more worthless and desperate than before. It was a feeling I could almost taste, and thinking about it now brings the most extreme feelings of anxiety because it all comes back to my mind.

The party's over

I remember one night I was out in Kings Cross. The party had ended several hours before and I was desperate for another line of cocaine, because I knew that stopping would force the realisation that I was a mess. Then I met a guy, with teeth missing, who was obviously a junkie (again, no judgement), and who said he could score me some cocaine.

I went straight to the ATM, withdrew $300 and gave it to him. He took my number. I took his. He was good-looking for a junkie and he disappeared in a taxi to score the drugs. I waited an hour, two hours, three hours... I don't know how long it was, but I remember thinking for a brief moment that was a taste of being homeless, and I realised how badly I had let myself go.

I got in a cab and went home, took a sleeping tablet and crashed out. I obviously never scored the drugs, nor did I get my money back. The next day the guy called to ask if I wanted to party again. I was sober, filled with shame, and I said no, perhaps another time. He didn't offer to return my money, or to get the gram of cocaine he'd promised me.

For months afterwards, he would call me at random times, such as 3.35pm on a Tuesday or 10.30am on a Thursday morning, to see if I was partying. Eventually, he stopped calling.

Purple pain

On one trip to Los Angeles, where I was in town to interview The Police — Sting *et al* — ahead of their Australian tour, I pissed against the wall what many would see as potentially one of the greatest moments of their life — seeing the late, great Prince perform in front of just 100 or so people at Hollywood's Roosevelt Hotel.

It was one of those late-night gigs — he was due to come on stage around 11 pm, which meant after midnight for sure as he was notorious for being late. I wasn't a major fan of Prince then, nor am I now — I like 'Purple Rain' as much as the next person, he just wasn't Madonna to me — but I knew it would have been a special night.

I don't think I truly appreciated the fact I'd missed out on this opportunity until after he died at the age of just 57 (a year older than my mum when she died) in 2016. Sure, I was pumped to go to the gig, but more because it was a very Hollywood thing to do and I was keen to soak up the experience and celeb-spot in the crowd.

I met another Aussie journalist mate for a drink at the Chateau Marmont hotel around 9 pm and we went together to the gig by taxi. I was well and truly sozzled by the time we got to the Roosevelt and I barely remember the night from then on.

More guilt and shame to add to the vault.

Prince didn't come on stage until well after 1 am; I know that because my colleague told me, by which time I was so drunk I can't actually remember seeing him perform. I recall simply this blurred short — very short — man shuffling across the stage with a big band behind him, smashing out the tunes. It was a history-making gig. I wasted something that could have been so good — that by all accounts *was* so good. And for what? A hangover, and more guilt and shame to add to the vault.

The sober light of day

Some nights I'd meet people and feel as if I'd become instant best friends with them. However, the next morning I'd be terrified about what I'd done or said in front of them.

One night, I was randomly photographed in Sydney by someone at a Kings Cross nightclub. I was clearly wasted, my eyes were pinging, and the image ended up on a friend of a friend's Facebook account. Oh, the trouble I went to in order to have that photograph removed! I had to call in all sorts of favours. I wonder if it still exists somewhere.

Another morning (or afternoon, I don't remember), I woke up in my bedroom in the house I was mortgaged to the hilt with and looked at the wall. I would always pretend (or try and trick my mind into believing) that my behaviour or excesses the night before hadn't been that bad.

This time though, there was a great big reminder on my wall. For some reason, somehow, a friend of a friend had come over. It was an actor from a big TV show at the time.

He, for whatever reason, thought it appropriate to sign my bedroom wall. It was probably funny at the time to whoever was partying in my room. I would have been entertaining people I didn't know downstairs or in the backyard around the fire pit. Or maybe I was with him and told him to do it. I don't think so but I honestly can't remember. I was so freaked out I painted the wall that afternoon, but you could still see the faint remnants of his autograph. It was a constant reminder that I couldn't say no to my demons. The act itself showed me how out of control I was at that time, which scared the absolute shit out of me.

That was one of the last times I got fucked up. A couple of times later was the last.

All aboard the nothing train

I was a mess, again alone, and the house like a bomb had hit after whichever random strangers had made it their home for a couple of days of partying. Pacing around my small concrete backyard, I called anyone and everyone in my phone. My sister in Jakarta. Her best friend in Canberra. My best friend from Canberra University. The cycle continued, call after call. Woe is me. I don't want to live. I am not worth anything. It was a pity party from hell, to the point that my sister's best friend, who is like a sister to me too, jumped in the car and drove to Sydney and spent the next few days with me.

She called Judy, who is like my second mum, and the two of them took me to the doctor the next day. There, the doctor told me I shouldn't drink or take drugs, that I had an addictive personality and I was spiralling out of control. It was hard to hear, but I knew it was time.

The realisation of what I was doing to myself hit me like a tonne of bricks. But at the same time, it also struck me that I could take control and change my life. Why spend thousands of dollars on doctor's bills, seeing psychologists and the like, taking antidepressant medication day and night, if I was going to mask my feelings with booze and cocaine? That's the moment I stopped. There wasn't a process or some grand plan.

Stopping also made me realise I didn't need to mask the pain.

I've never been to Alcoholics Anonymous (or Narcotics Anonymous). When I stopped, I just stopped. I am all or nothing and, for now, I accept the fact that I am on the nothing train when it comes to booze and cocaine — and I don't ever see myself stepping off.

It shocks people that I have been able to just stop. Being an all or nothing kind of guy made it easy in a way. Stopping also made me realise I didn't need to mask the pain as it only ever led to the inevitable self-loathing, further exacerbating the trauma that already sat there deep down to my core. I couldn't end up like Charlotte. In my mind, I needed to find a reason to not just survive but to live, even happily, for myself but also for her. And so I doubled-down, saw my psychologist more, got my medications adjusted after however many years of taking the same stuff, and got back on the 'get well' train.

Don't get me wrong, it wasn't easy, it just was. I had no other choice.

10

Losing Control: 3 am Drunk Dialling

I was notorious for the drunk dial when I got wasted. I'd call around to see who would answer, sometimes to see if they'd join me at the bar, and other times just to chat and have someone to keep me company. After a few drinks and with my buzz on, I would ring pretty much from A through to Z in my phone book, no matter what time it was or where in the world I was.

I once rang my boss, an editor at one of the biggest newspapers in the country, while drunk at a friend's wedding in Germany. Fortunately he found it funny, but it wasn't an ideal time to call as I was spewing into the bushes on my hands and knees. My friend had to confiscate my phone after that.

I'm sure countless of my closest friends, and acquaintances too, blocked my calls on occasion. My friends laugh about the drunk dialling now, but there was a serious side to it. The guilt and the shame the next day was almost too much to bear. I still feel shame thinking about it. While I could lie to myself internally about being out of control, this was an outward sign to others that I'd lost my shit. Also, I often had no idea what I'd said, and who I'd called. I'd even go into my call log and do a blanket delete so I wouldn't be able to remember, and if anyone brought it up afterwards, I'd just laugh it off as a joke or a pocket dial.

I still feel shame thinking about it.

In a way, drunk dialling is a cry for help. One time, when I was staying in a five-star hotel in Los Angeles, I was on a bender. Cocaine in LA is about $30 a gram, compared to $300 in Sydney. That's what it was then at least, though I'm not sure now as I haven't touched the stuff in years.

That night I had been out at the infamous Chateau Marmont — the celebrity place to hang out at 8221 Sunset Boulevard, where John Belushi famously died of a drug overdose on 5 March, 1982. Photographer Helmut Newton also died in 2004 after crashing his car pulling out of the hotel's driveway.

The Chateau Marmont is the stuff of Hollywood legends. I try to visit every time I am in LA. A pivotal scene in *A Star Is Born* (the Lady Gaga and Bradley Cooper version) was shot there. Heath Ledger was snapped by paparazzi there in 2006, in a grainy video surrounded by people snorting what looked to be cocaine.

'I'm going to get serious s--- from my girlfriend, we had a baby three months ago,' Ledger is heard saying in the video. 'I shouldn't be here at all.'

I related to those words of acknowledgement from Ledger because every time I was on a bender, I knew I was on borrowed time almost as surely the clock was ticking on someone calling me out on my bullshit. I knew I was on a trail of self-destruction, and the inevitable pit of self-loathing come-down was on its way sooner rather than later. I'd drag out that partying to put off those feelings. I too would tell those I was partying with I needed to stop. But hey, fuck it, I was already high anyway so why stop then. I'd deal with that shit later or it would deal with me.

The last (and only) time I stayed there (it's about $600 a night for a basic room), it was wall-to-wall Hollywood stars, from Justin Theroux at the bar to Isla Fisher taking a meeting, Joel Edgerton having coffee with his girlfriend and Jon Bernthal playing with his kids in the pool.

I got into the spirit of the Chateau Marmont this one night with a couple of LA-based friends — it would have been rude not to — but with an infamous 2am curfew in the city, everything shuts down early. You either kick on to a house party or go to bed. My friends had to work the next day, so I went back to my hotel room by myself and, you guessed it, drank the mini-bar dry as I made my way through my phone contacts.

I wasn't selective in who I would call. From TV stars to family members and distant acquaintances, anyone was fair game if their number was in my phone.

One actor back home in Australia on this occasion could only vaguely remember the call when I reminded her about it, but she didn't recall details. 'Phew!', I felt, as for me these calls are one of the greatest shames and embarrassments of my life—outward reminders of how fucked up I was.

I called my mate Charlotte Dawson. I rang two of my aunts, who were then in their late 70s (how kind of me, they would have been overjoyed and not worried about me at all!), a couple of my cousins and, of course, my sister. They didn't know I'd had a few lines of cocaine, but they knew I was drunk and probably suspected other stuff. I always said 'a few lines' because it made me feel better, but it could have been a few bags (a gram being in each bag). They were understandably worried about me.

Thinking back gives me serious anxiety to this day—they thought I was living the dream, and then these phone calls would show how rocky I truly was. It was after my mum had died from cancer at the age of 56, and I was a mess.

Her death brought up all my other traumas that had been festering inside me for years. Having bottled up my shit and kept myself going on an even keel, or so I thought, it was these drunk moments that saw me fall into a puddle of emotions as I'd lean into making some very bad decisions. Cocaine didn't help. I'd spill my guts about how shit I thought my life was, how much I missed my mum, how I still struggled and had nightmares about being abused. I was processing all this shit still, despite the fact I'd had years of therapy. I was never a part of AA, or a 12-step program. Therapy for me was a combination of counsellors, psychologists, psychiatrists and regular check-ins with my GP. That, on top of medication.

Getting drunk and doing cocaine was the last thing I should have been doing but when you place so little value on yourself, you just don't care what happens to you. I kept myself alive, in this self-imposed cycle of hell, for my sister and nieces.

When you place so little value on yourself, you just don't care what happens to you.

I'd ring people at random — going through my phone from A to Z and picking numbers.

One guy I rang said all the right things on the phone but then used my vulnerability against me by starting rumours in work circles that I was unstable and that I had threatened to kill myself.

It was malicious and nasty, and while I was on the edge and may have said some fucked-up loose shit, I knew I wasn't suicidal because I know now as I knew then that my family was keeping me alive. I was genuinely struggling though so the call would have been alarming, I understand that. But instead of checking up on me in the days and months that followed, he used the incident as a moment to gossip. Was it a laughing matter? If he was so genuinely concerned, why did he not contact me or a family member the next day rather than doing his best to damage my reputation?

This is another reason I do not drink. I lose control when I do. I accept that and don't blame anyone but myself. People do however find that hard to understand and when I say I don't drink, nine times out of 10 people look at me like I've got three heads. When they do get it, they assume I am an alcoholic.

I don't drink because it is my choice. It would be nice if that was more accepted in our society. Alcohol is such a huge part of our culture. We drink when we are happy. We drink when we are sad. We drink at cafés. We drink at pubs, restaurants, on the street, in the park and on public transport. It is just so entrenched in what we do. The reason I don't drink is not because I'm an alcoholic, although maybe I am. I haven't really come to terms with that, although I truly don't think I am. It is because I don't stop at one drink. I don't stop at five drinks. I stop maybe at 20 drinks (or when I've passed out). And five drinks leads to a cheeky line of cocaine, then a few bags. I can't say no. I don't say no. And it's a spiral. You already know the cycle.

I've spent too much money on psychologists and counsellors and antidepressants to waste that. I made it to the point where enough was enough and I chose to have no regrets.

11

The Reality of Reality TV

To be embedded is to be 'attached to a military unit during a conflict'. The term can be applied more broadly in journalism though. For example, covering entertainment, you could be embedded if you are 'attached' to a TV or film production.

I've been embedded several times for an entertainment journalism job; I even had the rare opportunity to travel on a two-week Forces Entertainment Tour of military bases in Afghanistan (Tarin Kowt, Kandahar and Kabul). A true combination of both meanings of the word in my working world!

I also did four seasons embedded in South Africa covering *I'm a Celebrity ... Get Me Out of Here!* Celebrities commit to living in a 'jungle' camp — I use the term jungle loosely — living on basic food rations of beans and rice. They compete in various physical, mental and gross eating challenges to obtain extra food items.

I was as embedded as you can get as an entertainment journalist. I worked on set out of a demountable shipping container for News Corp, writing stories for all our publications nationally. It generated a lot of content for us, because it ticked all the right boxes in terms of celebrity scandal, video and action-packed moments. That translated to stories in the newspapers, online and on social media.

One of the hardest parts of *I'm a Celebrity* was constantly treading that line between being embedded and doing my job as a journalist.

I was not being paid by Channel 10 or ITV, but there was certainly implied pressure that they had footed the bill for my flights and accommodation. To them, my job was to report on the goings-on of the show, the storylines, to interview the celebrities before and after they were in the jungle. I was compromised to an extent, but I always prided myself in trying to be impartial. But if there was a negative story to be written, then I would be the one to have to write it.

To say it was an interesting four years is an understatement. Each season I would spend anywhere from a couple of weeks to the full two months of production based on set. It remains a career highlight, but largely due to the experiences I was lucky to have had outside of shooting the show.

Honestly, the first year I believed *I'm a Celebrity* was this revolutionary TV format after years covering the likes of *Big Brother*, *The Bachelor*, *The Voice* and *The X Factor*. Reality television had become so predictable, basically a vehicle for usually pretty people to become influencers or as a launchpad to a radio or TV hosting gig. Once considered a controversial beacon to some, spearheading the new wave of a genre, reality TV had become tired and tiresome. I thought *I'm a Celebrity... Get Me Out of Here!* was going to deliver what it claimed it was going to.

The first year's cast included Maureen McCormack of *The Brady Bunch* fame (iconic!), chef Julie Goodwin, cricket greats Merv Hughes and Freddie Flintoff, comedian Joel Creasey, and radio host Chrissie Swan. All the celebrities seemed to be there for the right reasons and none of them really knew what to expect. They were going in blind, so to speak, as were we behind the scenes. What was a given was that celebrities were involved and that they would generate good content on screen and for general societal talkability.

As each season went on however, the format became more predictable and more manipulated in my opinion. I guess that is the case on all reality TV formats though as viewers and competitors understand better what is going on in front of the camera and behind the scenes.

The show was the real deal. Professional rangers — or 'Bush Boys', as they were commonly called on set — were stationed 24 hours a day, seven days a week around the production to ensure that big cats, hippos and other critters didn't get too close or cause any harm. It was legitimately in the wild. Baboons and monkeys were everywhere. And there were snakes, lots of snakes. I'd always check my bed before going to sleep to ensure there wasn't one tucked in under the sheets, something I was extra diligent about after one incident.

There was a group WhatsApp chat with various updates on security and so on, which was often filled with sightings of the most dangerous of snakes or some other (exotic to us) critters. This was a daily occurrence. One senior producer sleeping in a chalet awoke one morning to feel something cold lying in the bed next to him. He rolled over to discover it was a large Mozambique spitting cobra. Highly venomous. Deadly. Fortunately, he had his back turned as he jumped out of the bed and the snake spat its venom at him. Another crew member couldn't walk for more than a week after stepping on a highly poisonous scorpion in the shower one morning. The pain was excruciating, apparently.

As each season of *I'm a Celebrity* went on, I became more jaded. Sure, the experience of being in Africa never tired, but I found it harder and harder to reconcile the reality of what I was seeing with the manipulation and tactics engaged to create stories for good television.

I went into the whole thing naively, which I guess is a common theme for me. I genuinely thought the show was doing the right thing, it had heart and was basically fish out of water, strip away the comforts and bells and whistles of fame and really celebrities are just like us. That idea is the basis of my work on the *Mental As Anyone* podcast.

Towards the end of the fourth season, I faced the toughest dilemma during my time in South Africa.

Fiona O'Loughlin was a contestant. Fiona is a friend, I truly think she is an amazing woman. She has struggled a lot in life. She is a reformed alcoholic. She has had lots of medical issues, and I really struggled with the producer's decision to send her into the jungle as a contestant that year.

I was deeply troubled after doing an interview with Fiona before she went into the camp. I remember thinking to myself at the time that I thought Fiona was too fragile to compete on the show. Her hands were literally shaking when we spoke, which was understandable given she had just come out of a rehab facility a few months prior. For whatever reason, the TV channel decided on her inclusion, deeming that she was well enough to go into the jungle. It just did not make sense. It didn't feel right, and I said so at the time.

I still to this day do not think they made the right decision. It was irresponsible — dangerous, even. I believe the decision was made in favour of getting good TV over someone's life and wellbeing. That to me was the final straw, because it proved that there was really very little care for people's wellbeing. It really was all about ratings, not celebrities being like the rest of us when you strip life back. It was all about filming TV moments and not about the welfare of the people that were in the jungle.

In those final days of the season, it was discovered that Fiona had been drinking the hand sanitiser contestants were given to clean themselves in camp. That is how bad her alcoholism had become. And that is how much pressure and stress she felt at that time. I knew about this story and chose not to report it, which perhaps makes me look like a pretty shit journalist — I know plenty of journalists that would have written about it. However, I believed it was a volatile and dangerous situation, one that I felt close to because of my own mental health demons.

I still think it was the right decision not to publish the story at the time. It was the right time later, coinciding with the release of her autobiography, *Truths from an Unreliable Witness*. It was right because it was the time she chose; she was in control.

'I dropped my bundle emotionally but that is not the reason I did it,' she told me in an interview published in *The Daily Telegraph* in 2020. 'My mind started playing games with me. It felt so real, and it is so nonsensical now, but I felt that I was the schmuck and everyone in Australia was laughing at me and that was why I was so close to winning. I didn't know what was being edited and what was out there.'

The whole thing unfolded in the final days of the competition, when O'Loughlin was in the top three alongside singer Shannon Noll and boxer Danny Green.

'I think it was probably reckless of me (to do the show). That is the problem with addicts, we think we do but we don't have our own best interests at heart,' she said. 'I freaked and planned to do it. In the middle of the night I just f**king did it. I waited until everyone was asleep and I drank hand sanitiser. It was disappointing because it kind of gives you ... first the taste is so vile, it takes so long to get the taste out of your mouth, and then I think you get about 10 minutes of numbness, which is what I was after and then you sleep. I wish I could say it only happened once but that would not be the truth.'

The struggle I felt was in observing a woman who was seriously unwell, slurring her words and falling over in camp. To get through, she was allowed to sleep in the medical hut and given medication to sleep. This was not shown or communicated to viewers at home and only came out when she wrote about it in her own book. It wasn't reality TV; it was manipulated television. Decisions were made in the interests of maintaining credibility for the show, not the wellbeing of a human who needed help. It would have looked bad if the story had come out at the time; in fact, I think the show may have been axed. It most definitely should have been.

Interestingly though, Fiona felt that producers had made the right decision in covering up the hand sanitiser incident and not kicking her off the show. They basically held her together with sticky tape to get her to the finish line, and she ultimately won the series and $100 000 for her chosen charity, Angel Flight.

'If they'd pulled me out of the jungle and I'd had to explain why, I don't know that I was well enough at that point. That would have retreated me to going back to round-the-clock drinking. The shame of that would have been very dangerous.'

That was my last season embedded on *I'm a Celebrity ... Get Me Out of Here!* I declined the offer to go back and cover the next year. There were a few reasons for saying no, but ultimately the main reason was how I felt about what happened to Fiona. I'm a sensitive soul, and I really struggle with that

I'm a sensitive soul, and I really struggle with that at times.

at times, but the way she was treated did not sit well with me and it really made me think more broadly about reality television and mental health, particularly in the context of my own addiction and struggles.

12

Isolated in the House of Pancakes

In January 2010, I was flown business class from Sydney to Los Angeles to cover the annual G'Day USA Australia Week — a celebration of all things Australia in the United States. That year saw Toni Collette, Simon Baker and Greg Norman honoured in West Hollywood, right in the thick of the action. As well as Aussie names, there were always big-name supporters, which that year included John Travolta and Cameron Diaz.

As you might imagine, LA is a party place. If you tip well at a bar, you get good top-ups of drinks — and they freely pour the booze. Cocaine is cheap too, really cheap, at say $30 a gram compared to $300 or more in Australia for the same amount (good stuff, too).

After my mum died, I went through those years of excess, working hard and partying harder — and this trip to LA fell during that time. Partying hard never stopped me from doing my work, and I always showed up on time. I was always proud of that. Even if I had slept just half an hour, I would be at my desk by 9am no matter what.

The G'Day USA LA event at the Kodak Theatre was as expected — wall-to-wall celebrities, some high profile and others on their way, and lots of schmoozers. The highlight of the event (a work night for me) was Nicole Kidman and Keith Urban presenting Simon Baker his award with a spectacular, unguarded tribute, sung to the tune of Men at Work's global pub hit 'Down Under'. Baker was a big star at the time thanks to his gig fronting hit TV show *The Mentalist* and *The Devil Wears Prada* movie.

Guests kicked on afterwards, spilling out onto the terrace of the Kodak Theatre. The after-afterparty was where it was at though. Those keen to keep going pushed on to hotel suites at the Loews Hotel next door. We bounced from room to room. Former Miss World Jennifer Hawkins was there, as well as *Avatar* star Sam Worthington and ex-Neighbours star turned singer Holly Valance.

I'm not implicating anyone else at these follow-on parties at all, but I will admit that I had a line (or three, or more) of top-notch, premium LA, rip-snorting cocaine that night. It was taboo and everyone was extra cautious around me, being a journalist — despite my naive protestations that I was off duty. LA being LA, everything shuts down at its infamous curfew time of 2 am. I'm sure some people carried on somewhere, but I had outlived my welcome for that late-night debauchery and found myself standing as a lone figure in the corridor of the hotel. I was 'the journalist'.

I went down in the lift and got into a cab. This is where the sad part happened. I wasn't ready for the party to end so I got my yellow cab driver to stop off at a 24-hour IHOP (International House of Pancakes) — a pancake joint about half a kilometre up the road from my hotel. Desperate not to be alone, I begged, literally begged, the driver to keep the meter running and convinced him to come inside with me for pancakes at this generic chain diner that was open 24/7. I don't remember what he looked like. I definitely don't know his name. I wasn't even hungry. It would have been 3am and only one other table was occupied. I chewed this guy's ear off about anything and everything I could think of, with my cocaine high in full swing. I don't think I even ate any pancakes — the driver finished both plates for us. I paid the fare of US$250 or more and got out of the cab, creeping back to my hotel room for a few hours of interrupted sleep.

You can only imagine the shame and guilt I felt the next day when I woke up, my mouth red raw from talking non-stop and my throat full of post-party mucous. My way of dealing with that was to lie to myself, convince myself I hadn't done anything wrong. Everything was okay. It worked on the conscious me but deep down I knew I was struggling. I wasn't okay.

That IHOP moment was a turning point for me. I realised how sad I truly was. Had I finally reached rock bottom? One minute I was at one of the hottest parties in town — my high-school self would have died at the thought. Then, I ended up sat in a cheesy chain diner with a guy I couldn't even name who only spoke to me because I was paying the bill. How low could I go?

Had I finally reached rock bottom?

This sad story highlights perfectly the high highs and the low lows of my life. I cringe whenever I think about that night. I have never told this story to anyone due to the embarrassment and shame, and the fact it reminds me of how low I felt at that time. It wasn't one of my finest moments.

❉ ❉ ❉

In my job as an entertainment journalist, certain things are off the record and there are agreed pens-down moments. It is easy to get caught up in the hype and fanfare, to even believe you are more a part of that celebrity world than you really are. I like the pens-down rule too, because it makes it easier to let your hair down in the sense that you can just enjoy the experience. While most celebrities will tell you they hate fame, I think they must be lying to themselves if they don't admit to seeking gratification through that fame. I related to that, with my work, but also in being around these people and enjoying the excesses of that lifestyle. Plus, it made me, even if for a brief second, feel like I was worth something. A small-town Aussie guy hanging with global household names.

In truth, however, it only really ever amplified my feelings of loneliness and isolation, which, in turn, was a disaster for my mental health at a time when I was so not self-aware. Staying on top of my mental health and being in a good headspace is crucial to managing this complex tap-dance of a relationship where you are on the inside but feel on the outer.

This strange dance is perhaps something we can all see in our own relationships, personal and professional, whatever worlds we mix in.

With very few exceptions, the celebrities I interact with are not my friends — they are simply work acquaintances and colleagues. To them, I am an annoying necessity, an enemy of sorts — someone to keep close, but not too close. It is a strange dance.

Your TOOLKIT
for ADDICTION
DR JODIE LOWINGER

Addiction is a response to a complex mix of biological, environmental and personal influences and experiences. It happens when something, such as a substance, a behaviour or even a relationship, takes over and starts running your life. It can feel like you're stuck in a loop, chasing relief or escape, even if you know it's causing harm to yourself or others.

Addiction isn't limited to drugs or alcohol. In my work, I've seen the many forms that addiction can show up, like sex, food and gambling addiction, or even an addiction to things that might seem harmless at first, like social media or shopping. People experiencing addiction may be seeking the rush of excitement or comfort these substances, behaviours or relationships bring. Other times, people are trying to numb their pain or avoid difficult feelings. Or it may be another reason entirely. In JMo's case, it was a mixture of reasons. Whatever the cause, the pattern is the same — you get stuck in a cycle where the things you turn to for relief start creating more problems than they solve.

So, what's going on when something that might, at first, feel somewhat harmless becomes an addiction? The answer can be found in the brain. Your brain is wired to reward things that help you to survive, like eating, connecting with others or staying safe. But some substances, behaviours or even relationships can hijack that reward system, flooding your brain with feel-good neurochemicals and making it prioritise that thing above almost everything else. Over time, this rewiring makes it harder to say no, even when it's no longer enjoyable or helpful.

Addiction isn't just about the brain. It's tied to emotions, relationships and the stressors in your life. For many, it's a way to cope with pain, trauma or feelings of self-doubt. It can feel like a quick fix, but the relief is temporary, and the fallout (such as shame, guilt, damaged relationships or health issues) can be overwhelming and create an increased desire to turn to those substances, behaviours or people in an attempt to numb the pain.

The good news is that with the right tools and support, you can take back control. In this toolkit, we're going to explore what addiction is, look at why it happens, and share some tools to help you start to move forward.

Addiction isn't the problem, it's the symptom

One of the most pivotal moments you may experience when dealing with addiction is the realisation that something isn't right. It might come after a specific event, such as a partner expressing concern or a job being at risk, or perhaps you wake up one day feeling depleted and ashamed. For many, this moment is accompanied by a flood of conflicting emotions. At first, it can be common to deny, rationalise or minimise the problem. Thoughts like, 'It's not that bad' or 'I can stop anytime I want' might come up.

Acknowledging an addiction can bring up fear, such as a fear of what life will look like without the addiction, a fear of judgement or a fear of failure if you try to stop. But naming the problem can also feel liberating. Being aware of and acknowledging the addiction is a first pivotal step in taking back control.

In my work with my clients, some of the deepest feelings that come up when dealing with the challenges of addiction are shame and guilt. Shame is deeply tied to how we see ourselves, while guilt focuses more on the impact of our actions on others. Together, they can feel paralysing. For example, someone with sex addiction might feel deeply flawed or 'broken' because of societal stigma or personal values. Someone experiencing compulsive eating habits might experience shame around their relationship with food or their bodies. Shame whispers, 'There's something wrong with you,' which can make it hard to seek help.

Shame and guilt might also lead people to isolate themselves, believing that they don't deserve support or understanding.

Addiction doesn't happen in a vacuum; it often affects relationships, jobs and other responsibilities. You might feel guilty about lying to loved ones, neglecting commitments or hurting people who care about you. While guilt can motivate change, too much can spiral into self-punishment and perpetuate the desire to numb those difficult emotions through the source of the addiction.

One of addiction's cruel tricks is that it can make you feel like you're the only one going through it. It can damage trust and create conflict with loved ones, pushing people away when you might need them most. This isolation might stem from secrecy, or a desire to hide your behaviour from others to avoid judgement or attempts to stop the addiction behaviours. For instance, someone with sex addiction, or another form of addiction, might choose to withdraw from serious relationships.

Addiction creates an illusion of control. Many people convince themselves they can stop whenever they want or that they just need more willpower. When repeated attempts to quit fail, this illusion crumbles, leading to feelings of helplessness and frustration. Trying to stop but failing can feel like you're running on a treadmill — you're exhausted, but you're not getting anywhere. After repeated failed attempts, hopelessness can kick in and you may start to believe recovery isn't possible. Thoughts like, 'I'm too far gone' or 'I'll never change' may start to take over.

For many people I see, addiction isn't the problem but the symptom. It's a way to cope with deeper emotional pain or unmet needs. Some common roots include past abuse, pervasive anxiety or other traumatic experiences. Addiction becomes a way to numb feelings or escape painful memories. Addiction can also stem from a longing for connection. For example, compulsive eating might fill an emotional void, while drugs or alcohol can provide a temporary sense of escape from feelings of loneliness. Feelings of inadequacy or self-loathing can also fuel self-destructive behaviours. You might turn to addiction as a way to silence your inner critic, even if it's only temporary.

Addiction is often marked by a painful cycle of craving and regret. Cravings can feel overwhelming, like a tidal wave pulling you under. The cravings are both physical and emotional, driven by a need for relief, escape or pleasure. Giving in to the craving might bring short-term relief or satisfaction; however, the high is fleeting, often leaving you feeling worse afterwards. Regret and self-criticism kick in, leaving you feeling angry with yourself for not resisting, which fuels further shame and guilt. This regret often leads you back to craving, which perpetuates the cycle.

Even when you know addiction is harming you, the idea of letting go of your addiction can feel terrifying. Letting go might feel like losing your safety net, and you might wonder how you'll manage stress, pain or boredom without it. Admitting you have a problem can also make you feel vulnerable, especially if you're worried about how others will react and whether they will judge you. Acknowledging you have a problem with addiction can bring with it fear and uncertainty about the future and fear of failure or relapse, making the journey feel daunting before it even begins.

If you're experiencing addiction, know that you're not alone. Recovery is hard work, but with consistency and dedicated action, recovery from addiction is in your control. Progress isn't about perfection; it involves taking one step at a time towards a healthier, more fulfilling life. With the right support, patience and tools, change is within your reach.

A toolkit for overcoming addiction

Overcoming addiction isn't easy, but it is well and truly in your control. Recovery is a journey, not a one-time event, and the right tools and strategies can make all the difference. The tools I suggest here form a scientifically supported toolkit to help you to start navigating the process of change.

A first critical step is acknowledging and accepting the problem as a problem. Consider why the addictive behaviours aren't serving you. Reflect on your values and what a meaningful and fulfilling life truly looks like to you. Having a clear 'why' to motivate you gives you the power to commit to change.

Build awareness around the triggers. There are often patterns related to situations, emotions or thoughts that trigger the desire to engage in addictive behaviours. The first step in managing them is understanding what they are. Identify the cues, such as time, location and emotions, that trigger the unhealthy or unhelpful behaviours. Keep a journal or log of when you feel the urge to engage in your addiction. What happened right before? What were you feeling? Were you alone or with others? Once you've identified your triggers, you can begin to anticipate and plan for them.

Triggers can be:

- *Emotional*, such as stress, anxiety, loneliness, boredom or even excitement
- *Situational*, such as being in certain places, being around specific people or occurring at certain times of day
- *Physical*, such as fatigue, hunger or pain
- *Mental* (related to thoughts).

Limiting exposure to triggers is an important part of the process. Do you need to remove any items, people or situations from your life that tempt you to revert to old habits? Plan alternatives to either replace those triggers or develop new responses to them. For example:

- If stress triggers snacking, try taking a walk or practising deep breathing instead.
- If you're trying to reduce alcohol, and certain locations trigger drinking, suggest going somewhere else instead.
- If you're trying to eat better, replace unhealthy snacks in the house with healthy ones.

See if you can introduce reminders and tools to support the new habit, such as sticky notes, alarms or taking your gym gear out the night before.

Try to set clear and realistic goals. Depending on what you're trying to change, it can be good to focus on specific, manageable steps rather than trying to overhaul your entire lifestyle. Accountability can be helpful, so consider sharing your goals with a friend, family member or therapist.

Addiction rewires your brain to prioritise the addictive behaviour. Recovery involves creating new neural pathways, or healthy habits, that can replace the old ones. Don't be concerned about starting small. For example, if you're working on compulsive eating, this might mean identifying vulnerable times and replacing unhelpful actions with more helpful ones, such as going for a short walk when you get home. Set specific, small goals that are in your control. For example, instead of 'I'll stop drinking,' it might be more helpful to say, 'I'll reduce my drinking to weekends only for the next month.' Consistency is key.

Create new opportunities for stimulating dopamine or feel-good neurochemicals. One way to do this is celebrating small victories. Positive reinforcement strengthens new habits, so reward yourself for progress, no matter how small, whether it's taking time for self-care, listening to an episode of your favourite podcast or simply acknowledging your efforts.

One of the most important steps when addressing addiction is learning to treat yourself with compassion. It's easy to get caught up in self-criticism, but recovery is helped by kindness, patience and understanding. Recognising that addiction is a response to some underlying challenge, not a reflection of your character, can help you to approach the process with less judgement and more openness.

An important component in the toolkit is ways to regulate emotions. For some, addiction can be tied to experiencing difficulty with managing emotions. Learning to regulate your feelings can reduce the need to rely on addictive behaviours. Recognise the power of mindfulness as a scientifically supported tool that can help you to pause before acting on cravings. It's about staying present with your thoughts and feelings without judgement, giving yourself space to respond rather than react. It can be helpful to engage in daily mindfulness practice to build that 'mindful muscle'. Even

5–10 minutes of mindfulness meditation can strengthen your ability to manage cravings. There are many apps that can guide you through simple practices. Alternatively, when you feel overwhelmed, see if you can try grounding exercises like the '5-4-3-2-1 technique': name five things you can see, four things you can touch, three things you can hear, two things you can smell, and one thing you can taste.

Try practising 'urge surfing'. Urges are like waves that build, peak and eventually pass. Instead of trying to fight or avoid cravings, learn to ride them out. Sit with the feeling, notice where it shows up in your body, and remind yourself it will fade.

Addiction takes a toll on your body and mind. Taking care of your overall physical health and wellbeing supports your recovery. When I'm working with my corporate high-performance clients or my clients at The Anxiety Clinic, this is often one of the most fundamental starting points. Sleep, movement, nutrition and human connection are the foundation stones to wellbeing. Other wellbeing needs include relaxation and stress management, meaningful activities and acts of kindness, and compassion for yourself and others. (My book, *The Mind Strength Method*, provides you with a comprehensive wellbeing framework.)

Consider what exercise or movement you can introduce into your daily routine. Remember that consistency is more important than quantity: regular physical activity releases endorphins, improves mood and reduces cravings. Start with something simple you enjoy, like walking in the outdoors, and see if you can build from there. Fuel your body with nourishing foods. For managing compulsive eating behaviours, working with a dietitian can help you rebuild a healthy relationship with food.

Poor sleep can exacerbate cravings and emotional instability. When working with my clients, we map out a plan to manage challenges with insomnia and specific sleep goals. Don't suffer in silence if sleep is proving challenging for you — seek out the help you deserve.

Chronic stress is a major trigger for addiction. Often the most powerful tools to reduce stress and boost wellbeing are mindset tools, such as learning how to move out of worry and realign to practical action, alongside embracing the right breathing and relaxation techniques. Exercise and spending time in nature are powerful stress management tools in themselves.

Key to this toolkit is to build a support network of trusted people. Recovery is hard to do alone. A strong support system can provide accountability, encouragement and understanding. Lean on loved ones. Share your journey with friends or family members who you trust. Let them know how they can support you, whether it's checking in, supporting you through therapy or simply being there to listen. You might consider joining support groups who can offer a sense of community and shared experience. See if you can get recommendations or referrals from people you know to be helpful, and find the groups that work best for you.

Addiction can often mask deeper pain or unmet needs. Addressing these underlying issues can be transformative. It can be tremendously helpful to seek professional help from a clinical psychologist who can help you to feel empowered and support you with evidence-based approaches that are specifically tailored to the challenges that you are experiencing, such as Cognitive Behavioural Therapy (CBT), Acceptance and Commitment Therapy (ACT) or Dialectical Behaviour Therapy (DBT). Sometimes addiction is the byproduct of unresolved trauma. Trauma-focused therapy can help you process the trauma and respond in helpful and transformational ways. Therapy is not a 'one-size-fits-all' approach. Skilled therapists will often use a combination of scientifically supported techniques to best meet your needs. It's also important to recognise that while talking through your problems might be helpful, talking therapy alone is not typically sufficient.

Recovery isn't just about stopping addictive behaviours, it's about building a life that feels worth living. Addiction can pull you away from your values, but recovery is a chance to realign with them, whether it's being present for your loved ones, pursuing your passions or living authentically in line with what is meaningful to you. A clinical psychologist will be able to guide you using appropriate evidence-based tools and techniques. Therapy will also help you focus on your worth and build self-esteem to create an even stronger foundation for recovery. Think about what you want your life to look like in one, five or 10 years. Rediscover old interests, try new ones or perhaps find causes you're passionate about and get involved. Helping others can boost self-esteem and create a sense of purpose. Recovery is a chance for renewal and passionate alignment to the things that matter most.

Finally, know that relapse doesn't mean failure; relapse is part of the recovery process. As hard as a relapse might feel, reflect on the experience as it provides you with an opportunity to learn what works and what doesn't, rather than beating yourself up and judging yourself harshly. What triggered it? What can you do differently next time? Create a relapse prevention plan by identifying high-risk situations and developing strategies to handle them. For example, if social drinking is a trigger, plan to bring a sober friend or have an exit strategy.

Recovery is not about being perfect, it's about improving over time. Celebrate the days or weeks you went without engaging in the behaviour and use relapse as a stepping stone for future success.

Overcoming addiction is a challenging and rewarding journey. It requires courage, commitment and self-compassion, but you don't have to do it alone. With the right tools, strategies and support, you can break free from the cycle of addiction and build a life that feels meaningful and whole. Take it one step at a time and remember that every small win is a step towards lasting change.

How to help a loved one if they're struggling with addiction

Supporting a loved one through addiction can be challenging and emotionally demanding. Addiction doesn't just affect the person experiencing it — it ripples out to impact relationships, families and friendships. You may feel a complex mix of emotions, such as compassion, frustration, fear, anger or sadness, or even hopelessness. But while you can't fix the problem for them, you can play a crucial role in their progress towards recovery.

A first step to feeling more in control of the situation, as well as offering meaningful support, is to educate yourself about addiction. Addiction isn't a moral failing, a sign of weakness or a lack of willpower, it's a complex interplay of biological and environmental experiences. Addiction changes the brain's reward system, making the person crave the substance or behaviour despite negative consequences. It's also often tied to underlying pain, such as trauma, stress or mental health challenges. Educating yourself helps you separate the person from their addiction. It also allows you to approach the situation with empathy rather than judgement, which is essential for fostering trust and communication. Read reliable resources about addiction, such as books, articles or information from trusted organisations.

Talking to a loved one about their addiction can feel intimidating. A good overarching principle is to approach conversations with compassion. You might worry about saying the wrong thing or pushing them away. However, a compassionate, non-judgemental approach can make all the difference. Choose the right time and place for approaching discussions. Have the conversation when you're both calm and in a private, safe space. Avoid discussing the addiction during a heated moment or while they're under the influence. Focus on concern, not criticism. Use 'I' statements to express how the behaviours affect you, rather than blaming or accusing them; for example, 'I've noticed you've been drinking more lately, and I'm worried about you' is more effective than 'You're ruining your life with alcohol.' Give your loved one space to share their feelings and experiences, and practise avoiding interrupting, judging or offering solutions right away. Practise listening more than speaking as, sometimes, just being heard can be incredibly powerful. It might be helpful to practise what you want to say ahead of time, so you can focus on expressing care, concern and a willingness to support them without trying to control their decisions.

Be cautious of actions that unintentionally support or perpetuate the addiction. While it often comes from a place of love and wanting to protect the person, it can make it harder for your loved one to recognise the need for change. Examples of enabling behaviours might include covering for their mistakes, providing financial support that funds the addiction or making excuses for their behaviour. Instead, set clear boundaries around what you will and won't do. For example, you might say, 'I can't lend you money anymore, but I'm happy to help you find treatment options.' Reflect on your current behaviours and identify whether any might be enabling. Consider talking to a therapist or support group for guidance on setting healthy boundaries.

While your support is invaluable, addiction is typically a strong pull towards unhelpful behaviours, which can cause family and friends to feel that perhaps the individual doesn't care — leading to challenging emotions that can get in the way. Encouraging your loved one to seek help from a mental health professional can often be one of the most impactful things you can do. Consider suggesting meeting with a doctor or therapist as a first step. Avoid overwhelming them with demands for immediate, drastic action. Research treatment options in advance, such as local rehabilitation programs, outpatient services or support groups, and see if you can provide specific, accessible information to make it easier for them to take the next step. Whether it's driving your loved one to appointments, helping them with paperwork or simply being there for emotional support, offering small acts of assistance can make the process feel less daunting.

Remember that recovery is rarely linear. It often involves setbacks, relapses and moments of doubt. As hard as it is to watch, these challenges are a normal part of the journey. Seek ways to look after yourself to be patient with the process. Your loved one may deny the problem, resist help or relapse after periods of progress. This doesn't mean they're not trying — it's a reflection of how difficult addiction is to overcome. Do your best to stay consistent in your care and encouragement. Celebrate small victories and avoid shaming them for any setbacks they experience. Instead of saying, 'I can't believe you relapsed,' try, 'I know this is hard, but I believe you can keep moving forward.' Practise patience by focusing on progress rather than perfection, and remind yourself that change takes time — and that your role is to support, not to control.

Supporting someone with an addiction can be emotionally exhausting. To be a source of strength for them, you need to take care of yourself, too. Make time for activities that replenish your energy and wellbeing, whether it's exercise, hobbies or spending time with friends. Consider writing down three things you'll do each week to take care of yourself, and stick to them. Remember, you can't pour from an empty cup, so it's important to set boundaries around your limits. For example, you might decide not to engage in arguments when your loved one is under the influence. Joining support groups and connecting with the families of others in similar situations can also reduce feelings of isolation and provide access to valuable advice.

While compassion is key, it's also important to encourage personal responsibility. Recovery requires the individual to take ownership of their behaviour and choices. Ask yourself to what extent you rescue them from every consequence of their actions. Shielding them too much might prevent them from recognising the impact of their addiction. Support them in taking steps towards accountability, such as apologising to those who they've hurt or actively participating in treatment. When appropriate, gently remind your loved one of their goals and values, such as saying, 'I know you want to rebuild trust with your family, and getting help is a big part of that.'

One of the hardest things about addiction is that you can't force someone to change — they have to make the decision for themselves. As hard as it is, accepting this can help you let go of guilt, frustration and the need to 'fix' everything. Instead, focus on what you can do and practise letting go of what is out of your control. You can express love, provide resources and set boundaries, but you can't control their choices. Recognise that their recovery is ultimately their responsibility. This doesn't mean you don't care; it means you are respecting their autonomy.

One of the things that is in your control is the behaviours *you* choose. By modelling healthy behaviours, you can show your loved one what's possible. Examples might include taking care of your physical and emotional health, maintaining healthy relationships, and seeking help for your own stress or concerns. Seeing you prioritise your own wellbeing may inspire your loved one to do the same. It can be helpful to share your own self-care routines or personal growth efforts, while avoiding framing them as advice. For example, 'I've found meditation really helps me manage stress' can be more impactful than 'You should try meditating.'

Even if your loved one isn't ready to change, letting them know you're there with consistent love and support can plant seeds for future recovery. It can be common for people to resist help at first, but knowing they have someone in their corner can make all the difference when they're ready to take that step. You might say things like, 'I'm here for you whenever you're ready. I love you and want the best for you.' It might feel appropriate to write a letter or text expressing your support, while keeping it non-judgemental and focused on care and encouragement.

Helping a loved one through addiction is a deeply emotional journey, but it's also an opportunity to strengthen your relationship and support them in rebuilding their life. While you can't fight their battles for them, your compassion, patience and understanding can make all the difference. Take care of yourself, lean on others for support and remind your loved one that they are not alone.

Reflection prompts

Whether navigating your own addiction or supporting a loved one, taking time to reflect can provide clarity. Here are some prompts to guide your thoughts — you can write in a journal or simply work through these thoughts in your mind.

For individuals struggling with addiction

1. What are some small, meaningful steps I can take today to prioritise my wellbeing?
2. What emotions or thoughts tend to trigger my cravings? How can I respond to them differently?
3. What's one thing I've learned about myself during this journey so far?
4. What would life look like if I no longer felt controlled by this addiction? How would I feel?
5. What are three things I value most in life, and how can I take small actions to align with these values?
6. Who in my life can I lean on for support, and how can I strengthen that connection?
7. How can I celebrate progress, even if it feels small, to motivate myself to keep going?
8. What would self-compassion look like for me right now? How can I practise it daily?

For individuals supporting a loved one

1. Am I setting healthy boundaries that protect my own wellbeing, while still offering my loved one support?
2. How can I show empathy and compassion without enabling harmful behaviours?
3. What expectations or frustrations might be holding me back from being fully present for my loved one, and do I need to take action to let go of these expectations or frustrations?
4. How can I take care of myself this week to recharge emotionally and physically?
5. What's one way I can express my support and care for my loved one without pressuring them?
6. How can I communicate my feelings and concerns in a way that builds trust and understanding?
7. What steps can I take to educate myself further about addiction and recovery?

PALATE CLEANSER
The Ultimate Entertainer – Michael Bublé

I'm asked a lot who my favourite celebrities are that I've met. To be fair, it is easier to say my least favourite than my favourite, but I do have a top five of both (in my head, anyway. It's not something I share openly!).

Michael Bublé is up there among the best, responsible for one of the most random, yet fun, celebrity encounters of my career.

In 2009 I was flown to Vancouver, Bublé's hometown, to interview him for his new album, *Crazy Love*. How these things work basically is that the record label in each country nominates media to do interviews and, depending on the country and its size and the artist's footprint and fan base there, they are allocated a certain amount of time. The bigger the star, the smaller the junket and the fewer number of interviews granted.

Bublé was a big deal then, as he is now. I was doing the only Australian print interview, and Tara Brown did the TV spot for *60 Minutes*. Business class flights from Sydney to LA, then on to Vancouver … I thought I was the bee's knees, living the dream. These days, most interviews happen over the phone or via video link. This interview was during the glory days when I was a platinum frequent flyer.

I was under no illusion then (just as I am now) that the reason I got the interview was because of the publication I worked for. *The Sunday Telegraph* and News Corp's national Sunday papers had the biggest reach. As much as I'd like to think it was because I had a good reputation (and relationships most definitely do count), ultimately it is the reach of the proposed article that gets you through the door.

I was the first interview of the day in the Bublé junket. A rooftop set-up with a camera crew was in place to film each interview slot of 15 or so minutes. My interview style is pretty relaxed — it always has been. I'm not lazy, I just don't write formal questions and I like to keep interviews as relaxed and conversational as possible. I'm not one of those journalists that writes down a list of 20 or 50 questions and sits there ticking them off a list as they go through the motions. That to me is counter-intuitive as it leaves no room for listening and responding to whoever I am chatting to. It is not that I don't prepare for interviews, I just don't like to be restricted by a set of questions.

The Bube (as I call him) took a shining to me on this particular day. It might have been my Aussie accent or the Australian publicist I was traveling with. Or perhaps it was simply that I had a casual interview style, although I don't remember being that relaxed as I sat jetlagged in front of the crew filming the interview for online video, which wasn't my usual thing back then.

Whatever it was, when we'd finished filming, Bublé said something about maybe catching up later when he's done. I thought he was being polite and didn't think much of it at the time — I was just relieved the chat went well.

After the interview, I got in the lift and went back to my room, with its spectacular view of Vancouver Harbour. I thought briefly about going out and sightseeing on what was my first (and so far only) trip to Vancouver. Instead, I transcribed the interview, keen to capture some of the fresh emotion of the chat (and to keep myself awake in my jetlagged state). Sat on the bed in my undies, I switched on the TV and the room phone rang not long after. I picked up expecting it to be the Aussie publicist, but it was the Bube himself telling me his car was out front and that I should come down as we were going back to his place. I threw on some pants and a top and bolted out the door, excited, nervous, surprised and full of anticipation about where we were going and what we were going to do.

Bublé had a big black car, a rich one I remember thinking. I'm not much into cars but I knew it was expensive. He fanged out the driveway and we drove to his place, which could only be described as a large but humble family mansion.

It started snowing as we pulled into his driveway. Bublé, an American label exec and an Australian publicist were there — it was just the four of us.

It was a pens-down moment, so I was off the clock and of course I wasn't going to write any of that evening in my story.

I kept my cool as best I could, all the time thinking why he would have picked me and what a surreal experience it was. It took me in my mind back to high school me, picked on for not being cool enough. We walked into his house and sat around the kitchen bench on high stools. There was an older guy there, a family friend that worked for Bublé, doing bibs and bobs around the house. He poured me a glass of wine and we sat in the kitchen.

As I wanted to enjoy this night for the long haul, not spew and be sent back to the hotel in a taxi, I stuck with the red wine — white wine makes you go crazy, right?

Bublé is two years older than me so he would have been 33 at the time. Bublé was the ultimate entertainer. We moved into his large lounge room, which had a giant grand piano as the focus of the room. It was an awesome space, but I stayed cool. (Like yeah, I often sit around and chew the fat with a multiple Grammy Award winner on the regular.)

Bublé played his new album pretty much in its entirety, not in an egotistical way but genuinely interested to see our reactions. He also took requests. Like, wow.

True to form, I snuck off to the bathroom and rang my mum and sister. Slurring my words, it would have been morning where they were in Canberra, as it was late at night in Vancouver.

I remember thinking, even Michael Bublé's bathroom was just like a normal person's. Soap and toilet paper in the cupboard. Toothpaste and a toothbrush in the drawer. Did the Bube brush his teeth with these? There was normal cleaning shit in the cupboard too. Does Bublé clean his own bathroom? Of course not. It was a second bathroom so the toothbrush probably didn't belong to him but it was cool anyways to get that insight.

It was one of those surreal moments where I kind of had an out-of-body experience, looking down at myself and thinking, 'This is something I will never forget.'

It was a welcome release from the stuff going on with my family back home, with my mum dying. It was a pretty shitty time in my life. I didn't talk to Bublé about any of that stuff. We all just shared in the moment, enjoying good company.

At some point we went downstairs, where he had a home cinema and a games room. I took a photo of us by a foosball table — he is mad about sports. When I got back to my lovely hotel, I posted the pic on Facebook and crashed out.

I was woken up at 7 am, still drunk, by the Aussie publicist, who was calling to tell me to take the picture down. I had breached the pens-down rule by sharing the photo on my personal Facebook.

Sitting upright with the alcohol sweats, I felt terrible. I was hungover as fuck and also sad that I may have ruined my newfound friendship with Bublé. Of course, I immediately took down the photo.

I still have a souvenir from that night, a hand-knitted grey scarf made for Bublé by one of his two sisters. It is thick and scratchy in that big loop knit style. I don't wear it often as I somehow felt guilty that Bublé had given it to me in the early hours of that morning — like it was an accident and he may have regretted the next day. It showed how nice he was though, literally giving me something precious to him because it was snowing outside and I was completely unprepared for the cold weather.

The feature story I wrote about Bublé was published in *The Sunday Telegraph* and other News Corp newspapers on 11 October, 2009, two weeks after my mum's death. Reading the story today, I can't help but think of sneaking into his bathroom to call mum, desperate to share the moment with her as I knew she would have got a buzz out of it. And she did. We laughed about it on her deathbed.

I also related to much of what he said, feeling in some way we were kindred spirits in our own way in that we shared a similar sense of vulnerability.

'I'm still a work in progress, but I think I have more personal experiences to pull from,' he said in the interview, also talking about his body, which I related to.

'A couple of years ago I was a lot chunkier so I was a lot more self-conscious. I was really happy in a relationship and the relationship was with McDonald's. We made passionate love every night. I can't tell you how many double Quarter Pounders with cheese I must have put away.'

Jokes aside, Bublé had previously dated Hollywood star Emily Blunt and was then rumoured to be romantically involved with Argentinian actor and model Luisana Lopilato, who appeared in the video clip for his single, 'Haven't Met You Yet'.

Bublé has been married to Lopilato since 2011. They have four kids together, the eldest, Noah, who was diagnosed with hepatoblastoma, a rare liver cancer, in 2016.

Noah's illness forced Bublé to slow down with work as his son underwent chemotherapy and radiotherapy. He is a special man, one of the good guys who I am proud to now call a mate.

However, it was a decade before we caught up again and became friends. I had heard how he was going through mutual acquaintances, although we didn't cross paths until then.

Back in business in 2020, before coronavirus shut down the world, I caught up with Bublé in Sydney as he toured the country. He was proud to state he is a changed man.

'There is a reason why I am a different human being,' he said. 'I am grateful. I genuinely appreciate people so much. I am completely liberated as a human, as an artist, as an entertainer. I have been through the worst thing that could happen to you and now I sing karaoke for money and I am out there laughing and crying and dancing and I love every second.'

Bublé said he has sworn off social media for life, and he doesn't look himself up online. Bublé still has active Twitter and Instagram accounts but he doesn't access them personally. If there's something he needs to know, his team keeps him informed.

In a world dominated by apps and screen time, the diagnosis of his young son with cancer prompted the move.

'A lot of it was a philosophical change of really trying to choose to just be in the moment and to like wake up in the morning and to check myself and go, "hey dude, you are a lucky man, go out there and show your kids with your actions" because most of my life was spent being a narcissistic dick.'

We don't see each other that often, and I'm sure I'm one of many journalists he's formed friendships with over the years, but this relationship has been important to me for many reasons. Mostly because he's a great human, and, I have always felt we related to each other's stories of feeling 'other'.

PART III
SELF-ESTEEM

The dictionary definition of self-esteem is confidence in yourself and a belief in your qualities and abilities.

So many factors come into play when you're talking about self-esteem and its counter-negative, low self-esteem.

I sometimes wonder if we were all born equal with a clean slate, no shame, no guilt, no negative experiences, would we all be bursting with positivity? Obviously not.

Self-esteem is so varied, complex and … deep. It is a feeling, but to some of us, it is almost tangible.

For me, it ranges from how I feel about the way I look to how I feel about who I am as a person. They are the fundamentals of my everyday life.

I have always been worried about my weight. I have always thought I am ugly. I'm lumpy here, I've got too many chins, too high a hairline. Ugly. Not good enough. This is low self-esteem to me. The physical part, at least. How I feel on any given day about any of these external aesthetic factors, much of which I know logically I have no control over, can impact how life plays out for me at that time.

There are also the emotional, people-centred elements to self-esteem and self-worth.

If my brain doesn't work the same way as the person next to me on the train, then, again, that leads to me thinking I am 'less than' and therefore I take a hit in self-esteem because I skew towards the negative in that department. But I don't think I am unique here. I think we all feel this way and, knowing that, reminding myself of this, can be a soothing remedy to the craziness inside my brain.

This understanding, for me certainly, helps provide a greater perspective on my overall wellness and what's going on in my brain from a mental health perspective.

13

Body Conscious

Body dysmorphia is something I was diagnosed with later in life, but I have always had an unhealthy relationship with food. My weight has always fluctuated, and I have visceral memories from childhood through to now of being super self-conscious about my size. I was skinny as a rake as a young kid but as soon as I hit puberty, kaboom — the weight piled on. Even now, I am either super skinny or super fat — it is very hard to stay somewhere healthy in between.

When body issues are discussed publicly, teenage girls and young women are the main focus, and rightly so. I have seen the issue through the way women are portrayed in the media. The idolising of a particular type of body shape, along with a lack of diversity and unequal representation in the media, has long been an issue. Finally, over the past couple of years, the media is starting to embrace diversity in body shapes and sizes and to celebrate differences rather than encourage conformity.

However, it is not something men speak about often enough. For me, as a gay male (as a man, in fact; I am sure heterosexual males feel this pressure too), I have always felt fat and always been uncomfortable with my body and how I look. Body issues have plagued me my whole life. I know others can relate but it feels oh-so-isolating and lonely in my head when I think about my weight. I am no

Body issues have plagued me my whole life.

model and logically I know that is okay because, very few people are. I am pretty comfortable now with the fact I won't ever have a sixpack — those aspirations are in the past. My body and how I look is not something that has ever sat well with me. To this day, even now when I look in the mirror, all I see is *fat*. My double chin. My gross belly. Even when I am at a healthy body weight, all I see is fat, fat, FAT. I was at my worst with this as a teenager, during those formative years with all the pressure kids feel at that time.

The gay social scene has never helped with these demons for me, and I know others. It is well documented to be one where six-packs, tightly toned bodies and perfection are idolised. When you have underlying feelings of negative self-worth, these thoughts around body image are only heightened. It is something I think we are all aware of in the gay community and while there is a push for more celebration of diversity, there is a long way to go. That's why I have always struggled at gay events like Mardi Gras or Pride and sought a little help from alcohol or drugs to get me through those moments. Since giving up those substances, I rarely participate in shirts-off, party-style events, and to be fair I feel a lot better for it. I am, however, more involved in the community from an advocacy point of view, acknowledging our past and trying to fight for the rights of those to come. That is what is important, not a six-pack — although I would love both, if I'm honest.

Passing out

When I was a teenager, you could legally get a job at 14 and nine months. One of my first jobs was working at a men's clothing store. There was a young entrepreneur in Canberra called Christopher Palmer and he ran an eponymous clothing business. He would have been about 25 and was a star on the rise — that's how he pitched himself and how we all looked at him, not that he would stack up today I suspect on something like Heidi Klum's *Project Runway*. The local paper did stories about him though. His 'thing' was using loud, colourful materials for men's accessories like bow ties, neck ties and waistcoats. He also did braces and the lining of jackets. It was for guys who wanted to splash out with some colour at a wedding or function. Why couldn't men be fashionable too? It was really cool stuff and was well recognised as there was nothing else like it at the time.

Christopher Palmer had an office in a suburb called Mitchell, in the outskirts of the industrial estate in Canberra. Working at Christopher Palmer Menswear involved everything from working in the retail shop selling clothes, to packing orders and sending them out to customers. A lot of the business was digital retail, even back then.

During the first Christmas holidays after making it to 14 and nine months, I was working a lot of hours at Christopher Palmer as well as a couple of shifts a week at Kentucky Fried Chicken (now KFC). (I had two jobs at the same time because I put in several applications and got both these jobs. I was desperate to work and earn my own money.)

My body issues were pretty bad in my head then. I was obsessive and constantly thought that I was fat. I never got into the gym stuff, which was never really the vibe back then like it is now. I wasn't sporty and I wasn't a rugby league player, and I didn't run in the athletics team, swim in a squad or play football. Yet, I still wanted to fit in with the leaner, fitter, sportier guys my age. Maybe then I would have been more popular or just less of a loser, I'd think at the time.

I used to starve myself. Maybe this is a common thing that lots of people do. It shouldn't be, of course. I reached the point where I wouldn't eat breakfast and I wouldn't eat lunch. If I was lucky, I'd eat an apple or two Weet-Bix. I would only drink water because I stupidly thought if I was hydrated, I would be okay.

I used to starve myself.

One Saturday, packing boxes, I passed out on the floor at Christopher Palmer. That is the moment I realised for the first time in my life that I had a problem with my weight and my body.

My mum was called. I was embarrassed and taken home. I still felt disgusting inside. Fat. Ugly. It came to a head around this time and my mum forced me to see our doctor about it. My issues went far deeper than my relationship with food. I needed psychological help — but in those days, we didn't really have those conversations, even in a relationship so close as I had with my mum.

Later, as life has gone on, my weight — specifically my feelings about my body — is something I have discussed many times in therapy. Again, it is one of those things where logically you know the remedy (work out more, go to the gym, play footy, play tennis, swim, anything) but when you tell yourself constantly you are fat and ugly, it can be a hard slump to get out of.

It can lead to fixating on a particular issue. Just the other day a friend sent me a photo of a red carpet interview I did with Renée Zellweger. Rather than allowing myself to enjoy the moment, I spent hours fixating on my stomach, sending the shots to my sister and one of my closest friends to dissect and validate concerns of the fact I had been trying to maintain a healthy diet and yet all I could see was a fat gut.

Seeking therapy has helped to structure and implement strategies like focused breathing to handle these situations, although this is hard when it is a constant underlying issue. That is why, for me, ongoing therapy and check-ins are important.

Managing the obsession

It has always sat there with me — it has never gone away. These days though I'm aware of it and I know the triggers, so I try to keep on top of it. *Try* is the optimal word. I have little strategies to deal with my obsession, like not weighing myself.

> **We are all works in progress.**

We are all works in progress, so I am constantly finding new strategies that help.

Mirrors, for example, can be hard to avoid. I've never liked looking at myself in the mirror — all I see are my flaws. I am more comfortable with myself these days, but I still avoid a mirror on a bad day because it is triggering.

I like to distract myself when I am having negative thoughts. I cocoon myself on the couch and watch trashy reality TV, or put on some music and hit the pavement walking to sweat out my feels. I jump on the phone with a friend. Or sometimes, I just get into bed and sleep.

As for food in general, I am not a moderation guy. I am all in, or not in at all, as with most areas of my life. That means constant consideration and care when eating, always choosing the healthier option and not over-indulging.

Portion size has always been an issue for me too. I have to be super careful with this to ensure I don't overeat.

This is a constant battle for me. I lost quite a bit of weight a few years ago through old-fashioned exercise and healthy eating. Right now, I am at a stage of losing weight because I need to, and through COVID it was difficult (for many of us). I am currently working on that. My weight has yo-yoed my whole life so every time I stack on the weight, it sets me back mentally and I have to steel myself for the next bout of weight loss.

I wish there was an easy fix. Alas, we know the answer to that. Today you could use Ozempic (I've tried it), a magic injectable that suppresses your appetite, but the reality is that this is only a quick fix. And while I don't have an issue with this treatment, I think it should be used in conjunction with ongoing therapy to look at the root issues of what's going on for a person. A complicated relationship with food is rarely solved so easily.

I know weight-watching agencies can be used to measure the weight-loss journey — and for some people these work well. They make people accountable and provide a kick-start when it comes to shedding some kilograms.

In all honesty, though, they are pretty much a waste of money. Losing weight is not hard. You simply need to do more exercise and expel more energy so you burn more calories than you consume in food. An ex of mine used to say, 'No pasta, rice or bread after 3 pm.' We were together 20 or so years ago but I can still hear him saying that.

Usually, I try to keep my carbs to a minimum, and I tend to avoid lollies or drink soft drinks of any kind — although I love a lemon, lime and bitters — so I can keep to as healthy a diet as possible. The diet I am currently on is low carbs and higher protein with lots of vegetables. It can be boring, but hey — you can't have your cake and eat it too. Or can you? I wish I was the sort of person that could eat all the carbs in the world. So, carbohydrates are a problem for me, as is sugar in general. Mostly though, I just don't know when to stop. I never have. Like alcohol, or any other vice, moderation is difficult for me. It is all or nothing, so I choose (mostly) to be super-strict on my diet. Or if I overeat at lunch, I will eat a lighter meal for dinner. It is basic stuff others seem to have down pat, but I have always struggled with.

Sometimes I fall off the wagon, and I try not to emotionally beat myself up for that. The other day there was a giant bag of Minties going around the office. I didn't have one or even two. I would have eaten 20 and felt like shit afterwards — in my stomach and emotionally, because I would have known I'd let myself down.

And while I still see myself as a fatty when I am forced to look in the mirror, being strict and super-controlled works for the most part because I am aware of the demons brewing inside of me, fixating on food and leading me towards unhealthy behaviours like eating too much. I know if I go too far in that direction, I may then lean into starving myself, which is also not healthy.

My wonderful partner, Alex, keeps me honest (sometimes too honest!), but ultimately I do appreciate it.

Don't tell Alex but a couple of days ago I tricked myself into thinking I could have just one chocolate — a mini Reese's Peanut Butter Cup — but ended up eating 10. That's how I do moderation — I just can't, so I avoid the bad stuff altogether and I try to be aware of the triggers.

I try to go easy on myself when I do break the rules.

Being self-aware can be important too. For example, I am hyper-aware that my mind does sometimes play tricks on me and I do lie to myself about what I consume, so I try to go easy on myself when I do break the rules. By lying to myself, I mean making an active choice. For example, I love fresh orange juice with pulp, extra pulp even. I don't stop at a glass, and even knowing it is filled with sugar, I can easily drink a whole two litres in one sitting. I rationalise this to myself by saying it is natural sugar.

Sometimes I visualise myself as the Cookie Monster on *Sesame Street* scoffing down chocolate chip biscuits. That's me when I lose control. I feel disgusting and disgusted at myself.

For me, I know that my feelings about my weight and my body will be a constant lifelong battle. By not weighing myself and by focusing on eating as healthily as possible, I am doing everything I can to try and live my best life.

14

Hair Makes a World of Difference

While I'm always obsessing about my weight, my hair is a great cause of happiness.

It wasn't always the case.

For much of my life, I have tried to deal with my weight by exercising and eating well (not that I do enough of either of those — it is a work in progress, as I explore in Chapter 13), but over time I realised my increasingly receding hairline wasn't going to magically reappear.

My biggest nightmare was the thought of going completely bald. Seeing old-school television stars — you know who they are — showing off their toupées in a clichéd gag makes me cringe. So, too, does seeing old-school hair plugs. But the technology is much better these days. Apparently more blokes are having hair transplant surgery — they just don't talk about it (cricket great Shane Warne was the Advanced Hair 'Yeah Yeah' man).

After much deliberation, I took action in December 2012.

Having a hair transplant is a cause for embarrassment for many, but for me it's changed my life. When I'm asked about it, I don't shut down — I speak up with pride. My first consultation was at hair surgeon Dr Russell Knudsen's office in Double Bay, Sydney, and I left feeling pretty good. Dr Knudsen was and remains the best in the business.

'Baldness is an option, it isn't compulsory,' he said as he inspected my head. 'You can't cure baldness but you can control it.'

A few weeks later I was in the chair at Dr Knudsen's surgery — once I'd made up my mind, it was simply a matter of booking it in and hoping for a good result. I may never have taken the leap had it not been for a friend who had had the surgery a year or so earlier and for the fact I was asked to be a guinea pig on the procedure to write a story for the *Telegraph*'s weekend health and lifestyle lift-out, 'Body & Soul'. I probably would have done it anyway, as it was something I had been thinking about for many years, but the work-related-incentive certainly helped seal the deal.

The procedure was scheduled for a Friday morning to give me the weekend to recover.

The operation itself took about nine hours. I arrived just after 8am and was seated on what looked like a dentist chair, with a rug over my legs. The full-day surgery started with an injection of a local anaesthetic in the back of my head, and another at the front. I was also given sedation, so as rock music played from speakers overhead, I relaxed and slowly fell asleep as Dr Knudsen worked on my soon to be luscious locks.

Dr Knudsen took a large graft of skin from the back of my head, basically cutting from behind my left ear to behind my right ear. It sounds gruesome but it didn't hurt at all. It just means I'll have a scar if I ever choose to shave my hair off. In fact, I'm proud of it — it's like a badge of honour. (Sometimes, when my hair is shorter and people can see the scar, they ask if I had a car accident or a brain tumour or something before I admit the real story.)

After the graft was taken, a number of nurses worked with pieces of my scalp under a microscope, separating the follicles into clusters of one, two and three hairs. That's the natural way your hair grows, I was told. To get the most natural look, the hairs have to be transplanted in these compositions.

By about 5 pm I was tired and restless, but the whole day had gone well. In total, Dr Knudsen had transplanted some 2700 individual grafts, which translated to more than 5200 individual hairs. I was told that a percentage of the hairs would grow, while a large proportion would likely fall out and start growing a few months later. The whole process would take a year.

My case was severe and would have cost between $12 000 and $15 000 — it is a lot of coin, but money well spent considering how it made me feel afterwards.

I was lucky, I admit that — it was an amazing perk of the job to be a guinea pig for the procedure. A hair transplant costs a lot, there is absolutely no denying this fact, but in a world obsessed with looks and where people are having cosmetic procedures all the time, I think the money is well worth it. It is easy for me to say but the upshot in terms of confidence and self-esteem would mean I'd have the procedure 10 times over if I had to.

As I walked out of the surgery with a paper bag of painkillers, I bumped into another journalist who told me that her mum had recently had the same operation. I'd never thought women would need to have the procedure.

A rogue grey and a full head of hair

I was nervous about the recovery, mostly because I didn't want to look silly.

I was due to be the MC at a lunch two days later with a bunch of well-known faces and was a little anxious about wearing a baseball cap in the heat. I wasn't embarrassed, it was just uncomfortable and I looked a little icky without the cap, especially because I sweat heaps.

For the first week I wore a tennis sweatband around my head at night, which held everything together when I walked around the house. A week later I was on national TV doing my regular gossip segment on the Seven Network's *The Morning Show* and I wore a Christmas hat — thank goodness for Santa.

Many of the grafted hairs fell out within the first few weeks. I felt nervous and worried that I'd done something wrong and the hairs wouldn't grow as hoped; it was a strange feeling. Eventually, pretty much all the transplanted hairs fell out. I panicked, thinking that I'd endured the whole process for nothing, but my hair slowly began to grow back, just as Dr Knudsen said it would, though there was an awkward phase for a few months when the front of my head was filled with what looked like a baby chicken's fluff.

Having my first haircut a few months in was liberating. I felt like a new person and could only imagine how it would look when the stubble grew into full hair.

> **I felt like a new person.**

That's when my little grey hair came through. Someone suggested I pull it out. No way — I had earned every hair on my head. I search for that hair in the morning when I look in the mirror.

Several months later, I went for a check-up with Dr Knudsen, who said my hair was about 80 per cent grown.

'I can barely recognise you,' he said. 'I'm very happy with that.'

Inside, I was high-fiving myself because I couldn't imagine it being better than it was.

I love going to the hairdresser now. I even like going out of the house with messy hair and no product. It feels good. Seeing photos of myself then compared to now makes me laugh. I look like a totally different person.

During COVID, with lockdowns and little need for a haircut, I could tie my hair up in a (very small) tuft. I grew it really long, down past my shoulders during that time, and I now have something shorter but still with some length.

A new look, a more confident me

Even though I'm a journalist and use words daily for my job, it's hard to explain what the surgery has done for my confidence and how happy it's made me feel. It's confusing to me that many women are willing to have different cosmetic procedures — breast augmentation, face lifts, and so on — while guys are too embarrassed to look at their own insecurities and how best to better themselves. They certainly don't talk about it as often, although I think there is a growing sense of freedom around blokes speaking about hair loss. That is why I am as open about my hair transplant procedure as I am about the fact I live with depression, or my sexuality for that matter.

Life is complicated enough without hanging on to all the insecurities we inevitably have. Talking about my hair transplant has, I believe, made a difference. Initially, lots of men reached out to me to find out about the procedure, but even today I still have men contact me via email or social media on a regular basis asking about the procedures. I explain that while I'm no medical expert, the boost in confidence and self-esteem made the whole thing worth it for me.

Everyone that has come to me explains they have held on to feelings of shame, a fear of hair loss and a lack of self-esteem for a long time. They are desperate to know more.

Shame is such an awful, ugly emotion. If I can do something to help myself and others feel the opposite of shame — pride, dignity, admiration even — then why not?

Seven years later, I had a top-up op, so to speak. I went under the knife for a second round to thicken my hair. My hair was fine — in fact, I loved it — but I just wanted more of it. It was pretty much the same procedure, only this time I knew what I was in for (yes, there is some discomfort along the way that I was prepared for. The procedure has advanced even more now, so today's hair transplants are less invasive.) The results were great, and I was again really happy with the outcome.

I take finasteride tablets daily, as prescribed by my doctor. It can help stem the loss of hair but also promote hair growth. I am, however, thinking of maybe checking in with the doctor about my crown to see if I need anything there. Again, as costly as it can be, it is something I would consider money well spent.

The important thing is, today, I have hair and I love it, particularly that rogue grey sitting at the front of my hairline.

I've seen more and more grey hairs appear — I love them too.

Now, I don't really remember what it was like to have a receding hairline. When I look back at images of myself pre-hair transplant I see a completely different person, inside and out. I see someone with sunken eyes, bloated and sad-looking, trying to find himself.

I don't hate my looks as much as I used to. I guess the hair transplant was part of my transformation. I felt I was taking back control of my life — where I wanted to be in the world, and how I want to be seen. That is what I try to think about today when

I look in the mirror. It is important to acknowledge that while we can make changes cosmetically to our appearance (and why not?), anything in this space has to come with some form of self-reflection and work on improving our mental health, and there is of course much more to self-esteem than dealing with your physical insecurities.

15

From Rejection to Connection

Rejection — the fear of rejection and the perception of feeling rejected — is something I think about a lot. I often feel rejection, even when I have no need to.

It is something that has come up many times through therapy. I've worked out why, or at least one of the reasons why.

My mum and my biological father weren't together when I was born. They were dating when Mum fell pregnant with me and my twin sister. The story we know is that our father was in a break from a long-term relationship with the woman he ended up marrying and having kids with. That's what I have spent most of my life believing, and I've had no reason not to believe this. However, I realise that this is just my mum's side of the story.

I am well aware in life that there are three sides to every story — your side, my side and the truth.

Our father's last name was Perry, so my name would have been Jonathon Perry if they'd remained together, married and she took his name. Obviously that didn't happen. There is a Perry Park near my house, and as I walk the dogs past I often think about what life might have looked like growing up as

> There are three sides to every story — your side, my side and the truth.

131

Jonathon Perry. JP — that nickname sounds all right. JMo is better though — more dramatic, more showbiz.

Anyway, Mum and this guy, let's call him Luke (after the late actor Luke Perry from *Beverly Hills, 90210*) dated for a while. The story I know is that when Luke found out Mum was pregnant with twins, he left. That's a shortened version, but you get the gist. These things happen — as far as I can tell, the relationship was never serious. That was between them, and I don't judge either of them in any way at that point. I believe Mum would have been 23 at the time and there was no chance she was going to have an abortion. She was pro-choice but wanted to proceed with the pregnancy, and so my sister and I were born on 27 February, 1978.

Being a single parent back then was far less common than it is now, but she did it and she did her absolute best. Mum's parenting style was to treat my sister and I as friends. We could speak about anything, and we did. Even when I was overseas for work or on holiday as an adult, we would speak nearly every day, and when I was at home in Sydney, we would chat on average twice a day but sometimes more. I still know her phone number off by heart, even though she died 15 years ago.

She was my best mate. Mum was a teacher before we were born, working with high school kids in Canberra. We were born at Canberra Hospital, after which Mum moved to Sydney until we were nine to be closer to family and to return to studying for her PhD in Women's Studies at Sydney University.

We lived a basic life in a small house in Balmain — which is pretty rich now, but back then there were many working-class families in the area. Mum made sure we had everything we needed but we didn't have cash to burn, and we were by no means wealthy. That was the world to which I was born — my mum was a single parent who loved me and my sister immensely and gave us all the love that we needed. We didn't have name-brand clothes or expensive toys, but we never wanted for anything.

I was acutely aware from an early age that my father wasn't in our life, and Mum never hid that from us. She never made him out to be a monster or a bad person — he just wasn't in our lives. She also didn't sugar-coat their relationship: They were dating, she fell pregnant and they broke up. He didn't have anything to do with us, and it didn't seem like he wanted to.

I've seen my biological father all of three times in my life. Once when we were small kids, just toddlers, he came over to meet us and gave us a toy each (I don't remember what the toy was). The second time was around the age of 10 or 11 when we were living back in Canberra. We were at our local shops one day. It was a school day. While getting out of the car, we awkwardly bumped into him — all three of us (Mum, my sister and me). I knew who it was instantly from the photographs Mum had shown us, but he turned the other way and went about his business. Did he recognise us? I don't know. We didn't speak at first, our hearts racing with emotion. Later, knowing it was our dad, my sister and I chatted about the strangeness of our father living a couple of suburbs away and the possibility of seeing him again. We (well, mostly me because I was the more boisterous of the two and I'd often ask the questions for both of us) quizzed Mum on our origin story, how they dated and what our dad was like. Mum was always careful with her words, never speaking badly of our father, although I still always felt that sense of not being good enough, not worthy of his attention.

The third time I saw him, I was 17. I was preparing to go on a six-month student exchange to Hannover in Germany. Because Luke's name is on my birth certificate, I had to get his sign-off on the paperwork so I could go. It was beyond stupid — he'd had nothing to do with us and I didn't think had paid much child support, if any, so it was crazy that he had a say in what I was doing — but that was the way it was and there was no way around it. I made an appointment and met him at his work. I recall our meeting being for roughly 10 to 15 minutes. We exchanged pleasantries and he signed the form, and that was the third and last time I have seen my biological father in my life.

My sister, Alison, did try to reach out to Luke Perry (not his real name, remember) when my niece, Olivia, was born in 2003. Alison sent Luke a letter with some photographs of Olivia — who we believed to be his first-born granddaughter. It was nothing offensive, just a card with some photos inserted to mark what might be considered a milestone to celebrate. The gesture seemingly wasn't appreciated by our father. He rang Alison and told her in no uncertain terms that it was inappropriate for her to send anything to his house. He stated he wasn't interested in any contact then or in the future. Ouch, that hurt.

All this being said, I hate it when I see separated parents today playing their kids against their former spouse — it is so ugly and the people most hurt are the children themselves (who the parents usually say they are trying to protect). That was Mum's philosophy, so she never spoke ill of our dad. And that is why my sister reached out — he wasn't demonised in our household, plus, who wouldn't want to know they had become a grandfather, presumably for the first time.

While I've only met or seen him three times in all these years, he has unknowingly played a huge part in my mental health battle because, like it or not, and partly due to him, I have this massive fear of rejection. It is something my mum had too — not from him, necessarily, but she always felt like she wasn't good enough. I believe I inherited some of that sensitivity to rejection — the feeling that I am not good enough — from her, along with a bunch of other things (like my addiction to shopping — which I talk about in Chapter 21 — and maybe my broader depression).

This feeling of not being good enough is something that comes up constantly anytime I have a counselling session. It is at the back of my mind most of the time and is something I fight constantly because logically I know I *am* good enough. It is the first theme a doctor or psychologist notes in me when we meet for the first time, and I have worked on and continue to work on in my life. It has been a common theme when speaking to guests on my *Mental As Anyone* podcast too.

It is what has driven me in this pursuit, the idea that not feeling good enough or feeling 'other' is something I think we all relate to regardless of how amazing our lives might seem from the outside.

Oh, brother

In December 2008, nine months before Mum died, we were down the south coast of NSW, where we spent holidays every year over the Christmas break and I found Luke on Facebook. I'm a journalist, so researching this stuff is part of the job and not something

I find hard in general. It was in the early days of Facebook — Mark Zuckerberg had launched the website just four years earlier at Harvard University in the US, making it available to the general public in 2006.

I mulled over what to do for a few days after finding what I believed to be our two biological half-brothers, Matt and Paul (names have been changed). Then I decided to message the boys. As I wasn't sure if they knew we existed, I messaged Luke, too, as a courtesy to let him know that I had contacted his sons.

This is what I sent:

Luke,
As a courtesy, I've copied below a message I have sent to your sons.
Regards,
Jonathon

Hi Matt/Paul,
This is totally out of the blue but not really sure how else to get in touch with you.
I am not sure what you know about my twin sister — Alison (she is also on Facebook) — and I. Your father, Luke, is also our father. We are 30 years old. We have had no ongoing relationship with him, having only met him a few times.
We have thought about you and your brother over the years and pondered whether and how to get in contact. We'd love to meet you at some point although totally understand that you may have no interest. As I have said, I don't even know if you are aware we exist.
I guess the next step, if any, is yours.
Cheers,
Jonathon

Alison knew about the messages, and we didn't really know if we would get a response. Obviously, I was desperate for one. My mum knew about it too — not that we felt we needed her permission, but it was right to tell her. Her only fear was us being disappointed.

And she didn't want me to suffer with the rejection that had pained me for so much of my life.

The response was swift from our biological father, Luke, who appeared to have blocked us on Facebook. One of my brothers, Matt, didn't respond. The other, Paul, did. He was living in the UK at the time and was eight years younger than us, so at the time he was in his early 20s.

We were right — Luke hadn't told them about me and my sister. He was shocked. We exchanged a few messages and even spoke on the phone one time. He sounded like a great guy.

Paul moved back to Australia not long after we connected and said he was going to speak to his father about us. Then, he seemingly blocked us. I felt rejected again, but I wasn't angry — I hoped that there was a bigger picture at play. I felt it was a chapter of my life I deeply wished to complete — an open book I couldn't close.

Meeting the family

I couldn't fathom finding out I had a blood relative, whether a sibling or cousin or the like, and not wanting to meet them, regardless of the backstory. So I continued to hope that one day a Facebook message would pop into my inbox and it would be from one of the boys. I just hoped it wouldn't be too late: Time is precious, as we know from losing Mum when she was just 56.

On 15 January, 2024, I received a direct message unexpectedly on Facebook.

It was 10.26 am. I was working from home in my little office in the garage shed when my phone pinged.

> *Hi Jonathon, happy new year!*
> *I'm sorry for not responding to you and shutting you and Alison out all these years. Hope you both are really well (smiley face emoji).*
> *How are you going?*

Huh? What? Wait a second... The message was from my half-brother, Matt.

To say I was shocked is a complete understatement. Flabbergasted, yes. I've never been good at keeping it cool, so I didn't hesitate and immediately responded.

> *Hey mate, this is such an incredible surprise.*
> *I'm doing really well. I just got back from three weeks in Thailand on Saturday and dread being back at work today. I want you to know I don't want to cause you any pain or make things difficult, it's just that life is short and you are biologically our half-brother. I'd love to know more about you.*
> *How are you?*

I strangely then sent a thumbs-up emoji and, just as quickly and awkwardly, added, 'Sorry, didn't mean to send a random thumbs up.'

Wow, I was playing my cards well here … cool as a cucumber.

Matt then responded:

> *I agree! I know things haven't been easy for Alison and you and there has been pain. I would like to get to know you both. Not sure how and may take a little time but I am keen.*

Holy shit, we were off and running. Matt and I messaged back and forth. He explained that when I'd messaged originally, he and Paul had spoken about it but that it was all too much for them in their early 20s. Understandable.

We went back and forth about life, love, schooling, uni, travel … it was amazing. Paul is eight years younger than me and my sister, while Matt is ten years younger. Everything flowed so easily. At the end of our chat, as we both had to get back to work, we said we would organise a time to speak on the phone.

That was one of the best days of my life so far. I rang Alison, who is much less pushy than me, and we were both cautiously optimistic.

I was wary of being hurt and told Matt that, and in reply he assured me that 2024 was going to be a good year.

That was one of the best days of my life so far.

And it was, in that department at least. Matt spoke to Paul and we set up a WhatsApp chat group where the four of us could message.

A month later, the four of us met for the first time at a famous Canberra café called Tilley's Devine Cafe Gallery.

I felt a combination of nervous, excited ... all of the feels. I drove to Canberra for the weekend, where Alison and I travelled together to meet our half-brothers.

We were both anxious: What if they'd made a mistake, changed their minds and weren't interested in meeting up? But we had nothing to worry about — Paul and Matt were already there waiting for us.

Immediately, any tensions dissipated. We sat together for well over an hour talking about everything — our childhoods, our family situation, Alison's four daughters (Matt and Paul didn't just get us, they were suddenly uncles for the first time), where we'd holidayed growing up, school, work, partners ... it felt very natural, like we'd known each other our whole lives.

We spoke of the fact that whatever had happened between Mum and our dad was not our story, but we could pick it up from there. Alison and I don't speak ill of our dad, nor should we. It is something we both respected in our mum and something we have continued for that reason. Also, in all the therapy, all of the sessions I've done talking about abandonment issues, why would I want to carry that pain around constantly? It only hurts me in the end.

We laughed about the fact we had believed their names were Matt Paul and Paul Matt, which was the way they were named online. That was a joke, apparently, from a trip they took around Europe where, on a night out, they changed their names on social media and just kept it that way. Their real names are family names and much more original.

I sat there fascinated by their facial features, comparing in my head our likeness. There is a definite likeness between the four of us, and I know I look very much like my biological father.

I was pretty stoked when we asked a woman at the table next to us if she could take a photo of the four of us, and she noted: 'You look alike.'

We were all quietly happy to hear it, so we told them we were related but we were only just meeting for the first time. It was a moment I will remember forever.

That day we agreed we wanted to continue to explore the relationship but not rush anything. The next morning, Matt and his girlfriend met me, Alison and her family for breakfast. Things were moving quickly, and I wasn't complaining. We were all looking forward to what the future had in store for us.

And that is what we have done since, chatting regularly on our WhatsApp group. Paul isn't great at messaging — he never looks at his phone — but he chimes in every now and then.

Matt and his girlfriend have visited me in Sydney, staying at my place. They attended the launch of my *Mental As Anyone* podcast and we speak pretty much weekly.

It has helped bring an end to years of pain and feelings of abandonment.

It has blossomed into a very special and important relationship.

Internally, while this is the beginning, it has helped bring an end to years of pain and feelings of abandonment. Our brothers do not hate us. They do want to know us. It wasn't something we did. It was just life. Life works in mysterious ways. This was simply how it was meant to be.

Seeing my counsellor at that time, I remember an overwhelming feeling of joy coming over me — a heavy weight had been lifted, and while I wished we had met earlier, I was ready to carpe diem the shit out of that relationship.

> **It has helped using ... an end to years of pain and feelings of abandonment.**

16

The Things We Do for Love

I dated a guy once for four years and we were intimate maybe a handful of times during that period. Some relationship, huh? In true me style, I was so desperate to be loved and feel loved (and constantly chasing that dream scenario) that I stayed with him.

He was straight before our relationship. He claimed to have never been with another guy before me, which is such a cliché gay thing for me to be lured in by — someone who is supposedly straight but curious — leading me to chase the unobtainable. I guess it was worse than a catfishing situation (which is when someone creates a fake identity to lure someone into a relationship and then takes advantage of them) because this guy gave me just enough to keep me there but never more.

I was good friends with former *Australian Idol* winner Casey Donovan at the time and remain very close with her today. We lived together as flatmates throughout some of this time. She has spoken a lot about her years of being cruelly catfished, and I lived through some of that with her. She put it all in her book, *Big, Beautiful & Sexier*, which was quite a big deal at the time.

Now, I don't know what is worse: being catfished, or being in a relationship with a real person who you know isn't there for the right reasons. This guy earned his own money, all of which went on drugs and alcohol, and I would subsidise his other life bills — rent, electricity and mobile phone, whatever he needed. I bought his alcohol and cigarettes, drugs too when he asked.

This guy and I were friends mostly, and he wasn't a great friend at that. I convinced myself we had a strong connection and we became best mates — as much as you can be best friends with an alcoholic and a drug user. I don't think we really had any deep-level connection at all. It was almost as though I knew that I was a glutton for punishment and that I knew that it was never going to work, but because I didn't feel good enough, I didn't think I deserved anything more. Not having had a run of successful relationships at that time, I honestly thought that might be all I was ever worth.

> **It was all about me surviving rather than me being happy.**

It was all about me surviving rather than me being happy.

I met him while I was working on a story — he was a friend of a friend of one of the reality TV singers that I met along the way. We ended up starting to see each other pretty much straight away. I thought we had a connection, and there was certainly a sexual attraction from my perspective, but the reality was we shared little more than kissing, and that was only ever when he was drunk and stoned (high on marijuana).

I'm not sure if I ever believed he was truly into the relationship. Maybe I tricked myself into thinking that it was the real thing. I'm sure my family and friends knew it was a farce, but they were mostly supportive — although now, looking back, I kind of wish they had held an intervention. I'm not sure if it would have made a difference, but it must have looked toxic from the outside looking in.

All this guy cared about was the fact that I earned a steady wage and was able to help fund his lifestyle. He was a labourer who worked to live, not lived to work. He lived a fun life but was equally screwed up himself and doing nothing to help himself or others. Perhaps I thought I could save him.

Neither of us had found the right balance in our lives when it came to work–life balance or in the mental health space. Having been a workaholic most of my adult life, I admired the fact he seemingly made the most of life outside of work. I was drawn to him. That's what I thought in the beginning at least, but the reality was he spent most of his time fucked up on whatever drugs he was taking at the time — cocaine, ecstasy, marijuana, alcohol … anything he could get his hands on.

He was from Europe and in Australia on a working visa. His main — only — priorities in life were smoking marijuana and getting drunk. He was definitely an alcoholic and most definitely a professional pot head. I fell in love with a guy who wasn't lovable because, like me, he didn't love himself. He cared about his bong, beer and spirits. It was pretty sad

> **I fell in love with a guy who wasn't lovable because, like me, he didn't love himself.**

actually, but I don't blame anyone else, I allowed myself to get into that situation and I allowed myself to be there because I was so desperate for someone to love me back and reciprocate my feelings. Even though it was unstable, it was stable in some senses. It was consistently unstable is probably the better terminology. It was also my longest relationship to that point. Regardless, ours was anything but a healthy relationship.

One time, I paid for him to fly to Los Angeles with me for a holiday and at the last minute he cancelled. I wasn't able to get a refund on the flight, so I was down a few grand. I knew it was pathetic, but he strung me along with excuse after excuse. Deep down I knew what was going on, but I let it continue anyway. I didn't value myself any more than he did, so I was willing to take anything.

For a time there, I guess you could have called me a drug mule. I say that lightly, with a half smirk on my face, but it is true in a way. I would withdraw hundreds of dollars, sometimes more than a grand, and drive out west of Sydney to an industrial area near Liverpool, where I would be directed to park in an unused parking lot in the back streets and wait. There was an old car yard that was gated off. At a designated time a car would drive in, a beaten up old sedan covered in patched paint, with half the bumper coming off the front. It was like a bad scene from an even worse movie, and I was starring as the fish-out-of-water city guy doing a deal that could go wrong at any moment.

I remember vividly thinking, 'What if I get busted by the cops?' It would end my career. But I didn't care; I did it anyway. I only cared about keeping him happy — the boyfriend who cared about nothing but himself and getting high.

I had given up on my own life.

It is strange to think about now, years later, given my career means the world to me and always has done, and I am in the most loving and caring relationship with an incredible guy who is very successful in his own right. With my mum having died, I guess in many ways I had given up on my own life in a way and was living because I didn't feel I had any other option — I'd promised myself to stay alive for my sister and nieces.

With that in mind, being locked up didn't seem so bad. This relationship was filling the emotional void or hole that I felt I needed to fill. I didn't feel strong enough to face the world on my own, and I had never felt worthy of a 'real' or 'healthy' relationship, so I sought love and validation in any way I could find it.

Once the beat-up drug dealer car drove in, I'd follow, pull up my car and walk into what looked like an old mechanics building. It was dodgy as dodgy could be. This car yard was the kind with old *Penthouse* girlie magazine posters hung up inside, and the bikini girl calendars from several years prior were still hung up on the wall. There was an overwhelming smell of grease. It was musty too, that stagnant dust smell of an abandoned building.

Sometimes I would go alone, other times with my 'boyfriend'. This was an every-few-months thing, at least half a dozen times in total, probably more. I'd buy him as much as I could afford in that pay cheque cycle to keep him happy. He always said he would pay me back but never did. It most definitely wasn't my comfort zone, although I tried to fit in and seem as 'straight' as I could. I'd hand the money to the drug dealer, who would count the cash out loud, throwing the notes down on the bench in an exaggerated way in case any cash was missing. He fit the stereotype perfectly in his baseball cap, button-up tracksuit pants and jumper as he shoved the marijuana into my hands. The pot would come in zip-lock bags, usually four one-ounce bags (28g per bag), stashed in a supermarket plastic bag. Keeping my cool, I'd politely take the pot and rush out to my car to get home as soon as possible, praying the whole time I wasn't pulled over by police on the hour-long drive home.

It was a rush, a little high of sorts where I knew I was doing the wrong thing but kind of didn't care. I justified it knowing I wasn't dealing drugs to young teenagers. I didn't care about myself. My self-esteem was rock bottom, so any rush of emotion, the validation I'd feel at seeing him happy when I'd give him what he wanted, was worth it. He'd spare me a smile, a hug, a little affection, which satiated my desire for validation short term. Inevitably though, I was very quickly back to feeling like a piece of shit.

If I had been busted, I would have gone to jail, probably. All the time I felt like a drug runner on borrowed time. Am I going to be arrested for even admitting this? I never smoked the marijuana, not once, but I knew I was doing the wrong thing, and I carry that guilt and shame to this day.

I'd think that if he was happy, happily stoned, we were good. By keeping him stoned, pathetically, it kept whatever this abnormal relationship was ticking along, which was a very unhealthy way to be. I knew that and I was always close to a breakdown because I wanted something that I wasn't going to get. When I pulled away in moments of strength and clarity, he reeled me back in. He preyed on my vulnerability. But I was desperate to be loved.

When the relationship finally ended, it was because he broke up with me, not the other way round. I had been rejected again, but I was left feeling like that's what I deserved. He went back to girls after that and is, I believe, in an unhappy marriage now to keep his parents happy.

Now, I look back at this time with some shame but also gratitude because he did me a favour in the end. My life is exponentially better with my wonderful partner, Alex. No relationship is easy, but I was stronger as a result of what I'd been through and more mature emotionally, ready to commit to a future with someone who reciprocated. Through the pain of dating this guy, I'd found some value in myself—but I had to hit rock bottom to get there.

17

Race-Car Mind

I have to preface this chapter with the insight that it was the hardest part of the book to write, not because of any trauma but simply on the basis I procrastinated on this more than any other (which is ironic).

A million search results come up when you look for an online ADHD (Attention Deficit Hyperactivity Disorder) test.

You're bombarded with questions like, 'Do you find it hard to meet deadlines at work?', 'How often will your mind wander onto different topics?', 'How often do you find yourself fidgeting or losing something?' and 'Do your energy levels fluctuate?'

Okay, so I've done a bunch of these online tests and according to them, I have high-range or high-level ADHD.

The truth is, I think most people would come up with a positive ADHD diagnosis on the basis of such broad questions that are open to manipulation and interpretation. That is the danger of Dr Google and social media.

I have, however, been told for as long as I can remember that people think I have ADHD, bearing in mind that the term wasn't one used commonly until more recently.

When I was younger, kids were just told they were naughty, hyperactive or plain and simple attention-seeking.

I am impulsive. Sometimes forgetful. Often emotional. Distracted easily (like very, very, very easily). I unknowingly and unintentionally interrupt conversations. I'm told I often stop telling a story halfway through, or switch stories altogether without noticing.

I often answer phone calls in the middle of a conversation. One friend told me I am easily bored, and my attention is lost quickly on things I am not interested in. All these things can feel brutal and are hard to hear.

I regularly write stories with someone on the other end of the phone, needing validation that the angle I am taking is right. I read out the story to the interviewee or run my lead paragraph past a colleague at work, not for anything other than to validate that I am on the right track.

I second-guess myself constantly.

To be fair, it may be annoying for others, but I find it ultimately helps me because I don't have to fix things as often later. And it helps as a journalist to build relationships based on trust.

Even though I know on paper I am a successful journalist, and I can write a yarn, no problem, I often lack confidence in my abilities. That is the universality of this conversation. I find most people suffer from these self-doubts.

I'm told people find me a bit aloof, scary even, and some say they struggle to truly connect with me because I always seem busy, distracted or disinterested — when that is absolutely not the case. I am just trying to get by, to exist.

Funnily enough (for people like me who overthink everything and take everything personally), when you realise nothing in the world is really about you, it makes life easier to survive.

It wasn't a sudden realisation — it was just something that crept up on me and has been confirmed through life experience and self-reflection. We are really just tiny specks in one short lifetime in this monumental world.

Knowing what I know now about ADHD and my diagnosis, everything makes sense.

This is a realisation I have to remind myself of often. We've all been caught up in thinking we are the centre of our own universe, surely? It is quite freeing to let that go.

Isn't that just 'normal' behaviour? Evidently not. Is that just my personality? Evidently not.

Knowing what I know now about ADHD and my diagnosis, everything makes sense. Finally.

At the end of 2023, I sought an official diagnosis with the help of my incredible GP, Dr Jane Hunt, at Sydney's Holdsworth House Medical Practice.

She referred me to Dr Morteza Hayati at Sydney's Mind Oasis Clinic, where I had to undergo a series of tests — blood tests, surveys, online forms and the like. I remember it being very comprehensive, as it should be.

After the pre-appointment carry-on came an initial consultation with the doctor, followed by a follow-up appointment.

The symptoms of ADHD include low self-esteem, short attention span, personal boundary issues, poor multi-tasking ability, high stress levels and social anxiety. Tick. Tick. Tick. Tick. Tick. Tick.

I related to many of the facts listed on the Mind Oasis Clinic's website about ADHD. The website pointed out that ADHD is non-discriminatory in that it can affect anyone of any gender, age or background. It also went on to explain that ADHD was a genetic, brain-based condition that had nothing to do with lifestyle choices.

These points instantly destigmatised some of the negativities I had been feeling about going through the ADHD diagnosis process. They reinforced my views around mental health in general — that anyone can be impacted — but also helped me to feel less alone, and seen in something that I'd never really allowed myself to think of as a contributing factor to my struggles.

Dr Hayati is a respected psychiatrist of several decades' experience working both in Australia and Iran. Having experienced and gone through many psychiatric assessments over the years, the process felt very similar to any other for me.

We covered my extensive medical history, the various traumas I'd experienced in life, my relationships with family, friends and partners, self-esteem, rejection, addiction, we talked about drug and alcohol use, certain behaviours and my response patterns.

I felt safe, seen and heard. It was clinical and professional. They took me seriously, even when I wondered if I was wasting people's time. Honestly, I wasn't sure if I had ADHD or if my 'behaviours' were all from other mental health diagnoses I'd received over the years, from deep depression to traits of borderline personality disorder, extreme PTSD and the like.

At that point, I kind of bundled them all into one big messy pile in my brain.

> **I kind of bundled them all into one big messy pile in my brain.**

A second appointment with Dr Hayati confirmed his diagnosis that I did indeed have ADHD. It wasn't as simple as that — he said my case is complex but that it is ADHD.

Dr Hayati said it was a surprise I'd kept my life going so seemingly successfully given everything I'd been through. I could have ended up on the streets, or worse, he said.

To be honest, the rest of the diagnosis was all a bit of a blur. Hearing that I have ADHD, what medication I needed to take, so something I could tangibly do to manage it, was the most important thing to me at that stage.

Due to the various other medications I take, Dr Hayati determined that I couldn't be placed on stimulant medications to manage my ADHD as that would most certainly push me over the edge. Instead, I now take sodium valproate morning and night. It is a medication used predominantly for epilepsy but also mental health conditions like bipolar disorder and ADHD.

The meds took several weeks to take effect. While I didn't notice any obvious symptoms at first, there is one major ongoing issue that I find challenging. The only real symptom I have is shaking hands and forearms. It is a strange and weird experience.

In a job where I often speak publicly, the tremors can make holding a microphone or notes difficult. At one brunch event I hosted for Virgin Australia, Ovolo Hotels and lululemon around Mardi Gras, I had to declare my ADHD diagnosis because my hands were shaking so badly. I held the microphone hard against my chest to stop my hands shaking.

I felt embarrassed but I couldn't do anything but own it.

A positive or negative ADHD diagnosis is too expensive. Fact.

All up, I paid more than $2000 (online it states that the cost of an ADHD assessment in Australia can vary in price from $1500 to $3000) for my diagnosis with tests and appointments.

The costs associated with a diagnosis can make it simply impossible for many. Studies state 3 per cent of Australian adults have ADHD. Imagine what that would come to if everyone was able to be tested?

And once you have the diagnosis, regular check-ins with your healthcare practitioner are also expensive and not subsidised.

I spend hundreds of dollars a month on medications alone. Adding a $500 appointment to that in the current cost-of-living crisis is not realistic for most, I am sure.

This is a serious issue I believe we as a country, and more broadly as global citizens, need to rectify. The need is there, and the greater benefit would most definitely outweigh the subsidy costs. For me, I stretched myself and paid what I had to. The diagnosis was worth it because it gave me a point at which to put a full stop and start again. Now, I can move forward.

The fact is, too, that there remains a huge stigma around ADHD. In fact, I would say it is getting worse.

There remains a huge stigma around ADHD.

I am open about my ADHD as I am about my other health conditions. Why shouldn't I be?

So many people have questioned my diagnosis, asking if I truly have the condition or if it is just a fad that doctors are prescribing.

What a ridiculous proposition.

In actuality, due to the massive costs associated with diagnosis, I believe we are only scratching the surface on the number of ADHD cases here and around the world.

I've heard people express scepticism about ADHD, saying it is simply laziness or a lack of discipline. Some attribute the rise of ADHD cases to handheld devices and too much screen time. Some, many even, say that in today's world, we over-diagnose the condition.

These stigmas can only lead to things like people not seeking a diagnosis and in cases where they are, treatment adherence, depression, lowered self-esteem and other heightened symptoms.

Imagine if we had a positive, nurturing response rather than a negative one.

Understanding the zoomies at last

I was surprised by how emotional I was when I left Dr Hayati's office after my diagnosis.

I cried in the car when I rang my sister, Alison, and my partner, Alex.

I wasn't so much sad as overwhelmed by a mixture of emotions — frustration, validation and, most importantly, I felt seen on something that had plagued me at the back of my mind for so very long.

It explained so much and opened a world of understanding I'd not entertained before. It wasn't an excuse, but it gave me an explanation for some of the behaviours I'd exhibited, such as obsessing about things, over-thinking, struggling to collect my thoughts, difficulty sleeping, difficulty focusing, being too focused, trying to do a million things at once. The behaviours change depending on the situation or the moment.

I felt less alone. There was a reason.

Plus, it opened up a whole world of fun. Some of the funniest nicknames I've heard for ADHD include 'zoomies', 'race-car brain', 'captain distraction', 'squirrel brain' and 'human tornado'. 'Zoomies' feels right to me!

Also, who doesn't love an ADHD meme? Not to trivialise what is something serious, but here are some memes I found online that I totally relate to:

- ADHD is when you're on your way to grab a snack and decide to change careers, learn the drums and clean out your cabinets first.
- Sometimes I'll start a sentence and I don't even know where it's going. I just hope I find it along the way.

- All those jokes about my ADHD would probably piss me off if I ever paid attention long enough to see how they end.
- I'm not random, you just can't think as fast as me.
- One thing I love about my ADHD is my ability to hyperfocus for hours on something that interests me. I spent yesterday reorganising four old boxes of assorted plasters into one neat box.

I think humour helps destigmatise the condition and can build a sense of community. If we can't laugh at life, how else do we cope? That's what I think anyway. Community is a very broad term and there are obviously a lot of different sub-communities within any given community. But feeling connected with others, feeling understood together, cannot be downplayed. I felt this when I was first diagnosed and dived headfirst into the online world of dissecting what had been shared with me.

My friends, some of whom also have ADHD, laugh at our quirks. And we do that because it can be funny. If you don't laugh, you cry, right? It can also be extremely tough and isolating when you fight the fight alone so why not share the laughs and the pain?

Difference is to be celebrated because in doing so, we feel less alone ourselves. While the world can feel quite dark, particularly now, celebrating our differences can go a long way to ensuring these conversations continue in a safe and respectful way.

Your TOOLKIT for SELF-ESTEEM
DR JODIE LOWINGER

When helping my clients with their goals, whether as their executive performance coach, or as their clinical psychologist, one of the most fundamental questions I ask them to reflect on is: 'What is driving your behaviour at any particular moment — are you being driven by discomfort with uncertainty and a need for certainty and control, or are you being driven by the things that you value, and embracing associated assertiveness and wellbeing?' The first option is underpinned by worry stories such as, 'What if I'm not good enough?', 'What if they reject me?' or 'What if they judge me negatively? I need to know for sure that they aren't.' Whereas the second option is the ability to sit with the discomfort of uncertainty and say, 'Maybe they are or maybe they aren't; I'm worthy whether I get validation or not.' This is *self-esteem*. It is something we have seen that JMo has grappled with his whole life, as have many others.

Healthy self-esteem is the voice in your head that says things like, 'I'm worthy and valuable for who I am, not because of the reassurance I am given about who I am.' It is about accepting you for you — a human with strengths and imperfections — rather than conditionally accepting yourself based on what you achieve, how you look or how others perceive you.

In contrast, low self-esteem is a difficulty with being able to recognise your worth, or a belief that 'I need to get reassurance about whether I'm good enough because I'm doubting it within myself.' JMo recalls experiencing this from earliest of memories.

Your self-esteem influences how you interact with the world, how you handle challenges, how you connect with others and how you treat yourself. When you don't believe in your own worth, external validation can turn from a 'nice to have' into a 'need to have'. Belief in yourself becomes contingent on what others think of you and, as a result, your life can become shackled by a fear of rejection. You might find yourself holding back from sharing your thoughts, feelings or needs because you're scared people might not respond well. For example, you might stay quiet in a relationship, even when something is bothering you, or you might get caught up in people-pleasing to be sure that other people like or accept you, sacrificing your own needs in the process. When external validation is a must-have, life can feel like an unstable rollercoaster — you feel good when you get it, but you feel awful if you don't. The dopamine hit you get when you receive the external validation then reinforces your neediness, — you become addicted to the 'validation fix' to help you to feel stable again, but the doubt soon creeps back in so this stability is short-lived.

The fear of rejection can make you second-guess yourself and stop you from taking risks, whether it's applying for a job, making new friends or pursuing a meaningful relationship. It's a fear-driven, self-protective mechanism, but one that often leaves you feeling stuck, disconnected or unfulfilled. This constant need for approval can leave you feeling drained, resentful, anxious or overwhelmed. After a conversation, worry or rumination might kick in, where you overanalyse or replay the situation in your mind, wondering if you said something wrong or sounded stupid. *Hypervigilance* (a heightened state of alert and awareness) around a fear of not being good enough leads you to focus on all your perceived 'not good enoughs', which then reinforces the sense of 'not being good enough'.

It's important to remember that self-esteem exists on a spectrum. On one end, there's low self-esteem, where feelings of inadequacy and self-doubt dominate. On the other end is overly high self-esteem, which can look like arrogance or an inflated sense of self-importance. Healthy self-esteem is a balanced sense of self-worth that allows you to embrace both your strengths and your development needs. It helps you to stay motivated to live life in line with the things you value and to seek continual improvement and growth.

Self-esteem is influenced by many factors, including your experiences, your relationships, your cultural messages and the genes you are born with. Despite these background factors, self-esteem is not set in stone and is something that, with the right toolkit, you can nurture, build and rebuild over time.

In this section, we'll explore practical strategies to help you strengthen your self-esteem, quieten your inner critic and develop a kinder, more supportive relationship with yourself. Whether you're starting from a place of deep self-doubt or simply looking to give your self-esteem a boost, scientifically supported tools are available to help you cultivate healthy self-esteem.

It's time to quieten the inner critic

Life experiences of rejection can leave a lasting mark on your self-esteem. Rejection taps into our deepest fears of not being good enough or not being wanted. On a biological level, humans are wired for connection, so exclusion or rejection can feel like a threat to our very survival. Repeated rejection can make you hesitant to put yourself out there again. You might think, 'What's the point? I'll just fail or be rejected again,' which can lead to self-isolation and a shrinking comfort zone.

This is reinforced by the harsh inner critic, or the voice in your head that tells you you're not good enough. The critical voice is one of the most pervasive and damaging aspects of low self-esteem, perpetuating a cycle that further reduces feelings of self-worth. That inner voice might say things like, 'Why bother? You'll just mess it up,' or 'You're not as good as everyone else.' Over time, these thoughts can feel less like a voice and more like a truth you can't escape. Negative self-talk can come from earlier life experiences, such as criticism from parents, teachers or peers. Or maybe, like JMo, your parent (in his case, mother) also had a low self-esteem. It might come from other traumatic life experiences or perfectionistic tendencies driven out of a need for certainty.

Self-doubt is a hallmark feature of low self-esteem, and it can show up in almost every area of life. It's that internal voice that questions your abilities, your decisions and your right to speak up. In the workplace, self-doubt might hold you back from asking for a raise, applying for a promotion or speaking up in meetings. Self-doubt can also feed *imposter syndrome* — a belief that you're a fraud, even when you're highly skilled or accomplished. You might feel like your successes are just luck, and it's only a matter of time before people 'find out' you're not as capable as they think. Self-doubt can even make you question whether you're loveable or worthy of a healthy, fulfilling relationship.

Constantly berating yourself creates a cycle of shame and self-doubt. It can stop you from taking risks, building relationships or feeling good about yourself, even when you're doing well.

For many people, self-esteem is tied closely to body image, or the way you see and feel about your physical self. This is further challenged by a world that constantly bombards us with unrealistic standards of beauty and physical perfection. Messages about weight, diets and fitness can seep into our sense of self-worth. The curated, filtered images on social media can make you feel like you'll never measure up, even though those 'perfect' pictures are rarely real. And with the rising use of AI image generation, this can become even more of a challenge.

Body shaming, whether from yourself or others, can erode self-worth and leave lasting emotional scars. Hurtful comments about your weight, shape or appearance can linger for years. Even well-meaning remarks, like, 'You'd look so much better if you lost a little weight' can cut deeply — and often your most relentless critic will be yourself. You might catch yourself thinking, 'I'll be happy once I lose X kilos,' or 'I don't deserve love until I fix this about myself.'

When you tie your value to a number on a scale or the size of your jeans, it can create a cycle of shame and frustration. This connection can be a tricky one, especially in a world that constantly bombards us with unrealistic beauty standards. When your body image takes a hit, your self-esteem typically follows. For some, body image issues go beyond insecurities and into the realm of eating disorders or body dysmorphic disorder (BDD). BDD is a mental health condition where you become excessively preoccupied with perceived flaws in your appearance. It can make you feel ashamed and anxious, or even drive you to avoid social situations. Body image concerns don't just affect how you see yourself in the mirror. They can impact your confidence, relationships and willingness to engage in life fully, like avoiding the beach, skipping parties or hesitating to speak up in public because you're hyper-focused on your appearance.

Comparing yourself to others is also a major contributor to low self-esteem. Unrealistic beauty standards perpetuated by social media platforms create a constant comparison trap. Airbrushed, filtered images make it hard to see your own unique beauty or even feel normal. Whether you're comparing your achievements, appearance, relationships or life path, it's easy to feel like you're falling short. When you look at someone else's life, you're seeing their curated version, not the whole story. Yet, it's easy to assume they have it all together while you're struggling.

They create a bar so high that no matter how much you achieve, it never feels like enough. Cultural expectations can also place pressure on you to meet specific roles or milestones, such as excelling in academic study, being the perfect parent or looking a certain way. These pressures can create a constant sense of 'not being good enough'. When you believe that 'I need to be perfect in order to be good enough,' it creates a fear of imperfection and unrealistic expectations. The standards are always set too high, resulting in constant stress, a fear of failure and never feeling good enough. And then, even when you achieve something great, it still may not feel like enough.

Many of my clients who are struggling with self-esteem find it challenging to engage with people in an assertive way. Assertiveness (or confidence) doesn't come easily to people. We are wired towards being passive or aggressive, and for someone who fears being rejected or fears being judged negatively, 'aggressive' is not an option so they turn to 'passive'. This can translate into difficulties with setting boundaries — but you can be assertive without being aggressive. When you don't value yourself, saying 'no' can feel impossible. You might worry that setting boundaries will upset others or make them think less of you. This can lead to you feeling overburdened, resentful or invisible in relationships.

Low self-esteem can make you tolerate poor treatment or settle for less than you deserve. If you don't believe you deserve better, you might stay in toxic romantic, professional or personal relationships, as JMo has done at times. When you don't feel worthy of success or happiness, you might unconsciously self-sabotage or create obstacles for yourself. For example, you might procrastinate on important tasks, push away people who care about you, or avoid opportunities that could help you grow.

Low self-esteem and worrying constantly about how others perceive you or whether you'll mess up can lead to high levels of anxiety and depression. Common feelings include a persistent sense of shame about not being good enough, worthy or loveable. It can result in you feeling stuck, hopeless or unmotivated, which further erodes self-esteem. You might find yourself trapped in negative thought patterns, such as, 'I'll never be good enough' or 'Why bother trying?' These thoughts can spiral, making it harder for you to take positive steps forward.

For individuals who are neurodivergent, the connection between self-esteem and life experiences can be particularly complex. They might have wonderful strengths, such as creativity, problem-solving skills or deep empathy, but their gifts may be overshadowed by a focus on their challenges. Many neurodivergent individuals grow up feeling out of sync with the world around them. This sense of being 'different' can lead to feelings of inadequacy, particularly if they were teased, misunderstood or excluded, which can in turn cause hypervigilance around the fear of being rejected or judged negatively. These feelings of inadequacy can become difficult to manage in a world where we're constantly measured against standards that don't seem to fit into society's norms (such as being comfortable in social situations or achieving linear success). As a result, neurodivergent individuals might be tempted to mask their true selves to fit in or avoid judgement, which can lead to anxiety around their authentic identity and chip away at their self-esteem.

If you see yourself in any of these descriptions, know that you're not alone. Self-esteem is something we all wrestle with at times. The good news is that these patterns are not permanent. With the right tools, strategies and support, you can begin to quieten the inner critic, let go of fear-based comparisons, and build a more compassionate, balanced relationship with yourself. When you have a healthy sense of self-worth, you're better equipped to handle life's challenges, build strong relationships and pursue your goals assertively. It acts like a protective buffer, helping you to bounce back from setbacks and maintain a sense of stability. Self-esteem is about knowing that even when things don't go your way, you're still valuable. It's about treating yourself with kindness and respect, even when you make mistakes. And it's about recognising that your worth isn't tied to how you look, what you achieve or what others think of you.

A toolkit for building self-esteem

Overcoming the challenges of low self-esteem is about learning how to manage anxiety and build your tolerance to uncertainty, shifting your mindset, and creating space for a kinder, more supportive relationship with yourself. Here, I share some practical tools and strategies to help you get started with standing up to the inner critic, smashing imposter syndrome, and boosting your confidence, assertiveness and influence. (My book *The Mind Strength Method* takes a deeper dive into these tools and strategies.)

The first step in building self-esteem is quietening that relentless inner critic — the voice that tells you you're not good enough, that you'll fail, or that people will reject you unless you're perfect. While you may never completely silence that voice, you can learn to get some distance from it. Some people find it helpful to give their inner critic a name or persona. When it starts chiming in, you can say, 'Oh, that's [insert your chosen name here] again. I can choose whether to listen or not.' Pay attention to the way it sounds and the stories it tells you. Instead of trying to prove the critic wrong, see if you can practise sitting with the uncertainty of 'maybe I am, and maybe I'm not'. This helps to reduce the power that the critical voice might have over you and begins to quieten its impact.

Low self-esteem can grow when we focus too much on things outside our control, such as how others perceive us, unrealistic societal standards or past mistakes. See if you can move from focusing on the fear of a negative outcome to focusing on what's in your control by living in alignment with your values. Shifting your focus to what you can control is empowering.

Break down big tasks into small, manageable steps. Each time you complete one, it reinforces positive self-beliefs. Celebrate small wins and effort. Did you speak up in a meeting? Cook a healthy meal? Take a much-needed break? Those wins matter. Instead of aiming for perfection, aim for progress. Each night, write down three things you did that day, no matter how small. Over time, this habit can help rewire your brain to focus on your effort rather than being shackled to the perfect outcome.

See if you can practise self-compassion, a powerful antidote to low self-esteem. This is the practise of treating yourself with the same kindness, understanding and patience you'd offer a close friend. Remember, everyone struggles and makes mistakes — it's part of being human. Write down a list of common negative thoughts and challenge each one with a kinder, more balanced response. Instead of beating yourself up, remind yourself, 'This happens to everyone.' When you catch yourself being self-critical, pause and ask, 'What would I say to a friend in this situation?' Then, say it to yourself.

See if you can practise mindful self-awareness and pay attention to your thoughts and feelings without judgement. Notice when you're being harsh on yourself and gently shift towards more compassionate thoughts. An exercise might be writing a letter to yourself from the perspective of someone who loves and supports you. What would they say about you?

Can you practise healthier ways to respond when you compare yourself to others? Comparing yourself to others is a surefire way to erode your self-esteem as your negativity bias will focus on all your perceived 'not good enoughs'. (The *negativity bias* is an inherent focus on the negative, even when positive things are taking place — for example, one bad review standing out even if there are a hundred good reviews.) The key isn't to stop comparing entirely, it's to reframe how you approach it. Remember, not all comparisons are created equal. Fear-driven comparisons come from self-doubt, like scrolling through social media and feeling like you don't measure up, whether it's in success, intelligence or appearance. These comparisons often leave us feeling inadequate and stuck. On the other hand, values-aligned comparisons can be a source of motivation. Instead of making you feel 'less than', they inspire growth, like looking up to a mentor, a leader or someone whose journey aligns with your own aspirations. These comparisons help you reflect on what truly matters to you and encourage you to take meaningful steps forward. This is part of a value of continual improvement, underpinned by a healthy growth mindset.

You might want to consider taking breaks from social media, or unfollowing accounts that trigger feelings of inadequacy. Instead of measuring yourself against others, focus on your own growth. Someone else's success doesn't take away from your own worth. Practise being genuinely happy for others, while recognising your unique path. Each time you catch yourself comparing, pause and name three things you're grateful for in your own life. Gratitude can help shift your focus back to what's good in your world.

Can you see if there are ways to build a healthier social network? The people you surround yourself with play a significant role in shaping your self-esteem. A supportive, uplifting community can make all the difference. Spend time with people who celebrate your strengths and support your growth. Distance yourself from toxic relationships that drain your energy or make you doubt yourself. See if you can practise letting trusted people see the real you. Sharing your fears and struggles can deepen connections and remind you that you're not alone. And remember, there is strength in seeking support, whether from a friend, therapist or support group. You don't have to navigate this journey alone. Write down a list of people in your life who lift you up. Make a point to connect with at least one of them each week.

If body image issues are tied to your self-esteem, focusing on self-acceptance rather than perfection can be transformative. Instead of forcing yourself to love every part of your body, appreciate what your body allows you to do, such as walk, laugh or hug. When you catch yourself criticising your body, pause and reframe the thought. For example, replace, 'I hate my thighs' with 'My thighs are strong and help me move.' When you find yourself comparing your body to someone else, replace 'I'm not as beautiful as them' with 'I'm special and unique because of what makes me different.' JMo, for example, is constantly obsessing about his stomach and lack of sixpack. Curate your social media feed to include accounts that promote body positivity, diversity and self-acceptance. Consider writing down things that you're grateful for every morning to start each day positively. Over time, this practice can help shift your focus.

See if you can engage in powerful interactions to rewire your mindset. Remember that the way you think about yourself shapes how you feel and act. By challenging old patterns and creating new ones, you can gradually shift your mindset towards one of self-worth. Affirmations are short, positive statements you repeat to yourself to challenge negative thoughts. For example: 'I am enough just as I am.' Make a list of your strengths and revisit it often. When self-doubt creeps in, remind yourself of what you bring to the table. Gratitude shifts your focus from what's missing to what's present. This simple shift can help boost self-esteem over time. Start each day by saying one affirmation out loud and reflecting on one thing you're proud of.

Low self-esteem is cultivated by fear, such as fear of failure, rejection or judgement. Taking small, brave actions despite the fear can help you rebuild confidence and prove to yourself that you're capable. You don't have to tackle your biggest fear all at once. Break it down into smaller, manageable steps. For example, if speaking up in meetings feels intimidating, start by contributing one comment in a smaller setting, such as an informal conversation. Instead of seeing failure as a reflection of your worth, view it as an opportunity to learn and grow. Ask yourself, 'What did I learn from this experience?' And finally, again, focus on the effort you put in rather than the outcome. Giving things a go is an achievement in itself. See if you can set one small, actionable goal each week that stretches you slightly outside your comfort zone. Reflect on what you learned from the experience, no matter the outcome.

If low self-esteem feels overwhelming or deeply ingrained, working with a trained clinical psychologist can provide valuable tools and insights. Cognitive Behavioral Therapy (CBT) helps you to identify and challenge negative thought patterns and replace them with healthier ones. If your self-esteem struggles are rooted in past trauma, trauma-based therapy can help you process those experiences and rebuild your sense of self-worth. Group therapy or support groups can also be helpful. Sharing your journey with others who understand can be incredibly validating and empowering.

Building self-esteem is a journey, not a destination. It's about showing up for yourself, day after day, even when it's hard. It's about practising kindness, setting boundaries and celebrating the small wins along the way. Remember, you are worthy of love, respect and care — not because of what you do or how you look, but simply because you are who you are. Remember also that you don't have to suffer in silence when embracing this toolkit. Working with a skilled psychologist or mindset coach can help you to live life with confidence, fulfilment and success.

How to help a loved one if they're struggling with low self-esteem

Watching someone you care about struggle with low self-esteem can be distressing. You see their worth, but they can't see it themselves. While you can't 'fix' their self-esteem, there's so much you can do to support them on their journey to building a healthier relationship with themselves. Here's how you can help in ways that are compassionate, constructive and empowering.

It's first important to understand what self-esteem is and isn't. Self-esteem isn't just about feeling good. It's about having a *balanced* view of oneself, acknowledging strengths and weaknesses without letting either define a person's worth. Helping a loved one who's grappling with the challenges of low self-esteem isn't about reassuring them that they are 'good enough' or trying to solve their problems for them. It's about being a steady, supportive presence as they work through their challenges themselves.

Avoid dismissing their struggles with phrases like, 'Don't be so hard on yourself' or 'You're amazing, just believe it.' While well intentioned, these comments can feel invalidating. Your role is to support, not to rush. Patience and acceptance of the challenges that your loved one is going through is key. Instead, practise validation with phrases such as, 'It sounds like you're being really hard on yourself' or 'Well, I love you and am here for you no matter what.'

Low self-esteem often blinds people to their own strengths and achievements. See if you can be a mirror for their strengths by gently reflecting these back to them when they're struggling to see their worth. Instead of vague compliments like, 'You're great,' focus on giving specific compliments that they will hopefully be able to recognise in themselves. For example, 'Thanks for being so thoughtful, it makes such a big difference in my life' or 'You're so good at making people feel comfortable, that's such a gift.'

Reinforce acknowledging effort, not outcome — even if the result isn't perfect. For instance, 'I know that presentation was tough for you, but you worked so hard on it, and you have every reason to feel proud of the effort you put in.'

Aim to be thoughtful and supportive in your communication. When someone's self-esteem is fragile, even casual comments can have a big impact. While constructive feedback is still important as a normal part of a loving relationship, be cautious of not unintentionally criticising or reinforcing their negative self-talk. For example, instead of, 'Why did you do it that way?', consider saying, 'I wonder if there's another approach we could try.'

See if you can model self-compassion. If you're constantly putting yourself down in front of them, they might internalise the idea that self-criticism is normal or necessary. Show them what self-compassion looks like by being kind to yourself. For example, if you make a mistake yourself, say, 'That didn't go as planned, but it's okay. I'll learn from it and try again.'

While you can't do the work for them, try to be proactive by encouraging and supporting your loved one's efforts to build their self-esteem. Consider asking open-ended questions with this goal in mind, such as, 'What are some things you might try to help you to not be so tough on yourself?' Perhaps gently encourage positive habits such as journalling, exercise or mindfulness practices, and offer to join them if it feels right. For example, 'Have you thought about trying journalling? It might help you untangle from difficult thoughts.'

Another powerful way to help is to encourage your loved one to seek therapy. Professional support with a trained clinical psychologist can provide scientifically supported tools and insights that help to dramatically shift negative thought patterns and reduce the likelihood of them being bossed around by their critical inner voice. Again, it can be helpful to start by asking an open-ended question, such as, 'What are some things that you could do to help with the difficulties you're experiencing?' You could then follow this up with something like, 'Therapy really helped me when I was feeling stuck. If you ever want to explore that, I'd be happy to help you find someone great.'

Sometimes a loved one just needs a safe space to be vulnerable. People with low self-esteem might worry about being judged or rejected, which makes it hard for them to open up. By creating a safe, non-judgemental space, you can help them feel supported and understood. Practise listening without fixing. Allow opportunities for your loved one to vent, while resisting the urge to jump in with solutions. Focus on listening and empathising, with statements such as, 'I'm here to listen if you want to talk about it.' Be their cheerleader and let them know you're there for them no matter what. Remind them that it's human to be imperfect and that they don't have to face their struggles alone.

When your loved one expresses self-critical thoughts, you can help them reframe their perspective without dismissing their feelings. Instead of outright disagreeing, ask questions that encourage them to challenge their own assumptions. For example, 'What evidence do you have that you're not good enough?' Offer a different perspective and share how you see them in a way that feels supportive, not argumentative. For instance, 'I hear you saying you feel like you failed, but from my perspective, I see someone who worked so hard and learned a lot.' Consider helping them shift their perspective by asking, 'What would you say to a friend who was feeling the way you are right now?'

People with low self-esteem often struggle to set boundaries because they fear rejection or conflict. You can support them with learning to prioritise their own needs. Let them know it's okay to say no to things that don't serve them; for example, 'You don't have to agree to that if it doesn't feel right', 'It's okay to put yourself first sometimes. You don't have to please everyone' or 'You're allowed to say no. It doesn't make you selfish — it makes you human.' Show them what healthy boundaries look like in your own life. This can inspire them to set the boundaries they need.

Building self-esteem is a slow process, and it's important to acknowledge and celebrate the small victories along the way. Point out when you see your loved one taking positive steps, like speaking up in a meeting or setting a boundary. Let them know you're proud of their efforts. For example, 'I noticed you stood up for yourself in that situation, that's huge.' Find ways to celebrate wins, big or small, whether that's writing a note of encouragement, or just telling them how amazing it is to see how hard they're working on this.

Supporting someone with low self-esteem can be emotionally demanding, so it's important to take care of yourself as well. Remember, you can't pour from an empty glass, it's okay to step back when you need to recharge. Supporting your loved one doesn't mean sacrificing your own wellbeing. If you're feeling overwhelmed, consider talking to a therapist or taking time to reflect on and engage in actions to support your own needs.

Helping a loved one with low self-esteem isn't about fixing them, it's about walking alongside them as they learn to see their own worth. Your presence, patience, and encouragement can make a world of difference, even if progress feels slow at times. Keep showing up, keep offering kindness, and know that your support matters more than you might realise.

Reflection prompts

Here are some reflection prompts to help you or a loved one dive deeper into the journey of building self-esteem.

1. What are the most common things I say to myself when I make a mistake or fall short? Are these thoughts helpful or hurtful?
2. If I could speak to myself as a kind friend, what would I say instead?
3. What's one thing I can do to make my self-talk more compassionate?
4. What qualities or skills do others admire in me? Do I agree with them? Why or why not?
5. How do social media, culture or the people around me influence how I feel about myself?
6. Are there any connections, situations or relationships that make me feel 'less than'? How can I set boundaries or distance myself from them?
7. Who in my life uplifts and supports me? How can I strengthen those connections?

8. What is one recent challenge or failure I've experienced? How did I handle it? What's one lesson I can take from that experience, and how might it help me in the future?

9. How can I remind myself that mistakes are part of learning, not a reflection of my worth?

10. Are there times when I say 'yes' to things I don't want to do? How does that affect my self-esteem?

11. What's one boundary I can set this week to prioritise my wellbeing?

12. How can I remind myself that saying 'no' is an act of self-respect, not selfishness?

13. What are three things about myself, my personality, my abilities or my experiences that I'm grateful for?

14. What's one flaw or insecurity I've been holding onto? Can I reframe it as part of what makes me human or unique? If someone I care about shared this same insecurity, how would I respond to them? How can I offer that same kindness to myself?

15. How can I remind myself that imperfection is not failure, it's part of being real and relatable?

PALATE CLEANSER
A Visit to Narnia — Tilda Swinton

Academy Award winner Tilda Swinton got me in trouble once. I say that with a laugh but it is true. I was the most hated man in the room for a minute.

In 2005, I was the National Entertainment Editor at Australian Associated Press (AAP). I was flown to Auckland, New Zealand, for a set visit on *The Chronicles of Narnia: The Lion, the Witch and the Wardrobe*. It was a book (by C. S. Lewis) and story I had loved as a kid, so I was pretty damn excited to go on set. It was everything I'd imagined, with director Andrew Adamson creating this incredible Narnia world in giant sheds on some film backlot. They are incredible movie makers in New Zealand.

Set visits, whether for a film or television show, are chaotic days. You spend hours waiting around only to grab an actor for a fleeting few minutes here and there between takes.

This was a special international press day though so it was slightly more organised. There were about 10 of us journalists in total, all of whom had flown in from different parts of the world. Coming from Australia, I was practically a local. Others flew in from Europe and Asia. We were all excited.

This film starred four then relatively unknown kid actors — Georgie Henley, William Moseley, Skandar Keynes and Anna Popplewell — in the well-known story of siblings sent from London to a professor's country home to escape the bombings and trauma of World War II. There, they find a magic wardrobe that leads to a mystical land called Narnia, which is under the rule of the White Witch (played by Tilda Swinton).

To defeat the witch, the four children (Lucy, Peter, Edmund and Susan Pevensie) must join forces with Aslan, the lion ruler of Narnia, for the great battle between good and evil.

Tilda Swinton is a legit movie star of the Cate Blanchett level, whose breakthrough role was alongside Leonardo DiCaprio in *The Beach* in 2000. That remains iconic. She is the kind of actor I admire — one who is respected for their body of work ('the craft' if you will, although I hate that saying), not for the gossip headlines they attract (who they are shagging or feuding with) or their general level of celebrity.

'I am going to have children backing away from me for the rest of my life, and I am sort of prepared for that,' she said of playing the White Witch. 'It is a tall order to play the epitome of all evil. I will just be terrifying everybody forever but I am up for that.'

The set was truly spectacular.

'This is the story of a war child's consciousness,' said Swinton.

'It is a really important film for us to make now because many of your children … are being exposed to all this stuff … all of our children are war children now.'

It was this quote, or more my questioning, that led to Swinton's response that got me in trouble.

For Tilda's interview, we were in some sort of shipping container. It wasn't glamorous at all. It was a boardroom set-up, with all of us sat around a large table.

When you have 10 journalists and one talent for what would have been 15 or 20 minutes maximum, you have to keep things moving with each scribe getting probably one question each if lucky. It is hard, though, because everyone has the aim of getting enough content to write a feature and inevitably there are stupid questions like, 'What is your favourite restaurant in Vilnius, Lithuania?'

I was a relative rookie at this point and didn't know the way of the land, so as Swinton spoke, I lapped up every word. I was keen to hear the story behind the story, not just the stuff about how long she had to sit in makeup or how uncomfortable her costume was. I wanted to know who she was, what drove her, why she was there — these were the nuggets of information that excited me as a journalist.

I probed further on what she meant about 'our children' being war children now. Sure, the Gulf War in Iraq was a thing, but it didn't feel like a war that truly impacted me.

It was unusual for a star to wade into such a deep topic back then, particularly in such a light-hearted short chat with so many journalists. Swinton knew she was talking to the media, and every word was a gem, so to speak.

She said exploring fantastical worlds like Narnia was an important way for children to escape the harsh realities of today's world.

'They have their own war and they go into a war where they are parentless,' she explained. 'They have to grow up and take charge and they have to become kings of their own kingdom.'

My line of questioning wasn't appreciated by the other journalists, or the Disney publicist.

But Tilda really got into it, so much so that she grabbed me afterwards and invited me to her trailer to continue the conversation.

There, we got stuck into her thoughts on the Gulf War and other political stuff. Gosh, I'd love to talk to her today about Donald Trump, Russia's invasion of Ukraine and the ongoing Palestine/ Israel conflict.

That day, the look on the other journalists' faces as I went on to my unplanned, one-on-one extra interview was not pretty. They were furious and I was later berated by the publicist for breaking protocol. The thing is, though, I wouldn't change a thing and I didn't really have any alternative. Swinton invited me. That extra 15 minutes was priceless, and not only because of the story I got out of it. It was hardly an award-winning piece — I certainly don't have a Walkley Award for journalism on my mantelpiece — but it instilled in me the confidence that Hollywood stars had something more to say than guff about how much they like this and that, how lucky they are or aren't or whatever else they say when sitting through often painful press junkets, being asked the same things over and over again.

Of course, I apologised to the other journalists. I think I even offered them a transcript but inside, secretly or not so secretly, I was chuffed because it felt like validation in my messed-up head that I wasn't a shit journalist. Tilda liked my line of questioning and wanted to dig a little deeper with me. That was a good feeling.

PART IV
LIFE & DEATH

When is your time? Is it when you choose to die, so suicide or voluntary assisted dying? Or when your time is up, so illness or shock accident?

Is it when you feel pushed to your limits, like you have no choice but to take drastic action to ease the pain of life?

So many questions come to mind when I ponder life and death, particularly around mental health. Whatever way you look at death, it is confronting and hard to process for everyone involved. Is a suicide attempt a selfish act? Is death cruel when you aren't ready to say goodbye?

And how do those left behind, regardless of how someone dies, deal with their loss?

These are some of the issues I will be looking at over the coming chapters.

What is certain is that death is permanent, which makes the whole thing so much more complicated to process.

18

Overdose

The first time I tried to kill myself was more than a cry for help — it was a legitimate attempt. I was in pain and genuinely didn't see any other option for me at that point. People say that suicide is selfish and sure, I agree that there is an element of truth in that, but I don't agree that a suicide attempt is always selfish because it can sometimes feel like the only option. That was how I felt the first time.

A few catalysts led to me giving up on myself, including depression. My mum had suffered from depression for many years. Throughout years 11 and 12 of high school, my sister and I had watched as Mum had been in and out of hospital getting her medication right and having electroconvulsive therapy (ECT) — where they zap your brain to give you a shock and get your chemicals flowing. (That is my layman's explanation, but I can tell you it isn't like the old days you would see in movies where people are turned into zombies — as if they've had a lobotomy — from ECT.)

My mum's journey with depression made me well aware of what it was and how it manifested itself — for her, at least, because everyone is different. That is the thing with mental illness. If you break an arm or have cancer, you get a plaster cast or you have **People don't understand what they can't see.** chemotherapy and other treatments. With depression, it is less visible. I think there is still a taboo around depression because people don't understand what they can't see.

175

I hadn't yet been clinically diagnosed with depression at this point, although I knew that I was hiding stuff, even from myself. My mind felt as though it was running at a million miles an hour. Thoughts were erratic. My self-loathing was extreme. The deep, dark thoughts were taking over more and more. I did my best to maintain my bubbly upbeat exterior, but inside I was a cesspool of negativity. It felt so real I could almost smell it. That was in the back of my mind as my world crumbled. The fact that I had been sexually abused was always present at the back of my mind too. I had suppressed the pain of this experience for so many years, holding it below the surface to keep my shit together. At least, I thought I was keeping my shit together up until I finished high school and started my first year of university.

I was 19 and had a part-time job working at the department store Target the day of my first suicide attempt. Graham, my abuser, walked in (I describe this moment in Chapter 2). Seeing him face to face really fucked with my head. The trauma was real and hit me like a tonne of bricks. (I was later diagnosed with post-traumatic stress disorder, severe depression and anxiety, among other things — all related to being sexually abused. There was an underlying chemical imbalance too, but the sexual abuse really was the catalyst for my emotional turmoil.)

At the same time, my relationship with my first love — the guy that I thought was the great love of my life — was falling apart. It was a situation I couldn't control. He cheated on me — or I believed he cheated on me at the time. Whether he did or not was kind of irrelevant then and most definitely is now. I was barely an adult and emotionally immature, relationship-wise. The troubles in our relationship, and then seeing Graham, really pushed me over the edge.

Years later, I found out my first love felt I'd blamed him for my suicide attempt and that he carried the guilt of that for decades afterwards. I don't think I was emotionally mature enough, or strong enough in any sense, at the time to truly explain to him or others what was going on for me. I'd told him in brief detail that I had been sexually abused, but I didn't really have the ability to go through what all of that trauma meant. I didn't understand it myself. Perhaps selfishly, I never considered his pain as I was so consumed by my own. I feel guilty about that now, and while I have tried to reach out to him over the years, I wish I'd had the chance to sit down and explain because the last thing I'd ever wanted was to create more trauma for someone else through the extreme trauma I'd experienced.

That night I went to my family home, where I lived in a granny flat in the backyard. I knew what I was going to do. I had thought about it hundreds of times. This night I knew it was time. I said goodbye to my mum, hugged and kissed her more than a usual goodnight, and went to bed. It would have been 9.30 pm or 10 pm, not late.

Although I knew *what* I was going to do, I didn't know *how* to kill myself. Sure, I'd seen movies but they don't really go into detail, which is obviously a good thing. There weren't any how-to books either, and rightly so. I didn't have a gun. I didn't have poison or anything like that, so I planned to overdose on whatever medications I could find in the cupboard. Mum had some heavy-duty medications for her bipolar illness, so I opened the medicine cupboard and stashed as many packets as I could find. Fortunately for me, Mum didn't keep her hard-core medications in the main medicine cabinet. She kept those in her bathroom, I guess. So, I took everything I could find, not knowing what it would do but believing that if I took enough it would kill me.

I stood in the backyard. It was a freezing cold Canberra night. I had a bottle of water in one hand and the tablets in the other, swallowing as many as I could with each sip, dry retching as I'd try to keep what I'd swallowed down. Inside, emotionally, I felt an immense sense of self-hatred. I felt I was a failure and that I didn't deserve to live. This was my punishment.

I don't know how many tablets I took. It was a lot. I still struggle to swallow pills to this day because of what I did that night. I was calm. I didn't cry. After I had taken all the tablets I had stashed in my pockets, I remember overwhelmingly being devoid of any feelings or emotions. The only thing I could feel was a sense of relief, which came from feeling the pain, and the pent-up anxiety and stress and everything that I'd held on to for so many years, lift off my shoulders. It was almost a physical feeling. I thought to myself, 'This is my time to go.'

So I did let go. I walked to my bedroom and lay on my bed, thinking I would just fall asleep and not wake up. It was actually the most freeing feeling I've ever had in my life — kind of like when you're floating in water in a beautiful bath, a swimming pool or the ocean. That is how it felt for me at the time.

I know it might sound selfish, but at that point, the ramifications of what I was doing were the last thing on my mind. I genuinely believed in my fucked-up mind that the world would be a better place if I wasn't in it — and that my mum, my sister, and everyone I knew and didn't know would be happier without me. In my head it was my time to go, and so that was my steadfast mission.

Minutes later, I don't remember how long exactly, I started to feel groggy and nauseous. I started to panic. What had I done? What if it was painful? I hadn't said goodbye properly. I didn't write a suicide note. I rushed inside the house to my mum who was sitting in the lounge room smoking a cigarette and drinking a coffee at 9.30 pm or whatever time it was — it was never a bad time for my mum to have a cuppa. I wasn't emotional. I remained calm and simply told Mum I had taken a lot of tablets, unsure what I had actually taken other than a lot of paracetamol. Mum cried, panicking, and she grabbed me and screamed, 'What have you done?' The screech in her voice sits with me to this day.

Deep, dark shame was quickly starting to creep in.

I had been so full of peace until that point, but deep, dark shame was quickly starting to creep in as I began to realise how my actions were visibly impacting those I loved.

Mum took me to Calvary Hospital (now North Canberra Hospital), about 15 minutes' drive, and they sent me through to emergency, where they had to clear my stomach of any toxins. An alternative to stomach pumping, I had to drink a charcoal drink in a popper — just like the fruit juice poppers we had as kids. It didn't take long before the charcoal started coming out of what seemed like every orifice — my mouth, my nose, my arse. It was truly disgusting. I wasn't feeling full of peace anymore. I was still groggy but this was very real.

The lights were bright in the uncomfortable and cold emergency ward where doctors assessed patients. The doctors and nurses didn't think I'd taken anything too serious or life-threatening but were giving me the charcoal because they had to take these things very seriously.

Back then, mental health seemed to be a taboo subject that people didn't understand. That can still be the case today. I remember feeling that the people treating me were looking down at me, as if I had done something stupid (which I had) and thinking that I was wasting my life (which I would have done). At the time, though, I felt as if there should have been a more nurturing approach than one of frustration. To me, it almost felt like they looked with disdain upon me, but to be fair it was probably just a coping mechanism to deal with the high-stress situations they were dealing with. I see the waste now and have come to understand their disappointment over time, especially if they were seeing person after person coming through the doors with similar issues and requiring the same treatments, but I felt very lonely and would have found solace in a more comforting approach.

Exhausted, I drifted off to sleep feeling like it was all a dream, later waking to find I was still in the harsh emergency department, hooked up to some monitoring machines. Mum and my sister were there, crying. I felt immense shame for putting them through that experience. I still hated myself and I still felt worthless.

That was the first time I seriously tried to kill myself.

That was the first time I seriously tried to kill myself.

They moved me to a ward after 24 hours or so of observation, after my stomach was cleared and the charcoal had come out of me. I didn't feel regret what I had done because the pain was still there, and I saw no way out. I don't even know if I felt relief that it didn't work, as I had lost all will to live. I couldn't admit it to anyone but I felt at that point that I'd only done half the job. The next time, I thought, I would do it properly.

Too weak to stand on my own, an orderly wheeled me across to a psychiatrist's office in the new wing of Calvary Hospital. He was also my mum's psychiatrist, so we trusted him. There, after an intense session of an hour or so, he put me on my first antidepressant ever—Prozac, two tablets a day, taken in the morning. At that point in my life I hadn't taken any party drugs, with the exception of a few tokes of a joint in high school. Actually, there had also been a poor attempt at a bucket bong with my friend Debbie and her older brothers in their garage that saw me embarrassingly green out in Year 10 or 11. Alcohol was my only drug of choice at that point.

The psychiatrist admitted me to the psych ward — yes, the psychiatric ward, which seemed serious in my head and made me think of *One Flew Over the Cuckoo's Nest* and people wearing straitjackets. The reality was very different — it was a quiet ward, just like any hospital really, but the people were emotionally rather than physically unwell, and we were locked in. It didn't feel like a jail, though. It felt safe. The clock ticking on the wall at the end of the corridor, near the nurse's station, was my only master of sorts as it dictated where I needed to be and when. Breakfast, lunch, dinner, therapy sessions.

I was in a room with four beds, although only one other was occupied. There would have been about 20 others in the ward of 10 rooms — each room had four beds, but the ward wasn't full of patients at the time I was there. The psych ward was just a place where I sat in my pyjamas or tracky dacks all day, every day. They made us attend therapy sessions, from art and crafts sessions through to group therapy sessions where you'd talk about your feelings. I excelled in arts and crafts. For example, I made a crystallised fish that took pride of place on the front of my mum's fridge until her death, when my stepdad brutally threw everything out.

In the group therapy sessions, however, I kept quiet, cautious. I wasn't up for much talking. It was all too raw to be honest. Plus, I was still processing my emotions from the suicide attempt. Subconsciously, I think I was hyper-vigilant about keeping my emotions protected as I wanted to get out of there as soon as possible and I didn't want them to know how fucked up my head really was.

I felt free for the first time in a long time.

There was a common eating area and a TV and reading room, otherwise I'd be on my bed or in therapy sessions. Even though I was locked in this ward, only allowed to go to the hospital café if I was signed out by a 'sane' person, I felt free for the first time in a long time. I was allowed to just be — nothing was required of me other than being there and being present. I didn't have to make phone calls. I didn't have to be at work or studying. I didn't have to worry about Graham or anyone else. Obviously, there was a lot on my mind, but I would talk if I wanted to talk, and if I didn't want to talk, I didn't have to. I could simply go through the motions. Food was cooked for me, I didn't go anywhere and I didn't need any excuses. There was no explaining for me to do. Just being. Again, of course I worried about all the things from before but while I was in there, everything was outside and I was cocooned in the relative safety of the ward. My mind was numb. I didn't even care if anyone knew that I was in the psych ward. My thoughts were simply on the routine they'd given me for that day. I was medicated too, so that helped keep me calm — and kept the shame and anxiety at bay.

One day, I was sitting in the corridor talking to another patient, a girl. She was in a wheelchair and I had a go in it. A male nurse pulled me aside and told me he thought I was faking my depression, suggesting that I should just 'harden up'. Shocked but lacking any fight, I told him I was legitimately depressed and he scoffed, 'Why are you playing around in a wheelchair then?'

I could sit in a wheelchair, barely playing, and still be depressed — they're not mutually exclusive experiences. I'd overdosed and a doctor had assessed me and admitted me to the ward. For him to question that when I was at my most fragile felt pretty shit.

On the ward, I was with people who were feeling the same sort of thing. It wasn't a pity party — we were all there doing what we had to do. Some were trying to get better. Others 'had' to be there because they were forced by family or doctors, or they'd done something like me (suicide attempt) to get themselves there. Some had more visible mental health issues than others, but each of us had our own issues that we were dealing with. It wasn't unusual for other people to think we were making it up or that the only treatment needed was to 'snap out of it'.

It struck me that most people on the ward had been admitted for treatment of depression, anxiety, bipolar, schizophrenia — all the usual mental health things. There was an extremely skinny young woman, maybe in her late teens, shuffling along the corridor who was obviously suffering from bulimia or anorexia. Many of the others seemed to have conditions that were drug-induced, where they may have had a bad chemical reaction, or perhaps the drugs had escalated a pre-existing condition. I'm not a doctor. I wasn't there to judge. My head was full of my own shit, and it was a relief to be with others also suffering. I could fly under the radar a little in that I was one of many patients dealing with shit and I was in a place where my story was not unique. Of course, it was a sad place in many ways because it was a ward where people went between losing their shit and, I guess, getting their life back on track. It was a middle ground. And while some got back on track, others didn't. I wonder where they are now or if indeed they are still alive.

I spent a week in hospital, seven nights in the psych ward, which I wear metaphorically as a badge of honour because it is part of my story. I am no longer ashamed. I am proud of those seven days because I took a major step forward by accepting treatment and acknowledging that I was suffering and needed help.

This is where I think I first started to learn how to manage my illness, recognising I am a work in progress. While not completely aware of what was going on in my head, I did realise then that this was not a phase or just a series of bad days. Seeing others battling their demons, understanding that I wasn't just 'crazy' in a horror movie sense and that I had to deal with the trauma, was a huge step. It made me more self-aware in general, although I knew it was only the start and I was in for a rocky road ahead.

I try not to have regrets at all in my life.

I try not to have regrets at all in my life, not even being sexually abused, because everything that has happened to me or that I have created or done, has led me to become the person that I am today. Because of this, I don't regret my time on the psych ward or even the reason why I was there.

Returning to normal?

I slowly slipped back into my 'normal life', whatever normal is. I was living with my mum. My boyfriend, my first love, and I were still working out whatever we needed to work out. He blamed himself for my suicide attempt, which is one thing I do regret. He and I had sex in my hospital bed when I was still in there and my room buddy was out in the common area. We pulled the drapes and went at it for a couple of minutes — not full sex but getting off. It was a strange desperate feeling of trying to connect, attempting to reclaim our relationship in that moment of raw passion after what I'd done.

Seeing Graham was also on my mind once I got out. I started seeing my psychiatrist once a week for intensive psychotherapy, and my medication was starting to kick in. He diagnosed me with a bunch of stuff, all medical jargon I didn't really understand other than the D word — depression. Still, suicide was something that I had in the back of my mind as an option because I still didn't value my life. I still didn't believe that the world was a better place for my being in it.

I still didn't value my life.

In my head, I was alive because I was too scared, too useless and too chicken to even be able to kill myself. I was holding on, cruising through until the day that I'd find the strength to go through with actually killing myself. In my mind, it wasn't a matter of if but when.

Another night, about a month later, that time arrived. Mum had locked up all the medicines in the house so I couldn't access them. There was literally a lock on the medicine cabinet. It was a requirement the doctor had set. Mum tried to watch me like a hawk, but there were times when I would convince her that I was well enough to go for a walk or grab something from the supermarket. This time, I found Mum's hidden stash of heavy-duty drugs she used to treat her mental health issues. And again, I went outside to do the deed. This time I was more distraught emotionally, and I took lots and lots of tablets, packets of paracetamol again, plus whatever else I could find from anywhere I could find it. Tears were rolling down my face. The pain felt physical. I didn't take Mum's medication in the end because I couldn't do that to her. The guilt would have killed her. But I made sure I took more of the other stuff so I would do it right this time.

Mum found me in my room. 'Oh Jon, you've done it again. What are you doing? I love you. I love you,' she cried, terrified as I lay groggy on my bed. I am not sure how she lifted me or whether she simply guided me to walk in my stupor, but she put me in her car and drove to the emergency department of the hospital. They pumped my stomach again. Having your stomach pumped is really fucking awful. Then I was given another charcoal popper drink. Yuck. They kept me in hospital for observation again for 24 hours, but this time they discharged me to go home after getting the clearance from my psychiatrist. That was the second and last time I tried to kill myself.

Everyone is different in how their mental illness manifests itself.

I've thought about suicide and ways to kill myself many times since but never seriously enough to follow through with it in any meaningful way. Suicide ideation wasn't a term known commonly back then. It is hard for me to describe or explain what was going through my mind in those moments. To the doctor, I described my worst points as 'episodes'. Again, everyone is different in how their mental illness manifests itself. An episode for me was when my mind — my inner voice — was going a million miles a minute and I couldn't control it. That inner voice came at me so fast — just normal thoughts at first, then getting more manic as the thoughts arrived faster and faster. The thoughts included suicidal ideation but also just fast, fast thoughts about anything and everything — a shopping list, what's on my schedule for that day, anything.

I sometimes feel the voices coming on to this day, but I know what to do when I feel that. I taught myself mostly, plus discovered some strategies through speaking to therapists, so many therapists. It only takes a second. The realisation is the main thing that stops it. I kind of meditate, focusing on my breathing. I take deep breaths…focus. Everything slows down. It is simple but it works for me although, if I'm truly honest, I am terrified of the day it doesn't work anymore.

Getting back on track

Now, in my 40s, I am mostly happy to be alive. I gave up drugs and alcohol years ago, and the support from my family and friends encouraged me to stop being abusive to myself and abusing my body. Actually, I asked for their help because I couldn't see a way of getting myself out of the depressive dark cycle of self-abuse I was caught up in.

I have a great GP, who is a constant help. I check in with her regularly on my mental health.

About 10 years ago, I went to my GP in a moment of crisis. I could feel my life spiralling out of control. Mum's death is what pushed me to my limit at that point in life.

I see these moments as episodes I've had during my life. The first was around the ages of 18 to 22, then the next came in my mid-30s after Mum died. This time, I was on a downward spiral and I could see no light to escape into.

My GP referred me to a new psychiatrist in Sydney. My previous psychiatrist was in Canberra, so I needed someone I could check in with regularly in Sydney, particularly in times of crisis like this. It had been more than 15 years since my first depression diagnosis, so it was time for another assessment anyway. He was a nice guy, kind of cute actually, and I felt in control as I was taking these steps. Throughout the years, when I've felt myself going down a bad path, I will touch base with my GP first and look at my options as to whether I need more intensive help from a psychiatrist or just a bout of counselling to manage whatever issue or feelings I have at that time, with the aim of getting back on track. I see it as a 'health management' issue and I try to get in early before things get out of control.

The new psych diagnosed me with a bunch of stuff—mostly things I'd heard before but with new twists and medical treatments as times had changed dramatically since my last chronic episodes—but it was in one ear and out the other. All I wanted to know was how to get back on track and what medications I needed to take to be me again. The diagnosis was severe to me—post-traumatic stress disorder, severe anxiety and depression, traits of borderline personality disorder...blah, blah, blah. I say 'blah' not being flippant but because they are/were just words. It was how I *felt* that mattered—getting back to a sense of normality was the most important thing.

He upped the ante on my Prozac, so I went to taking three tablets in the morning instead of two. And he added Seroquel to the mix. Seroquel is a pretty heavy-duty antipsychotic drug but it helped me sleep because it helped shut down my mind, which I was struggling with at the time. Without eight hours of sleep, I am fucked.

I had to wean myself onto my prescribed daily dose of Seroquel over about two weeks, so I flew to Jakarta for three weeks, where my sister was living with her family. I had to increase the dose every few days, starting with a quarter of a tablet, then increasing to a half, then a full tablet, then two. I was told to expect strong side effects — drowsiness, mood or behaviour changes, nausea, stomach pain. I was okay for the most part, although I had moments of my mind racing and would go through light-headed stages. I slept a lot those first two weeks. By the third week, I was pretty much back to my now normal self.

Once the medications kicked in, literally for the first time ever in my life that I could remember, I wanted to be alive. I was happy. What a beautiful thing to finally feel at the age of 35. My suicidal ideation subsided then, although I have had dark days where depression and anxiety has threatened to take hold. Wanting to live, the great freedom of wanting to be alive, is such a joy and I wouldn't trade it for anything. I do have more than a slight fear at the back of my mind that I could go back to those shit times because my brain is out of my control, but I am grateful for being alive. And I will continue to do what it takes to keep it that way.

I've subsequently weaned off Seroquel and now take the less intense agomelatine to help me sleep at night.

Up until that point of taking control by getting on top of my medications and overall health, I was convinced I too would die at the age of 56 like my mum, and her mum before her. It wasn't an if but a certainty in my mind. I couldn't see a life after that age and would count down how many years in my head I had left to stay alive. What a fucked-up way of thinking. Now, though, most of the time I want to live until I'm 80 or more. How good is that?

Depression, despite all the work I and many others have done to get rid of the stigma, is still a dirty word. That is why I am so open about my battles. But some people simply don't understand depression. You might as well say you've got the plague. Friends, very close friends even, often try and persuade me to get off the medication. Someone just recently told me to switch to CBD oil to get off my medication. It would make me lose weight, he'd say. 'Do you know how bad anti-depressants are for you? Do you know what they are doing to your body? You will lose so much weight, do you understand?'

I am used to this lecture. Other friends have even tried to get me to give up my antidepressants because they believe it is a 'choice' to feel that way. One friend suggested I go to South America and do an Ayahuasca retreat — where you hallucinate, piss yourself

> **I need help and there is no shame in realising and admitting that.**

and vomit everywhere to find yourself. I am sure that is great for some. But, for me, no thanks. For some reason, they think it is bad that I am on medication. I don't see it that way at all. Antidepressants help me to realise my full potential. Each to their own, I guess. I have no intention of not taking the medications. I can't just buck up and be positive. That is not my path. I need help and there is no shame in realising and admitting that. I feel empowered now that I understand the help I need.

Knowledge is power. Knowing what is going on with my head and body to me is power. I feel in control when I am on top of my mental health.

Each to their own, though. What works for me is not going to work for everyone. My hope, or dare I say suggestion, is that people find their own path and what works for them. Life is hard enough when you are juggling these things without having to deal with the added input of every Tom, Dick and Harry wanting a say in your health.

Find a GP who advocates for you, someone who has your best interests at heart. And most importantly, do your thing, whatever works for you — whatever makes you feel most empowered.

I look at my mental health battle the same way I do my sexuality and the fact I am a survivor of sexual abuse. I have done a bit of work in the mental health advocacy space with different not-for-profits and my *Mental As Anyone* podcast, and my view is that by sharing my story, I hopefully help to reduce that stigma just a tiny bit more so the next person may find it that little bit easier to manage their mental health and to accept their true self.

19

Listen Up: Abuse and Power

I would have been 10 the first time I remember thinking about trying to kill myself. I was in Year 4 of primary school. That is pretty sad looking back at it now. It was a pretty lame attempt and to be fair, I am pretty sure I didn't intend to follow through with it but the pain and self-loathing was there to the point that I wanted it all to come to an end.

I have no idea how I would have coped in a world of social media — it is much tougher for kids now with all the apps and online bullying. But, gosh, it was hard when I was a kid too.

I've always felt different, like I didn't fit in.

It started during the first year my twin sister Alison and I were in different classes. We were inseparable, as twins often are; we had the same friends and did everything together. I guess we were each other's safety blankets. Alison was put into a Year 4/5 mix class with one teacher, and I was put into a Year 4/5 class with a male teacher by the name of Mr Brown.

I think it was probably the first time I'd had a male teacher and I was quite excited about that given I had not had many male role models in those earlier years of my life. The problem was that Mr Brown was a pretty troubled man, which as a kid was very confusing. Teachers were supposed to be perfect. They had their shit together. Mr Brown, on the other hand, was very aggressive and abusive. He singled out me and two other students in the class and took his stress out on us. The more he treated us badly, the worse we acted out. We weren't the best-behaved students, but we weren't by any means the worst. His way of dealing with that was physically and verbally abusing us. As an example, one day he restrained one of the other two students, with her arms pulled behind her, then threw her across the room. With me, it was much the same. It was very physical and verbal abuse. And it was normally when we'd be held back for being naughty or for doing something wrong or making a mistake with our homework — that's when he would do these things to us. He would tell us we were stupid, that we were worthless and a waste of time. He swore at us, too — fuck, shit, other words. But he was careful — when others were around, he would just tell us off, gaslighting everyone by making out we were really poorly behaved kids.

Despite the way he behaved towards me, I was desperate for him to like me. I've always wanted to please people and to impress people, to be liked and validated — it continues to be an issue for me to this day. I remember desperately wanting Mr Brown to think I was okay, even though he was such a bully. I was always trying to get his approval, while also being a naughty 10-year-old.

I can feel the pain of the child me, desperate for help. I remember the stress of all of that hit me pretty hard as a kid. Overwhelmingly, I wanted his approval, but also that of others. I didn't want to be seen as the naughty kid, but I found myself in this bad cycle of abuse where he would use his power over me, mostly mentally but also physically. It was a dark period of my life, very dark. Thinking about it now, it is almost like a physical darkness comes over me. I can feel the pain of the child me, desperate for help.

At some point, Mum realised I was troubled. I wasn't acting 'normal' and she knew that I was having difficulties adjusting to class. At first, she thought it was the stress of being separated from my twin sister and that I needed time to adapt to the change. Mum had numerous meetings at the school, where the picture was painted that the other two students and I were wayward and needed structure and discipline. Mum was made to feel bad for being a single parent, that she was not harsh enough with me, which in turn they said had led to me being troubled and acting out. That was the implication, anyway.

#

One night, I kept sneaking outside. Mum had a girlfriend over at the time and they were having dinner. They were in the other 'good' lounge room. I kept coming inside and then going out the back glass sliding door to the shed in the yard. My mum asked, 'What are you doing?' and I made up some excuse.

There was an old petrol can that we would use to fill the lawnmower with fuel, and I kept going outside to inhale the fumes. I was going back and forth inside, outside, inside, outside. I was acting kind of stoned. I was high. Eventually, Mum noticed that I smelled like petrol. I denied it and told her I had mowed the lawn after school. Later, she followed me outside and found me in the shed, sniffing a petrol can. It would have been about 9 pm.

When Mum found me, I was semi passed out and high from inhaling the petrol fumes. That was how troubled I was. This could have happened to any curious kid, I guess. It was a weird moment for me. I didn't set out to sniff the petrol, but when I did, it gave me a rush and a high that relaxed me.

I cringe when I think about it — I was full of shame, guilt and embarrassment. I knew it was a shameful thing to do, even at that age. I didn't know what petrol sniffing was. But it felt good and I didn't really understand what I was doing or the consequences of my actions.

Mum took me to the hospital and the doctors said I needed psychological help. I also felt ashamed that my mum was made to feel like a failure. The system was broken then, as it is now.

The system was broken then, as it is now.

Around that time — it was probably towards the second half of the year — things were still pretty shit at school and getting worse. Mr Brown portrayed me as the brat child, and no one needed much persuading to believe it. It was easier to blame the kid than look at the bigger issue. Things were becoming more volatile in class. Without the context of what was going on, or knowing that Mr Brown was abusing us, it would have appeared that three of his students were becoming increasingly difficult and disruptive. (Perhaps we were, in a way, but there was good reason.) One day, fed up, I stormed out of the classroom and went and sat in the middle of the busy road in front of our school. Someone had to pull me out of the way of a big public bus because I had put myself right in front of it. Looking back now, that moment, and my petrol sniffing incident, were the first times I realised I was struggling with mental health issues. They were more cries for help than legitimate suicide attempts. It was about numbing the pain.

Sure, there were extenuating circumstances (the ongoing abuse from Mr Brown was a big factor), but I knew things weren't right. Mum pulled me out of school immediately after the bus incident and it all blew up from there. Mum was amazing, of course, but to others, instead of being given sympathy as a victim of a toxic situation with my teacher, I was treated like a difficult child. Friends disowned me; I felt like a pariah, which only exacerbated everything and made my self-loathing and lack of confidence worse. I changed to the local Catholic school, St Joseph's Primary, which my mum thought would have more structure and more discipline, to get me back on track.

For my remaining time in primary school, the fear of my new school friends finding out my past haunted me daily. Rumours started to spread from the old school that I was crazy, unhinged even, and that I had sat in the middle of the road outside the school as a bus came my way. It was a horrible sickly feeling of fear, regret and shame that I can still feel in the pit of my stomach today. What was I going to say at 10, that my teacher had gaslit me and was abusive? Yeah, right.

# # #

Mum didn't leave it there with the school though. She made a complaint but from what I remember it was swept under the carpet. My sister was happy in her class with her friends, so she stayed on through to Year 6. There was no point in uprooting her and making her life difficult. I remember feeling shame for embarrassing her in front of others, and now I realise how hard it would have been for her when everyone in the school thought her brother was crazy.

We later found out that Mr Brown had been moved on from the school after several of the other parents complained about his behaviour. On investigation, we were told that he had previously been banned from teaching in the state of New South Wales altogether. The story went that he had lived and worked in New South Wales while he went through a messy divorce. We never found out the full details, but he appeared to have been abusive to students there too as he struggled with his divorce. How this did not come up in a school check when he applied for a job in the Australian Capital Territory still absolutely blows my mind, but there it was. We were collateral damage, as he took out his stress on myself and a couple of other students.

I was lucky to have a mum that believed in me — a woman who advocated for her children, believed in them, dug deep and asked questions. Mum spoke to my sister and I freely, obviously not about stuff that would hurt us, but I remember her including us in the conversations, not treating us as 'other'.

> **I realised the importance of listening to alleged victims.**

From this whole experience, I realised the importance of listening to alleged victims because I believe through my lived experience that there is nearly always some level of truth to what they are saying. Of course there are exceptions, but where there is smoke, there is generally fire, right?

20

Death Rattle

My mum died five months after my uncle Barry's death (at Easter, on Good Friday). Her cancer was everywhere — she was literally riddled with it. To her credit she put up a good fight because, well, she wanted to live. My mum, Trish, was only 56. I was 31 at the time. It was a tough five months of what felt like round-the-clock chemotherapy and radiation. At one point they were giving her normal chemotherapy, and then they drilled a hole in her skull, the size of a 50-cent coin, and poured the chemo drugs through a hole directly into her head because the cancer had spread around the brain. There was cancer behind her right eye too, and in her lungs, kidneys, liver ... pretty much everywhere.

Months earlier, the doctor had told us Mum could last a few more years if we were lucky and the treatment worked. None of us were prepared for just a few months.

We celebrated Mum's 56th birthday on 6 September, 2009. Three weeks later, she died.

It was a special birthday as we knew Mum was fighting for her life, but we had no idea her death would come so soon. We invited my other uncle, my aunt and cousins, and people from all around Australia. It was a nice big family barbecue. Mum was frail, she'd lost her hair and was wearing a turban-like thing, but you wouldn't have thought she was about to die. She had a light smattering of makeup on, enough to give her some colour as her skin was almost a greyish beige from fighting the cancer. It was a special day and I'm glad we did it, but I wish we also had known it was our last hurrah, so to speak.

From then on, she got sick, really sick, really quickly, and went downhill rapidly. Mum was in and out of hospital during those five months. Her immune system was pretty shit so even a small infection meant hospitalisation. I was on and off small propeller planes what felt like every other week, travelling back and forth on the short flight from Sydney to Canberra. I'd get a phone call and have to rush off with little to no notice. My closest work colleagues, Shandelle Battersby and Claire Harvey, were rocks at this time and would often console me as I'd break down into tears in the office. I'm sure I wasn't doing my best work at this time, in fact I knew I wasn't, but it wasn't an issue and I'd often spend weeks doing what work I could remotely from Canberra, tap-tap tapping away on my laptop, while sitting next to Mum's hospital bed or beside her during her chemo treatments.

When she was admitted to hospital one time, we thought she would come out again but she never did. She was in a private ward of Canberra Hospital in Woden. She was exhausted, and by the time she was transferred to palliative care, she was fighting to the last breath. Talking was an issue from the day she went to hospital that time though. That is what put her in the hospital this stint. One day she woke up at home and just couldn't speak properly. A normal sentence would come out sounding like gobbledegook or gibberish. The doctor wasn't too worried and put it down to the intensity of the chemo process. But just after her birthday, it got really bad. It was like her brain was saying one thing and what was coming out of her mouth was another. It was hard to watch, especially in someone who was still so young. My god, I feel like I will be 56 in a minute.

We honestly all thought it was just a phase of the chemo and she'd be good again soon.

While Mum was in hospital, my sister and I wheeled her outside to meet up with one of our closest girlfriends, Jodie Roff (one of my sister's best friends, who is like family to all of us), who was there visiting a family member. Though Mum had given up smoking, by this point the cancer was everywhere, so as far as we were concerned, she could smoke as much as she wanted if it made her feel any better. She could even have three packets a day — heck, she could try magic mushies, smoke marijuana or consume anything else if it made her feel better. Where I previously would have been at her about smoking, I told her I didn't give a shit if she lit a cigarette or 10.

Until that point, Mum had been able to light a cigarette, but this time she put the ciggy in her mouth wrong. It was the wrong way around completely — so the brown bit was sticking out of her mouth and her brain just didn't compute what she was doing wrong. We had to help her. You cry or you laugh and that was the final time we all laughed together, giggling together at the silliness and sadness of the situation that we couldn't do anything about.

Stuff like that was constantly happening towards the end, and it was really hard to watch. Mum went downhill quickly when she was admitted with difficulty talking, and the doctor just said, 'Look, this is happening much faster than we thought in the brain. And you don't have much time left.' They couldn't give us a number of days, weeks or months. It was just soon.

Hypnotherapy with Helen

Mum smoked like a chimney her whole life, two packets of cigarettes a day — probably more some days. She always had a ciggie in one hand and a coffee in the other. If it wasn't coffee, it was a glass of coke (the soft drink, not cocaine). She loved her ciggies and coffee. Now, on special days like birthdays, Mother's Day and Christmas, my sister and I go to her memorial stone, light a cigarette and pour a latte over the plaque on a river stone by the creek at Norwood Park Crematorium. It is cheesy to admit but we play Bette Midler's 'Wind Beneath My Wings' on my phone and sit there remembering Mum. It may be silly but it's something we do. I cry every time, even now so many years later, and it is the only time I can listen to that song.

Mum's first experience with cancer was fighting breast cancer. At the time, I was interviewing Helen Reddy, the superstar Aussie singer of the 60s and 70s, and she told me how she practised hypnotherapy. I was fascinated. It was a lovely, casual chat with a remarkable woman. In passing, I explained to her that my mum had cancer, that she smoked and I had been trying to get her to look at holistic health options on top of the chemo. Helen asked me to give Mum her number. I wasn't expecting it, but it was a positive experience in what was a really shitty time. And so Mum rang her. She would drive from Sydney to Canberra once a fortnight over a period of several months, and go to Helen's apartment for hypnotherapy treatment. Helen, who won a Grammy in 1973 for her feminist anthem 'I Am Woman', didn't charge a cent — and not because I was a journalist. It was simply something she did for people to help them because she could. She didn't need the money. She was genuinely happy to help.

Thanks to Helen, Mum gave up smoking for quite a while after the first stint of breast cancer. She would chew nicotine gum like it was nobody's business, but she didn't smoke anymore. My grandmother, Beryl, had died of lung cancer; because Mum smoked so much, she often joked that smoking would kill her too. Mum also predicted that she would die young, like her mother, but at the back of my mind I put that down to her depressive outlook on life rather than some sort of crystal ball intuition.

I feel immense gratitude to and for Helen Reddy, who has since died of dementia (she was 78). I am not sure she realised how much she did for my family. It wasn't just about the smoking; it was a psychological thing. The hypnotherapy seemed to help my mum think more healthily. Mum took up swimming at that time too, she'd go and swim laps every day. She had never been a great swimmer, but she went to the local pool with her paddleboard and taught herself to swim. It was really good for her — she was in the best physical health she'd been in for as long as I could remember in my life. She was eating more healthily. Her skin glowed. As someone who had never really valued her life, plagued by depression herself, it was wonderful to see Mum not just fighting to live but wanting to be here. The hypnotherapy dramatically changed Mum's mindset — she was happy, despite the fight she was going through. And I genuinely believe Helen's support played a major role in helping Mum recover from that first bout of cancer.

A family fallout

Those last weeks before Mum died, my sister and I would talk about my stepdad. If Mum was broken from her illness, he was the nail in her coffin.

We had fallen out with our stepdad earlier in the year, so it was really difficult having to see him. Why we had the falling out is not my story to tell, but suffice to say we timed everything so the crossover with our stepdad was as limited as possible.

Long before, he had spoken about being physically violent in previous relationships with women but always painted himself as the victim. This was discussed openly in the family. To him, he was a reformed man.

I honestly, hand on heart, believe that Mum was in a situation of coercive control, which made it too painful for her to admit, feel, see and admit that he was a violent, narcissistic man. She was too sick to face it. But in those last two weeks, in a moment of clarity, she told me that she didn't know how to get out of the situation — she was just too sick.

I found out after Mum had died that my stepdad had been violent with Mum too. She had confided to my sister and my aunt that this had happened on multiple occasions. This time, he had her on the ground kicking her at one stage. She would have weighed 60kg, him upwards of about 150kg. I had no idea at the time other than that they were fighting and Mum was upset — she moved out and stayed a few days at a hotel one time, and I naively believed it when she told me her puffy eyes and red blotchy face was from crying. He'd often put Mum's visible distress down to her mental health struggles and would gaslight her even in front of me.

Mum would put her keys in a bowl on the kitchen bench each time she'd arrive home. One time, I witnessed my stepdad pick up the keys and move them to another part of the kitchen. I called him out for it there and then to which he stood his ground and made Mum think she was going crazy. It was infuriating.

There were the usual things with a blended family that my sister and I were too young (around 12) to understand, but there was a mixture of resentment and excitement towards our two stepbrothers. Excitement because we finally had siblings (this was long before we

199

found out about our half-brothers) and resentment because it felt like they received preferential treatment when with us as they could do no wrong to our stepdad and we could do no good. In hindsight, as an adult, it is easy to see they were dealing with their own shit and would have understandably resented us. They had their own trauma.

One time, on a beach holiday, we were all staying in a cabin — my mum, my stepdad, my sister, myself and my two stepbrothers. One of my stepbrothers and I fought the whole time. I would have been 13 and he would have been a few years younger. He kept annoying me, punching my shoulder, so I hit him back after warning him several times to stop. I didn't punch him hard but he put on his best crocodile tears, milking the moment, and all hell broke loose with my stepdad coming at me, clocking me fair in the face and decking me to the floor. My stepdad was six foot plus and I was a kid. It was brutal. He was a man with a temper. I ran away that day … for a few hours. From then on, it became a case of managing my stepdad's temper and doing my best not to cop another blow-up.

After a violent outburst, he would go to the opposite extreme and engage in what they'd call 'love bomb' behaviour these days where a person smothers you with kindness. He would obviously feel bad and would shower us with small gifts like chocolate or yummy food but it wasn't long before the cycle would flip and he'd be back angry again.

As kids, we didn't speak to Mum about it because we wanted her to be happy.

My sister and I dealt with it very differently. She was introverted and withdrew, never questioning or crossing the line as she went into her shell, while I was more extroverted and pushed him on things I didn't agree with. That meant we would often butt heads metaphorically but ultimately I was always careful and my sister and I felt constantly as if we were treading on eggshells.

Later, when I realised the extent of my stepdad's violence, I struggled to reconcile Mum's situation with the knowledge that she was a raging feminist and had brought me up to be that way too. How did that sit when she was in a relationship with a man who was abusive to the core? I don't think of Mum as a battered housewife; she was a warrior and always stood up to him when she had the emotional strength to do so.

I think the challenge for him, and partly what attracted him to her, was the thrill of chasing that power over Mum. While Mum was strong from the outside looking in, she was vulnerable too, as we all are. She suffered from bipolar and I believe he saw an opportunity to prey on that weakness. I think he saw it as a game. He was a narcissist.

It felt like a full-time job pandering to his ego. He retired from work and made a lot of fuss about 'running' the household, telling us how hard he worked to do the shopping and cooking. We'd have to praise his cooking or all hell would break loose.

In reality, Mum was working fulltime, bringing in all the money, and he was living a good life. They even had a cleaner.

When Mum had cancer the first time, we had a family chat with her, my stepdad, my sister, me, and our stepbrothers. It was at our family home growing up, where we had lived long before Mum met our stepdad. We discussed what would happen if she or our stepdad were to die. Their wills left everything to the other of the two, so if he died first, everything went to Mum; if Mum died first, everything went to him. Their wills were structured so that when they had both died, their inheritance would be split a third to me, a third to my sister, and a third split between my stepbrothers (so they received a sixth of the estate each). Out stepdad openly acknowledged that my mum had brought more property and money to the relationship. My grandfather believed that you had to have an education and that you had to own your own home: If you had those two things, then you would be able to manage life in a reasonable way. So, Mum had a house thanks to my grandfather's help, and she received a second house when he died — an apartment she inherited in Sydney. Our stepdad brought nothing to the relationship, maybe some furniture, but the whole house was furnished with our family's antiques. Later, he contributed a small house in Canberra to the family when his mother (we called her Oma — German for grandmother) died a couple of years earlier.

My stepbrothers were getting their inheritance from their mum as well as their split of my mum and stepdad's lot, so the arrangement seemed fair. (Our stepdad often spoke of his guilt at leaving them and how he left everything to them to make up for that.)

The week before Mum died, she and I talked about her will because I was worried that, given our deteriorated relationship with our stepdad, he might change his will and take everything once Mum died. I was more worried about our family antiques, photo albums and the like, but the money would also have helped me and Alison to pay off a small house, which would have made a difference to us both. I explained these concerns to Mum and she agreed that when she got out of the hospital that time round, she would see a lawyer to make sure it was all sorted and there would be no loophole to exclude us.

Unfortunately, she died a few days later — a few horrifically tough days. My sister and I were sleeping there at the hospital. When they knew there was no point in any further treatment, we still didn't know if it was a few weeks or months (we were hoping the latter), so they said that she was to be transferred to Clare Holland House, a palliative care facility. She was sleeping more and awake much less. The hospital organised an ambulance. Her body was shutting down.

Just before the doctor told us, I had to pull my shit together (from the emotional mess we were all feeling watching Mum deteriorate) and do a phone interview with former Miss World Jennifer Hawkins in one of the lounge rooms in the ward. I told Jen I was at the hospital and that my mum had cancer. Jen was lovely, and said, 'I'm sorry to hear that,' and we went straight back into plugging whatever product it was I was talking to her about — spring water, tequila, some fashion brand or whatever. I thought at the time how ruthless the business was but that I was happy for the distraction. Jen was perfectly polite and has always been lovely — it was just a realisation moment for me about the business more generally.

That was like two days before Mum died. They organised the palliative care to this beautiful place by Canberra's Lake Burley Griffin. I went in the ambulance with Mum. I cradled her head in my hands the whole way. It was a short drive of no more than 30 minutes, and I whispered to Mum how much I loved her the whole way as I held her head with one hand and rubbed her forehead with my hand. She was asleep and never woke up. My aunt Gwen drove down from Sydney, as did my uncle John, both coming to say goodbye to their baby sister. There was a procession of close family who came to say their farewells. It was heart-wrenching.

The night Mum died, my sister and I were sleeping on fold out armchairs, the uncomfortable type they have in hospitals where you barely get a wink of sleep. It didn't matter as every long breath Mum took we feared would be her last. It was about one o'clock in the morning when she died. The death rattle had started. It's that weird thing you hear about — people told us we would know when Mum was about to die because of this death rattle. My mum had also told me about the death rattle because she heard it when both her parents had died.

To me, the idea of a death rattle conjured thoughts of some sort of horror movie. In reality, a death rattle sounds even more tortuous. It is very strange — it sounds made up, even — but it was exactly as Mum had described it when she died. It's when someone is dying that they can't swallow or cough to clear the saliva but it doesn't cause any pain to the person. I think of it as the lung cavity being empty, rattling around with each deep, long, laboured breath. A death rattle can last anywhere between 24 and 48 hours.

My sister and I were trying unsuccessfully to sleep, full of despair with each breath as the nurses told us it was only the early stages of the rattle so we had time and 'would know' when it was about to happen. What that meant we didn't truly know. How would we know? Would we know? We didn't want to waste any time so we rang our stepdad and he came to the hospice. The three of us were with Mum when she died — my stepdad at the foot of the bed, me and my sister on either side of Mum, with me on her left and my sister on her right. We took turns saying goodbye, all crying. To this day, I harbour some strange guilt that I may have helped Mum go faster. Of course I didn't do anything. She was dying though, and I could feel it as I held her. I felt the rattle and held her tight. We held Mum tight as she took her final breaths, trying to make her feel comforted while also letting her know she didn't need to hold on. We both whispered into her ear, kissing her cheek, telling her we love her and she could let go, that she had fought hard but didn't need to keep fighting.

It is the only time I've been with someone when they've died. It was just the most surreal, weird thing, especially as it was someone who I considered to be my best friend and who I loved so much. I felt empty and that hole stays with me today. The pain eases but it is always with you.

We were exhausted and crying, and we stepped out to let the nurses tidy Mum up and 'prepare her body'. Such a strange term.

It was excruciating waiting outside Mum's room. What were they doing? As we walked back in, delirious and devastated, devoid of any energy but also feeling some relief that she was out of pain, the nurses pressed play on some strange whale music. God knows how that was going to make us feel better when someone had just died. I still can't listen to some of Mum's favourite artists we played for her while she was 'sleeping' in that palliative care room. Geoffrey Gurrumul Yunupingu. Patsy Cline. The Flying Pickets. *The Big Chill* movie soundtrack. They played this sort of whale screeching, like whale mating calls you would see in a David Attenborough documentary. It was odd at best.

The nurses had put a light covering of makeup on Mum's face, which was also strange. And she was cold, like ice, which seemed to have happened so fast. It was one of the hardest days of my life, hardest moments of my life, and my sister and I hugged each other, looking at her and wondering where she had gone. Could she see us? We didn't and don't believe in a god, but we still wondered if her soul was there with us.

Alison went home to her place, my stepdad went back to the family home — as did I, back to my kid bed, where I took a sleeping tablet and crashed out into a bizarre dreamland of happier times, trying to escape the pain of Mum's death.

As far as we know, our stepdad did cut us out of the will. We saw nothing of our inheritance — none of the antiques or photo albums. The last we heard, our stepbrothers offloaded everything to the local tip when our stepdad was in jail.

21

Inherited Qualities: Shopping 'Til You Drop

When all else fails, shop. That's what I do. That's what my mum did. It has always been my way of filling that void of not feeling good enough within myself. And it usually always helps, even if only for a few minutes. The initial buzz wears off quickly as it is only a temporary fix or distraction from the actual problem.

I take everything to the point of addiction, even shopping. Like, I don't just shop, I shop for a bargain to the point of hyper-focus and don't stop until I get the dopamine/adrenaline hit. Then, I come down afterwards, feeling flat. It is a good point of reference for me. I know I am feeling a bit topsy-turvy, that my mental health is not great, when I excessively shop.

By excessive shopping, I mean buying new socks when I have a drawer full at home, buying new undies when I have dozens of them too. I must have 60 t-shirts at home — all different colours and sizes to fit me at every weight. I have business shirts too that have never been opened, at least a dozen of them — good quality ones too. That's even after a clean-out of my wardrobe — eight garbage bags went to Goodwill. My eyes light up when I walk into a Westfield, and I rarely walk out without a purchase — usually something I don't need.

I justify my shopping by thinking that I need things in a different size or colour, or whatever. However my mind rationalises my excessive shopping, I know it is a good measure of when I am not necessarily on a straight, even track.

You could say I am my mother's son.

You could say I am my mother's son. Mum was the same — she loved to shop more than anyone I've ever met. She never had a lot of money when we were growing up. She would save up and buy special things, and always good quality so that whatever it was she bought, it lasted. She would spend any money she had on me and my sister. And when she did have some regular cash coming in, such as when she progressed her career in the public service, she would buy herself nice things. When she bought shoes, they were made from expensive Italian leather. Millers of Manuka, a former boutique luxury shop in Canberra, sold her favourite brands, including Escada and Jaeger. She would buy herself a power suit each year. My sister and I would sit there for hours as shop assistants brought out new season collections for Mum to go through. It did our heads in.

Mum was so happy when she was shopping. Today, I wish I had been more patient with her on those shopping days — it was nice to see her smile.

At Mum's funeral, I talked about how amazing Mum was, how she was our best friend and that Alison and I loved her so much — the usual things you would expect in a eulogy. It was a very sad occasion, but I tried to be funny and got some laughs. Because everyone knew that Mum loved to shop, I made everyone aware that I had inherited that trait too. (My sister is the opposite; she doesn't get the spending bug like I do.)

In the days after Mum died, I shopped until I dropped. I bought anything and everything I liked, filling a hole of grief with instant gratification that barely lasted a moment before the hole needed filling again. I read the full list of items I bought at Mum's funeral. It was extensive. People laughed.

The list included R.M.Williams boots and a suit, even though my work rarely calls for me to wear one. I remember being at the factory outlet mall in Canberra. There was a homewares store where I bought this can opener, some super-duper gadget. The bonus was that it was on sale, so I had to buy multiple can openers because it was such a good price. I remember giving them out to a few people after the funeral.

I wasn't coping well. It was more than a bit weird. It was funny though.

So yeah, I am my mother's son, and shopping for me is one way, albeit an unhealthy way, to deal with stress. If I dig deep to look at what is behind my desire to shop, I think it is the instant gratification that appeals to me — I value being able to buy and own something that no one can take away from me. The things I buy are concrete, tangible things.

I don't have the full speech, but here are my draft notes for my speech at Mum's funeral.

Mum, you'll be happy to know since your passing, I've bought a new suit, two pairs of shoes, a new cutlery set, some socks, tracky dacks, some work shirts, two Ralph Lauren jumpers and 20 five-in-one can openers — everyone gets a prize.

In true Mum form, always shop to make yourself feel better.

Mum passed on her love of beautiful clothes, Italian leather shoes and fine Egyptian cotton bed linen.

Her closet at home is a sight to behold.

My collection of some 40-odd pairs of shoes is nothing to hers but is more than most guys, and Mum had about 100 pairs.

We used to call Mum the Imelda Marcos of Australia because she's got hundreds of pairs of shoes.

Mum loved Christmas. She would spend the whole year stocking up on gifts she'd see around the place. One Christmas stocking wasn't enough though — we did pillowcases, and lots of them. Thanks for your generosity, Mum — you've left us a stockpile of presents to last the next three years.

But it wasn't all about shopping; Mum had a strong sense of social justice and was committed to making a real difference to people's lives through her work as a public servant. And she believed education was the key to the future.

Travel was one of Mum's greatest joys. From Bali when we were six years old to Sri Lanka and Europe as teenagers and Malaysia and Thailand after that.

Mum took her first trip overseas to China in her thirties but saw travel as a way of opening our eyes and educating us.

She was passing that love of travel on to Livy (Ali's first daughter). We all holidayed as a family in Malaysia when Livy was a year old.

Mum took Ali and I to Euro Disney when we were 15 and just a few weeks ago, we sat Livy down and told her the four of us, Mum, Livy, Ali and I, would be going to Disneyland in LA and then spend some time on the beach in Hawaii this coming January. Mum was really looking forward to that trip.

We'll still go, Mum, with you in our hearts.

Livy was truly the apple of Mum's eye. To say she loved her is a gross understatement.

Mum, you are our best friend, as you always will be. We love you.

Your TOOLKIT for LIFE & DEATH

DR JODIE LOWINGER

Grief is the emotional and psychological response to loss. It's what happens when someone or something that matters deeply to us is taken away, like JMo in losing his mum or feeling abandoned by his father. While we often associate grief with the death of a loved one, it can stem from any significant loss. This might include the end of a relationship, the loss of a job, a major life transition or even a broken dream. Through my experiences helping adults, children and adolescents to work through the challenges of grief, I can say that people's experiences of grief aren't always linear, and they don't necessarily follow a neat timeline. Grief shows up in different ways for different people. Dealing with grief requires validation, compassion and patience with regard to the unique experiences that you or a loved one might be going through.

Grief can make you feel like you're on an emotional rollercoaster. Some common ways grief might show up include emotional responses, such as sadness, anger, guilt, relief, confusion or even numbness. You might even feel a mix of emotions that seem contradictory: one moment, you might feel overwhelming sadness; the next, you're angry, relieved or feel numb. Physical symptoms of grief include fatigue, headaches, changes in appetite, trouble sleeping or even a weakened immune system. Behavioural symptoms might include withdrawing from others, struggling to focus or feeling restless. Grief is a full-body experience that can affect your emotions, thoughts and your physical health.

Even if you're surrounded by people, grief can make you feel isolated and lonely. You might think, 'No one really gets what I'm going through,' or feel pressure to put on a brave face for others. There are also spiritual impacts for many people, where grief may shake your beliefs or make you question your purpose in life.

Acute grief is the immediate, intense reaction to loss. This is the raw, all-encompassing pain that often comes right after the loss occurs. It's like a wave crashing over you — intense, overwhelming and impossible to ignore. Over time, the waves might become less frequent or less intense, but they can still catch you off guard, especially during anniversaries, milestones or quiet moments.

Some people experience complicated grief, where the experience of grief doesn't ease over time. It might feel like you're stuck, unable to move forward or accept the loss. A person can also experience *anticipatory grief* if they begin grieving a loss before it's fully occurred, such as when a loved one is diagnosed with a terminal illness. Sometimes, multiple losses stack on top of each other, known as *cumulative grief,* leaving little time or space to process one before another hits. All these experiences are highly responsive to therapy, so it's important not to feel like you need to soldier on or struggle alone. Be sure to seek out the help you need.

Suicide is the act of intentionally ending one's life. It's a complex topic, often misunderstood and surrounded by stigma. If you've ever experienced suicidal thoughts, you know how they can feel like a dark cloud you just can't shake. These thoughts are frequently not about wanting to die as much as they are about wanting relief: relief from the pain, the pressure or the constant noise in your head. JMo wrote about first feeling relieved before ultimately panicking when he attempted suicide. Having these thoughts doesn't make you weak or hopeless — they're a sign that you're in distress and are deserving of support.

Suicidal thoughts can range from fleeting moments of wishing life were easier, to more persistent, detailed plans to end one's life. Passive suicidal ideation might include thoughts like, 'I wish I could disappear' or 'Life would be easier if I weren't here,' without specific plans or intent. Active suicidal ideation involves thoughts that include planning or intending to take action to end one's life. Regardless of the level of these thoughts, ensuring that a safety plan is in place and moving towards practical action to help are essential.

Grief and suicide are complex, painful and deeply personal topics. Grief isn't just something to 'get over', and suicidal thoughts aren't something to 'snap out of'. Both require time, compassion, and the courage to seek or offer help. In this toolkit, we'll explore practical strategies for navigating these challenges, whether you're grieving, struggling with suicidal thoughts, or supporting someone else through their pain. While these tools and strategies can be helpful regardless of your situation, it's important to be aware that grief and suicide are two separate struggles. Keep your own experience in mind as you read on; this toolkit is here to help you, however you may or may not be struggling.

Remember, it's okay to feel what you're feeling and it's okay to ask for help. You don't have to do this alone.

You are worthy of care and support

Suicidal thoughts often come with feelings of shame, guilt and isolation, as though you're carrying a secret you can't share. You might think, 'No one would understand' or 'I don't want to burden anyone.' Suicidal thinking is influenced by biological, psychological and social factors:

- Mental health conditions, such as depression, bipolar disorder, post-traumatic stress disorder (PTSD) and other mental illnesses, can heighten suicidal thoughts, especially if untreated.
- Trauma or significant loss can leave deep emotional scars, which increases the risk.
- Chronic pain or illness can lead to ongoing physical pain or feelings of hopelessness that may contribute to suicidal thinking.
- Social isolation and feeling disconnected from others can amplify loneliness and despair.
- Stigma or fear of judgement can prevent people from seeking help and make them feel even more trapped and vulnerable.

The important thing to note is that no matter what that voice in your head is saying, the thoughts are not a reflection of your worth or how much you're loved — they're a signal that something in your life needs attention and care and that you are worthy of seeking out the help you need. Having helped many people grappling with suicidal thoughts, I can share first-hand that reaching out for support will help you to feel more in control and move beyond that big black cloud to a life that feels better. Just taking that first step to seek out the help you deserve will make a profound impact.

Losing someone to suicide can create a unique form of grief that's heavy with questions, guilt and, sometimes, anger. This kind of loss, often referred to as *suicide bereavement*, can feel isolating because of the stigma that still surrounds suicide. If you've lost someone to suicide, you might find yourself grappling with thoughts like, 'Could I have done something to stop it?', 'Why didn't they tell me they were struggling?' or 'How could they leave us like this?' These are natural, human responses, but it is important to recognise that, as in JMo's case, suicide is most typically the result of intense pain that the person felt they couldn't escape, not a reflection of how much they loved or valued their relationships.

Understanding common misconceptions about suicide can help you to approach the suicidal thoughts or suicidal behaviours of others with understanding rather than judgement. For example, a person might hold the fear that 'talking about suicide will give someone the idea'. However, research shows that asking someone directly about suicidal thoughts doesn't increase risk; in fact, it can actually save lives because it opens the door to support. Another commonly held myth is that 'People who talk about suicide just want attention.' Rather, talking about suicide is often a cry for help, not attention. It's a way of expressing deep pain. A third misconception is that 'Once someone decides to die, there's nothing you can do.' The fact is that suicide is preventable. As mentioned, many people who feel suicidal want the pain to end, not necessarily their life. Intervention and support can make a profound difference.

Both grief and suicide carry a heavy weight of stigma, which can make them even harder to navigate. But when we talk openly and compassionately about these topics, we create space to break down stigma and build understanding and helpful action. If you're grieving a loss, struggling with suicidal thoughts or supporting someone who is working through these difficulties, you're far from alone. These experiences are part of our collective human experience, and help is available. Whether through therapy, support groups or trusted loved ones, there are ways to process grief, address suicidal thoughts and move towards healing. The feelings and experiences can be overwhelming, and you may feel like there's no way forward, but remember — you are not weak or broken, you are navigating something deeply painful and you are worthy of care and support.

Depression and anxiety often go hand in hand with grief or suicidal thoughts. They can amplify feelings of hopelessness, making it even harder to find a way forward. Depression can make everything feel harder, such as getting out of bed, eating or taking care of yourself. It's like a fog that dims everything around you. As I highlight in my book, *The Mind Strength Method*, the voice of depression can trick you into thinking that your problems are permanent ('nothing will ever be good'), pervasive ('nothing is good') and personal ('I'm no good'). Common feelings include worthlessness, emptiness and a loss of interest in things you would otherwise enjoy.

Anxiety can show up as constant worry, racing thoughts, or even physical symptoms like a racing heart or shortness of breath. You might feel like you're on edge all the time, waiting for the next bad thing to happen.

Depression and anxiety can create a vicious cycle. Depression makes you feel stuck, while anxiety keeps you worrying about everything you're not doing. It's exhausting, but depression and anxiety are also mental health challenges that you can work through and are highly treatable with the right tools and support.

When you're dealing with grief or suicidal thoughts, guilt and shame often come along for the ride. These feelings can be especially intense if you've lost someone to suicide or feel like you 'should' be handling things differently. You might find yourself thinking, 'What could I have done differently?' or 'This is my fault.' Guilt can be a heavy burden, but it's important to remember that no single person is responsible for someone else's actions or feelings. Shame often comes from the stigma around mental health and suicide. You might feel like you can't talk about what you're going through because you'll be judged or misunderstood. But keeping these feelings bottled up only makes them more powerful.

In the aftermath of loss or during periods of deep emotional pain, it's common to question your purpose or your beliefs — even the meaning of life itself. This existential questioning can feel unsettling, but it's also a natural part of processing what you're going through. After a loss, you might find yourself searching for answers that may never come, such as questioning why something has happened, or feeling a sense of injustice. When you're feeling hopeless, it's easy to wonder whether anything really matters. This sense of futility isn't a reflection of reality — it's a symptom of emotional pain.

Both grief and suicidal thoughts can create a sense of distance between you and others. You might feel like no one understands or worry about burdening people with your feelings. It's common to withdraw when you're struggling, whether because you're overwhelmed or because you think no one can help. But isolation can make things feel even harder. You might long for someone to talk to but worry about how they'll react. Will they judge you? Will they say the wrong thing? These fears are valid, but most people want to help — they just might not know how.

In the midst of grief or pain, you might have moments where you laugh, feel okay or even experience joy (as JMo did even in hospital). These moments can feel confusing, or you might feel guilty for 'moving on'. But these breaks from the pain are a sign of healing, not forgetting. Feeling good doesn't mean you've stopped grieving or struggling. It just means you're human, and humans are capable of holding multiple emotions at once. Give yourself permission to feel those moments of relief. They don't diminish the depth of your loss or struggle; they're a reminder that healing is possible.

Grief and emotional pain take up a lot of mental and physical energy, which can leave little room for anything else. Whether you're grieving, battling suicidal thoughts, or dealing with depression and anxiety, it's common to feel stuck, like you're not moving forward—no matter how hard you try. This 'stuckness' can feel frustrating and demoralising, as if you're failing somehow, but it's not permanent—it is a part of the process of healing. Healing isn't linear; it's a winding road, with ups, downs and plateaus.

A toolkit for coping with grief or suicidal thoughts

If you're facing grief, loss or suicidal thoughts, these feelings, while deeply painful, are a natural response to what you're going through. They don't define you, and they don't have to last forever. With the right tools, support and patience, it's possible to find relief, connection and hope. Here, I share some tools to help you navigate these complex challenges.

When emotions feel like a tidal wave, grounding techniques can help you anchor yourself in the present moment. These strategies are particularly helpful during moments of intense anxiety, sadness, or when suicidal thoughts creep in. Grounding isn't about fixing the problem, it's about finding a moment of calm so you can engage in more helpful actions. One example of a helpful grounding practice is the '5-4-3-2-1 technique' (which I have mentioned before in this book). Look around and name five things you can see, four things you can touch, three things you can hear, two things you can smell and one thing you can taste. This exercise redirects your focus to what's around you rather than what's swirling in your head.

Breathing exercises can also be helpful grounding techniques; it is a strategy I know JMo uses a lot. One example is box breathing, where you breathe in for a count of four, hold for four and exhale for four. This helps to re-engage the parasympathetic nervous system and take you into a greater state of calm. You can experiment with longer exhales to further calm your nervous system and send a message back to your brain that you are safe.

Engaging your senses can also interrupt spiralling thoughts and bring you back to the present. For example, splashing cold water on your face, holding an ice cube or lighting a scented candle can be helpful.

When suicidal thoughts hit, it's hard to think clearly. That's where a crisis plan comes in — a simple, pre-prepared guide to help you get through the toughest moments. Having a plan ready when you're feeling okay means you don't have to rely on willpower or decision-making in moments of distress. An example of some elements in the crisis plan might include:

- Writing down warning signs. Consider what thoughts, feelings or behaviours signal that you're struggling. Knowing your triggers can help you recognise when to take helpful action.
- Listing your support network, including trusted friends, family members, therapists or helplines. Write down their contact information so you can reach out without having to search. Include emergency contacts so if things escalate you know who to call for immediate help. Include crisis hotlines, local emergency services or a trusted professional to contact if you need to.
- Identifying coping strategies. Write down activities or tools that help you feel calmer or more connected, like taking a walk, journalling or listening to music.

It's important to give yourself permission to lean on your support system. When life feels heavy, connection is vital. It's easy to pull away when you're struggling, but leaning on others is a critical step to help lighten the load. Share what you're feeling with someone you trust. You don't have to have the 'perfect' words — just letting someone know you're struggling can be a relief. Whether it's asking a friend to check in on you, joining a support group or seeking professional therapy, letting others in can make a big difference. Let go of feeling the need to be perfect. The people who care about you want to be there for you, even if all you can say is, 'I'm not okay.' Connection reminds you that you're not alone and that others care about your wellbeing, even when you're struggling to care for yourself.

Our minds are tricky — they can convince us of things that aren't true, especially when depression, anxiety or grief are involved. Reframing negative thoughts doesn't mean ignoring your feelings — it means challenging thoughts that might be overly critical or unhelpful. Notice when a negative thought pops up, like 'I'm worthless' or 'I'll never feel better.' To get some distance from your thoughts, ask yourself, 'What would I say to a friend who had this thought?' See if you can replace the thought with a kinder one. For example, 'I'm worthless' might become 'I'm struggling right now, but that doesn't define who I am.' Thoughts are powerful, but they're not facts. Challenging negative thoughts creates space for hope and self-compassion. If you continue to struggle with managing the spiral of negative thoughts, consider working with a clinical psychologist.

When life feels overwhelming, even basic tasks can feel impossible. The key is to start small and celebrate progress, no matter how tiny it might seem. Instead of saying, 'I need to clean the house,' try 'I'll spend five minutes tidying one corner.' Small wins build momentum. Celebrate effort, not perfection. Did you get out of bed? Eat a meal? Text a friend? These are wins, especially on hard days. And most importantly, be kind to yourself. If you can't do much, that's okay. Rest is part of healing too. Small, manageable steps help you rebuild confidence and remind you that progress, no matter how slow, is still progress.

Writing can also be a powerful way to process emotions, especially when they feel too big to say out loud. Write whatever comes to mind without worrying about grammar or structure. Let the words flow freely. This can help you express what's hard to say. Journalling gives you a safe space to explore your thoughts and feelings without judgement. See if you can practise gratitude journalling to help you reinstate some of your serotonin and feel-good neurochemicals. One way to do this could be to write down three things you're grateful for each day. They can be big or small, such as a sunny day, a kind word or your favourite snack. Letter writing can also be helpful. Write a letter to someone you've lost, to yourself, or even to your feelings to help you process your grief. Mood boosters are covered in detail in my book, *The Mind Strength Method* so if you want to do a deeper dive into practical ways to help yourself or a loved one to feel better access these via audiobook or hard copy.

Your mental health is closely tied to your physical wellbeing. While it's not a magic fix, taking care of your body can make it easier to manage emotional pain. Even if you don't feel hungry, try to eat something small and nourishing. Your brain needs fuel to function. Gentle movement, like a short walk or stretching, can help release tension and boost mood. Grief, depression and anxiety can mess with sleep, but creating a calming bedtime routine, like turning off screens and using relaxation techniques, can help. When your body feels supported, it's easier to navigate emotional challenges.

If you're grieving, finding ways to honour your loss can help you feel connected and bring a sense of meaning. Creating a memory box can be a helpful way to process grief rather than shut it down. Fill the box with photos, letters or items that remind you of your loved one. Consider writing a letter, poem or journal entry about what the person meant to you and celebrate their life. Light a candle, visit a favourite place or do something they loved in their memory. Honouring your grief allows you to process the loss and keep the connection alive in a meaningful way.

Sometimes, the weight of grief, depression, anxiety or suicidal thoughts is too much to carry alone. Reaching out to a clinical psychologist or doctor is a sign of strength, not weakness. Professional support offers tools, perspective and a safe space to navigate your struggles. Cognitive Behavioural Therapy (CBT) or other scientifically supported strategies can help you reframe negative thoughts and process grief and loss. If depression or anxiety feels unmanageable, medication might also be a helpful tool. Talk to a healthcare professional to explore your options. While there are opinions both for and against medication for treating mental health, it's important to do what's right for you. You should raise any concerns with your healthcare professional and allow them to help you make an informed decision If you're in immediate distress, crisis hotlines can provide support and guidance. They're there to help, so don't hesitate to use them. (The Resources section at the back of this book provides some crisis hotlines you may find helpful.)

When things feel dark, it's hard to believe they'll ever get better. But feelings are temporary, even the most painful ones. Healing takes time, but it's possible. Think about a time when you overcame something hard. What helped you get through it? Imagine what life could look like if the pain eased. What would you want to do, feel or experience? Take your experiences one day at a time. Focus on getting through the next hour, the next day, the next small step. Hope isn't about knowing exactly how things will improve, it's about believing that improvement is possible.

Navigating suicidal thoughts, depression, anxiety, grief or loss is one of the hardest things anyone can face. But you don't have to do it alone. With the right tools, support and small steps, it's possible to find relief, connection and even joy again. Remember, it's okay to feel what you're feeling and it's okay to ask for help. You're not alone in this. Keep going, one moment at a time. You're stronger than you know.

How to help a loved one who's grieving or experiencing suicidal thoughts

Supporting a loved one who is grieving or struggling with suicidal thoughts can feel challenging. You might worry about saying the wrong thing, doing the wrong thing or making the situation worse. You don't need to have all the answers or be a perfect support system. Showing up with compassion, patience and a willingness to listen can make a world of difference. Here's some suggestions to help you navigate this challenging time while supporting the people you care about.

It's human nature to want to take away someone's pain. But grief and suicidal thoughts aren't just problems to be solved. Often the most powerful way to help is being present without trying to 'fix' things. Let your loved one cry, vent or sit in silence. Sometimes all they need is for someone to be there. Avoid saying things like, 'They're in a better place' or 'Everything happens for a reason.' These well-meaning phrases can come across as dismissive. Instead, try saying, 'I'm so sorry you're going through this' or 'I can't imagine how hard this must be for you.' Acknowledge their feelings without judgement. Saying, 'That sounds really painful' can feel more supportive than 'Don't think like that' or 'You have so much to live for.' Remind them they're not alone through statements such as, 'I'm here with you.' Your authentic connection is one of the most helpful things you can provide. Just being there shows them they're not alone in their struggle.

When someone's grieving or wrestling with suicidal thoughts, they don't need your life wisdom, they need a safe space to let their feelings out. Listen actively. Avoid interrupting or jumping in with your own experiences. Use reflective phrases like, 'It sounds like you're feeling…' to show you're truly listening. Don't try to minimise their pain with comments like, 'At least you still have…' or 'It could be worse.' These statements, though well intentioned, can feel invalidating. Being truly heard can be incredibly healing. It lets your loved one know their feelings are valid and they're not facing this alone.

When someone is deep in grief or struggling with suicidal thoughts, even basic tasks can feel overwhelming. Offering concrete, practical help can be a lifesaver. Offer to cook meals, run errands or help with daily chores. Instead of saying, 'Let me know if you need anything,' try 'I'm bringing dinner over on Tuesday, does pasta work?' Help them navigate logistical tasks like funeral arrangements or paperwork if they seem overwhelmed.

If your loved one is experiencing suicidal thoughts, encourage small, manageable steps. For instance, 'Let's take a walk together' or 'How about I sit with you while you call a psychologist?'

Offer to help them find resources, like therapists or crisis hotlines, and even go with them to appointments if they're comfortable. When everything feels like too much, even small acts of support can lighten the load and help your loved one feel cared for.

Don't be afraid to talk about suicide. Many people worry that bringing up suicidal thoughts will 'put the idea in someone's head', but talking openly about suicide can reduce stigma and help your loved one feel safe enough to share. Consider starting the conversation with statements and questions, such as, 'I've noticed you've been really down lately. Have you been having thoughts about hurting yourself or not wanting to be here?' or 'Sometimes, when people feel overwhelmed, they think about ending their life. Is that something you've been thinking about?' If they say yes, stay calm and thank them for trusting you enough to share. Then, ask open-ended questions like, 'Can you tell me more about what you're feeling?'

Sometimes, the best way to support a loved one is to help them connect with professional resources. Suggest grief counselling or support groups where they can share their experiences with others who understand. Encourage them to seek professional help and offer your support with the process, such as by saying, 'I think talking to a clinical psychologist or doctor could really help. Can I help you make that happen?' Most importantly, if you have any concerns about their immediate safety and feel that they might be in danger, don't leave them alone. Call a crisis hotline or emergency services for help. Talking about suicide reduces shame and opens the door to support. It shows your loved one that you care enough to ask the hard questions. If they're resistant, offer to help them make an appointment or even go with them. Professional support provides tools, insights and resources that go beyond what you can offer as a friend or family member.

Grief doesn't have an expiration date. Your loved one might seem fine one day and then break down the next. This is normal. Be patient with their process, even if it feels slower than you expected. Don't rush them with phrases like, 'Aren't you over this yet?' or 'It's time to move on.' Avoid comparing their grief to others' experiences. Everyone grieves differently. Instead, let them know it's okay to grieve for as long as they need. Be there for the long haul. Grief doesn't end after the funeral or a few months—it's a journey, and your continued support matters. Allowing your loved one the space to grieve in their own way shows respect for their process and strengthens your connection.

While you can't force someone to 'feel better', you can gently encourage healthy ways they might try to help them cope with their pain. Suggest creative outlets like journalling, drawing or gardening. These can help them process emotions without feeling pressured to talk. Gently encourage them to honour their loved one in meaningful ways, like lighting a candle or creating a memory book.

If your loved one is experiencing suicidal thoughts, ensure that they have a crisis plan. This might include emergency contacts, grounding techniques and safe spaces to go when they're struggling. Suggest small, manageable activities to get them moving, like a short walk or listening to music. Healthy coping strategies provide an outlet for pain and a way to regain a sense of control.

Supporting someone through grief or suicidal thoughts is emotionally exhausting, and it's easy to neglect your own wellbeing in the process. But you can't pour from an empty cup—you need care and support too. It's okay to take breaks when you need them. Let your loved one know how you are feeling, such as by saying, 'I care about you deeply, but I also need time to recharge so I can be there for you.' Talk to a therapist, join a support group or confide in a trusted friend. Supporting someone else doesn't mean you have to carry the weight alone. Prioritise self-care and make time for activities that replenish you, whether it's exercise, hobbies or simply resting. Taking care of yourself ensures you have the emotional energy to continue being there for your loved one.

Supporting a loved one through grief or suicidal thoughts is one of the most challenging things you can do, but you don't have to have all the answers or fix everything for them. Just showing up, listening and reminding them they're not alone can make a world of difference. Remember to care for yourself, too, because your wellbeing matters just as much. Together, you can navigate this difficult journey, one step at a time.

Reflection prompts

Take a moment to pause and reflect. Whether you're grieving, supporting a loved one or facing your own inner struggles, these prompts are designed to help you process your thoughts and feelings in a compassionate, non-judgemental way.

1. What emotions come up when I think about this loss? Can I name them without judgement?
2. What's one small thing I can do today to take care of myself as I navigate this loss?
3. What would I say to a friend who was feeling the way I am right now?
4. What are three things — big or small — that have brought me even a flicker of comfort or relief recently?
5. Who can I reach out to, even if it feels scary or vulnerable, to share how I'm feeling?
6. If I imagine a future version of myself who's found a way through this, what would they want me to know?
7. How can I show up for my loved one in a way that feels meaningful to them?
8. When have I faced challenges in the past, and how did I get through them?
9. What's one tiny step I can take today towards healing, even if it's as simple as breathing deeply?
10. How can I honour the parts of myself that are struggling while also making space for growth?
11. If I could sit down with my future self, someone who has found peace and healing, what wisdom might they share with me?
12. If I could speak to my heart right now, what would I tell it? And if my heart could speak back, what would it say?

PALATE CLEANSER
Princess Leia — Carrie Fisher

I knew Mum had had both girlfriends and boyfriends at different times, but I didn't know what 'gay' meant when I was a kid. It was all the same to me. I knew I was different from the other kids at school because I fantasised about both Princess Leia *and* Luke Skywalker when I was seven years old. (By fantasised, I mean I thought of them as attractive in the way a small child would — nothing sexual.)

A fabulous turn of events later in my life was that, in my early thirties, Hollywood actor Carrie Fisher became a friend of mine. I even have a pet snake, an Australian Children's python (*Antaresia childreni*), named after her. A Children's python can grow up to around 140cm and is known to have irregular blotched colour patterns, usually in brown and tan but they come in several colour variations. They are semi-arboreal and mostly nocturnal.

Fisher wasn't really a friend in the true sense of the word, she was more of an acquaintance really, but she rocked my world for the short while we were friendly.

Fisher had written several books about her years of drug abuse, her mental health battles, and the trouble she had dealing with fame and Hollywood.

I think she recognised that I, too, was damaged.

We'd previously met a few years prior when she was doing her stand-up show, 'Wishful Drinking'. We met again in 2013, when she travelled to Sydney for an appearance at the Supanova convention (conventions are where stars of the present and years gone by meet with fans, sign autographs and press the flesh).

Before her flight to Sydney, she called me from Los Angeles International Airport while she was picking up supplies from a convenience store in the convenience area. We chatted on the phone as she was about to board her flight. She was not thrilled about the long flight, as a nervous flyer, but she was full of sass and energy. We hit it off as she spoke of her collection of Princess Leia memorabilia.

'I can always find some weird souvenir of me,' she said of appearing at conventions. 'I'm sure I will find some humiliating piece of merchandising of me as a shampoo or something and meet a lot of nice people, so what could be bad?'

She continued, clearly amused at the thought: 'I think it is funny. I wish merchandising was aerobic so I could be thinner but it's not so it might as well be funny. Lego me was really weird. The soap of me I really like. They have a robe of me and the cookie jar of me I hadn't seen until very recently, so that was nice. Who knew I was going to grow up and be a cookie jar, so imagine my glee.'

Some 36 hours or so later, catching up at the Shangri-La Hotel in Sydney, she took my number and said we would catch up later that day if I was free. I was flying to Los Angeles myself the next morning and didn't really think much of it. Surprisingly though, that evening her assistant called and told me, 'Carrie would like to see you.' I never expected the call when she took my number, I just thought she was being polite.

Most stars dread appearing at fan conventions, probably because it is a reminder of glory days past. But it is a quick money-earner, and comes as a reminder that these stars still matter to people, even if their heyday was many years ago.

Also appearing at Supanova that year were the likes of Margot Kidder (Lois Lane from the original *Superman* films, who I was also excited to meet), David Hasselhoff (The Hoff), Karl Urban (*Xena: Warrior Princess*, *The Lord of the Rings* and *Star Trek*), and James and Oliver Phelps (twins who played Fred and George Weasley in the *Harry Potter* films).

But for me, Fisher was the biggest drawcard. Then, at 56, she was Hollywood royalty — the daughter of singer and actor Eddie Fisher and acting sweetheart Debbie Reynolds.

She was a bonafide, bigger-than-life superstar.

To most people, she will always be Princess Leia, with her cinnamon-bun hairstyle from the epic *Star Wars* franchise.

When I think of her, I remember the time she invited me to her bedroom for a good old chat like two girlfriends catching up after a long time apart, where no subject was off limits.

Just to meet her was a buzz, but to call her a friend — to have her phone number and email in my phone — that was really something else to me.

The image of Carrie Fisher opening her hotel room door wearing a long nightie, barefoot, with no makeup on and her hair pulled back with a cream-coloured band will be etched in my mind forever. Her skin was perfect, as if she had just moisturised.

On this night, I curled up at the foot of her hotel room bed, creased with laughter as she told tale after tale of her wild and incredible life.

She was a born performer, even sat on the bed.

In some ways we both knew it was naughty — breaking that third wall controlled by publicists and managers — but Fisher wasn't one to be told what to do.

I'm sure the moment wasn't as life-changing for Fisher as it was for me. She most likely found me cute and amusing and, as I said, I suspect she recognised similar damage in me. We had both experienced trauma. It was unsaid but implicit.

I don't know how long I was there for — the truth is, I was so enamoured with her that all I know for sure is that her assistant called to invite me to come over to see Carrie Fisher at around 6 pm, and I wasn't home until after 10 pm.

What I do recall are her stories of a woman living her life to the full, with Hollywood as the backdrop.

She was excited to show off her shopping from earlier in the day in The Rocks, including a Chinese biology sculpture-like object that looked like it would sit well in an acupuncturist's office.

Fisher was one of those people everyone seemed to know instantly— her life was open for all to see, which was in large part her problem. She was candid about her depression and the many medications she was on, having revealed years prior that she suffered from bipolar disorder.

'It is a balance issue with my meds, I manage it,' she told me, as I shared some of my own story of depression and mental health issues.

She didn't hold back on her drug use, either, speaking frankly about the fact she smoked marijuana for the first time at the age of 13 and went on to abuse alcohol, cocaine and other drugs such as LSD (lysergic acid diethylamide).

She did not go into minute detail — each tale was just part of her story, a rich tapestry of highs and lows. She almost assumed I knew the whole story, I think, as she referred at times to her several books detailing her colourful life.

Despite the darkness of some of the topics and a tinge of sadness, she made her stories hilarious with big arm gestures. And I shared my own personal stories with her.

She gossiped shamelessly. She described Hollywood giant and Oscar winner Al Pacino as a 'cranky a**hole'. Pacino, of course, was in a long-term relationship with Fisher's close friend Beverley D'Angelo, star of the *National Lampoon's Vacation* films, with whom he has twins.

She spoke of her mum, the legendary Debbie Reynolds, as if she was just a slightly eccentric old lady, and she told me about her half-sisters Joely and Trish, as well as her brother, Todd.

Fisher's ex-husband, songwriter Paul Simon, wrote a number of songs about her, most notably 'She Moves On'. She was clearly proud of that fact and enthused about Simon's musical brilliance.

Her weight loss and yo-yo Hollywood dieting also came in for scrutiny as we cosied on the bed. She said she found people's interest in her weight amusing. Again, having previously chatted over the phone about it, Fisher also spoke of her fascination with Princess Leia merchandise from the *Star Wars* films.

Fisher was in on the joke of conventions. She was singing for her supper, so to speak, and unashamed about it. At the time there were some negative articles about fans being charged to pay $80 for an autograph and photo with her. She didn't care. She had to make a living somehow and this was before the revamped JJ Abrams *Star Wars* franchise put her back in the spotlight.

'I think of it as kind of lap dancing in a way,' she said in her wry way. 'I'm doing my lap dancing down there and it is fun.'

When I finally left that night, she gave me a gift — a teddy bear that looked like *Star Wars'* Chewbacca, made out of Australian alpaca fur. She said she'd found it in a small store in The Rocks that day and had thought of me.

On the swing tag attached to the bear, she had written a personal note, which would be one of my most cherished possessions, but for the fact my dog, Lily, took a liking to the bear, slobbered on the note and rendered it almost illegible.

'Hey, Jonathon,' it now reads: '(Something something something) Chewie down...under his pants (something something). Carrie Fisher.'

Somehow I think this funny, eccentric, fragile yet tough woman would have got a big laugh out of Lily's gift-tag sabotage.

As she bid me farewell, she summoned her cute male assistant back to the room. Looking back, maybe she just wanted him to get laid. Whatever she was thinking, I went downstairs in the lift to her assistant's room, and we fooled around. What a perfect ending to a perfect night.

CONCLUSION

I have never really laboured on mental health labels. I use depression as a blanket term, mainly because it is all-encompassing but also because it is easier than explaining the minutiae of my mind. Plus, it really isn't anyone's business unless I choose to share it with them.

I had to contact my doctor to find out my exact diagnoses, as there have been different variations over the years. They're really just words — my focus is on how to live the best life I can now.

My intention with this book has been to provide some insights into my life — a seemingly successful one on the surface, while underneath there has been considerable trauma and difficulty to overcome.

As the book's title suggests, I wanted to flag the fact that no matter how different we may seem — no matter where we come from, or what our sexuality, religion or skin colour is — we are all battling our own shit.

We are all, indeed, *Mental As Anyone*.

A life lesson from Kate

The great Hollywood actor Kate Winslet was in Australia not so long ago for her incredible film, *Lee*, in which she plays World War II American war correspondent Lee Miller. It was a passion project for her that took nine years to bring to the big screen.

Interestingly, Kate Winslet — she of Rose in *Titanic* fame — has to fight her own battles on the work front, and presumably personally too.

We caught up twice when Winslet was in Sydney, the first occasion on the red carpet at the Randwick Ritz cinema as she entered a premiere screening.

I'd come face to face with the Academy Award winner once before, back at the Toronto Film Festival many years earlier, but that was a press conference and not a one-on-one interview.

This time it was just her and I talking, albeit with a throng of people around us clamouring to take a photograph of the massive global star.

As a side note, I really need to stop swearing in a professional sense — but when I met Kate Winslet I just couldn't help myself. I was so overcome by the film and her insanely powerful performance that my exact words were: 'Congratulations, this film is fucking amazing.'

She didn't seem offended; instead, she responded with a laugh, 'My god, you know when you are in Australia when the journalist says that.'

A day later, at the Intercontinental Hotel overlooking Sydney Harbour, I had a full 15-minute interview with Winslet for a more in-depth feature on the film.

Again, she exceeded my every expectation. So often with these interviews you leave disappointed. This time, I most certainly did not.

I'm often self-deprecating during interviews. That is partly who I am but also (to let you in on a secret) I find it helps when you show your own vulnerability as it encourages the person you are interviewing to open up themselves.

There is a lot of nudity in the film, so I spoke about the bravery it takes as an actor to appear naked on screen. It wasn't gratuitous nudity; rather, it was empowering. I also mentioned my *Mental As Anyone* podcast and that I was in the final throes of writing this book.

Now, when you do these interviews, they run a tight ship and interviews run back-to-back. There's management and publicists and lots going on, with a queue of other journalists waiting their turn in the corridor or a room nearby. So, when our time came to an end, I thanked Kate (I think I can call her that now) and thought that was it.

It takes a lot to shock me. I don't overwhelm easily, but Kate took my hand and dragged me out of the room into another, where a team of people were buzzing around.

One noted, 'Kate, you don't have time, you've got your next interview.' But she was unfazed and said she wanted to talk to me privately — that she needed to give me a 'pep talk.'

There was no other room spare, so she took me into an ensuite bathroom and shut the door. It was tiny — literally a toilet on one side, a sink on the other.

In the middle of this tiny space, she held my hands and gave me a quick lecture. By lecture, I mean a kind and wonderful moment of sharing a snapshot of the wisdom she's learned over decades of having her body, image and talent analysed in the public eye.

'If you're having a bad day, do what you need to do, stick crystals in your pocket if that is what you have to do,' she said with stern kindness.

Then she told me not to worry about my body or weight: 'It is exactly as it is meant to be.' She also said it was a great interview.

With that, we walked out of the tiny bathroom. We said goodbye and I went back to the office, while she headed into another interview.

In that brief moment, I understood that how we see ourselves is not always how others see us, and sometimes you simply have to do what it takes to get through the day.

They're great lessons.

My tips for positive mental health

Some years ago, while writing a story about my journey, I shared a number of tips on positive mental health. Here, I share them with you with some slight updates, hoping that they provide something helpful you can use in this crazy, often toxic, world we live in.

• Take regular breaks from social media.
• Be kind to yourself.
• Switch your phone to airplane mode when you go to bed (or even better, 30 minutes before).

- Go for a walk (preferably without your phone).
- Phone a friend.
- Take a bath — it helps me, even a quick soak.
- Find something you enjoy to help you wind down, like yoga, a sport, tai chi, scuba diving or reading a book.
- Be honest with yourself.
- Consider getting a pet. This may not work for everyone, but my beloved Lily, who has since left us, really helped me through my darkest days. When I couldn't see reason to get out of bed myself, I had to do so for her.
- Develop a support network — a trusted few people you can check in with on a regular basis.

Overwhelmingly, at this point, I want to say I hope this book has helped make you feel less alone in your thoughts. Difference is something to be celebrated. Life is for the living — it has taken me decades to get to the point where I want to live, and I want that for all of you. No matter how dark things may get, there is light at the end of the tunnel. You can make it. You can do this. You are worth it. Whatever your path, however your journey unfolds, I wish you well.

RESOURCES

Do you need help? If you're in Australia, try contacting one of these services for help.

- Lifeline: 13 11 44 (lifeline.org.au)
- Beyond Blue: 1300 22 4636 (beyondblue.org.au)
- Kids Helpline: 1800 55 1800 (kidshelpline.com.au)
- headspace: headspace.org.au
- SANE Australia: 1800 187 263 (sane.org)
- Butterfly Foundation: 1800 334 673 (butterfly.org.au)
- The Anxiety Clinic: 02 9389 3339 (theanxietyclinic.com.au)

You can also try the following apps:

- ReachOUT
- Smiling Mind
- Calm
- The Check-in
- ReachOUT
- WorryTime

Gotcha4Life (gotcha4life.org) is a not-for-profit foundation dedicated to building a mentally fit future through their work with schools, sports clubs, workplaces and communities across Australia. Visit their website to find out more about their work.

If you're in New Zealand, try contacting one of these services:

- Lifeline: 0800 543 354
- Depression Helpline: 0800 111 757
- Youthline: 0800 376 633
- What's Up: 0800 942 787
- 1737 Need To Talk: Call or text 1737

The following apps could also be helpful:

- Groov
- Small Steps
- Headstrong
- Wellbeing Support.

If you're outside Australia or New Zealand, try these services:

- International Association for Suicide Prevention: Free hotline in more than 50 countries: www.iasp.info/crisis-centres-helplines/
- Find A Helpline: findahelpline.com
- Mental Health Helplines: International Director: HelpGuide.org
- United For Global Mental Health: unitedgmh.org/support
- World Health Organisation: www.who.int/news-room/feature-stories/mental-well-being-resources-for-the-public

Some apps that could be helpful are:

- Headspace
- Calm
- MindShift
- Breathe2Relax
- Simple Habit

ACKNOWLEDGEMENTS

This freaks me out — there are so many people to thank and only so much space. And what if I forget someone?

So, please take this as a blanket thanks to everyone who has positively impacted my life … ever.

Of course, I do need to name-check a few.

Trish, Mum — not a day goes by I don't miss you like crazy. The pain never goes away but it does get easier with time because I've learned to focus on the positive memories rather than the gaping hole in my heart. Your bravery in being open about your mental health, even when it felt as though the world was against you and the fight seemed impossible, inspires me and drives me each and every day. I love you to the moon and back times infinity. I just wish I could tell you in person one more time.

Alex, you changed my life completely and made me believe in love in a way I didn't really think possible. I love doing life with you, even when times are tough. Thank you for putting up with my idiosyncrasies and for trying to understand them when life is a lot.

Alison, my twin, side by side we have taken on the world. We are worlds apart in so many ways — people tell us constantly how different we are, but truthfully, inside, which is what matters, we are two peas in a pod. I love you infinitely.

Olivia, Grace, Chloe and Bella — you are everything to me. Whatever life throws your way, I will always be there by your side. I love you lots and lots like jelly tots.

Stuart, thank you for being a mate and brother — but most importantly, thank you for being there for Alison and the girls. You are a wonderful man.

Judy, my second mum and bestie, thank you for the constant support, emotionally and in sharing your wisdom. Ali, Stu, Alex, the girls and I would be lost without you.

Matt and Paul, this is the beginning of something special, I can feel it to my core. I'm eternally grateful we have finally found each other.

Lily, Bruiser, Marcia, DanDan, Lotus, Tequila — ILYSM.

Maureen — you gave me a safe space to write the majority of this book at Villa Costa Plenty. Thank you for your love and generosity, then and always, from the day you were at our birth.

To Jordon Lott and the wonderful Wiley team (Renee, Chris, Lucy, Leigh, Ingrid, George, Markus, Clare, Lulu, Marie-Anna and Priyaa). When you know, you know. After others tried to convince me to fit this square book into a round hole, you just got it. Thank you for your guidance and patience.

To my friends, colleagues and bosses at News Corp, particularly *The Daily Telegraph* and *Sunday Telegraph* teams led by Ben English and Anna Caldwell, thank you for allowing me to be me, even in my most manic of states. And Campbell Reid, you're a legend, mate.

Kerry, you were able to step back and look at the bigger picture when I struggled. Thank you for your warmth and kindness — this certainly has been a rollercoaster, and I'm thankful to have been on it with you.

Lucie McGeoch and Sarah Stinson, wow! I don't know how I could ever begin to repay you for the guidance you've given me on this. From start to finish, your encouragement has been incredible. Book publishing is a very different beast from what I'm used to and so in times where I've struggled to stay positive, you've always picked me up and given me the confidence to keep going. Plus, you are bloody creative, smart, fabulous women filled with extraordinary ideas. I am tickled pink to have you as friends.

Amanda J, your words of support, constant encouragement and love during the writing process will never be forgotten.

Adriana too, thank you for your support through this—you are a mighty warrior of a woman and I love you. I can't wait to read your book one day.

Dr Jodie—you knew instantly where this story needed to go. Your incredible hard work, understanding, patience and thoughtfulness is more appreciated than I can ever say in words. And massive respect for your ability to put the psychological jargon so many of us find confusing into 'real people' talk. You are making a difference.

David Champion. You are family, although I am not sure if you're more brother or father (ha). I actually don't know where you get all of your energy from — you're funny, witty, ridiculously smart, wise, worldly, generous and kind. Thank you for always being there for me and others. I hope I've been there for you as much as you have for me.

Marsy, we've been through some journeys, you and I—from Rock Eisteddfod (I said a 'boom chicka boom') to baby making. You've gone above and beyond, somehow managing to read my crazy mind and help turn this *Mental As Anyone* vision into something extraordinary.

Morgs... 15 years, who would have thought? We've been to the highest of highs and the lowest of lows—and oh, what a ride it has been. I am so grateful for you and proud of the impressive person you've become. You are wise beyond your years.

To my closest university mates and lifelong friends, Katie, Zoe, Leah—there has never been any judgement, just love, laughter and some tears too. I love you unconditionally.

Veronica M—the regular texts about life in general, the podcast feedback, always checking in, your honesty and friendship over what is now three decades is truly special. You are a remarkable woman, V.

Jane E—your unwavering friendship and career guidance, even in the toughest of times, has been phenomenal. You have always believed in me and I am immensely grateful.

To the Morans, the Hammonds, the Keasts, the Williams' and the broader family, I love you. The Perrys, too.

Dr Jane Hunt — you are a legend. You're caring, thoughtful, warm and helpful. You are just the best GP, and without your direction and sometimes tenacity, I would not have made it to this point.

Maria Lewis — not only do I love your incredible *Who's Afraid* book series, you will always be a dear friend. You don't know it, but you gave me the confidence to buckle down and just write in the first place. Hopefully you are as proud of this work as I am of yours.

Louise D, it has only been a short while but already you have impacted my life so greatly. I am looking forward to so many more years of life and friendship.

Marlia, Gina and Camo — thanks to the best lawyers in the media business.

Darcy and the crew at ProPodcast, thank you for turning *Mental As Anyone* into the podcast it has become. You got it from the beginning — these stories matter.

There are so many others I need to name-check: Casey, Colette, Mick O, Sapphire, Clare, Sam, Tanya, Mary, Guy, Gus, Anthony D, Zara, Caitlin, Cat Donovan, Dale, Christian Gilles, Edwina, Sarah, Sonja, Tracey, Rajh, Caroline, Brendan, Sarah, Nova Entertainment, Lian, Sally, Jodie, Sophie, Shandelle, Claire, Candice, Susan Leon, Arrnott, Sam, Olympia, Dietrich, Christiane, Mario, Timm and Simon.

And to everyone else that is part of my life and this book's journey, you know who you are and you know what you did, so thank you from the bottom of my heart.

Printed and bound by CPI Group (UK) Ltd, Croydon, CR0 4YY

10/06/2025

14686748-0001